Dialogues of Dispersal

Dialogues of Dispersal
Gender, Sexuality and African Diasporas

Edited by
Sandra Gunning, Tera W. Hunter and Michele Mitchell

A Gender and History Special Issue

Blackwell Publishing

First published as a special issue of *Gender and History*

BLACKWELL PUBLISHING
350 Main Street, Malden, MA 02148-5020, USA
108 Cowley Road, Oxford OX4 1JF, UK
550 Swanston Street, Carlton, Victoria 3053, Australia

First published 2004 by Blackwell Publishing Ltd

Library of Congress Cataloging-in-Publication Data

ISBN 1-4051-2681-7

A catalogue record for this title is available from the British Library.

Set by Advance Typesetting Ltd, Oxon
Printed and bound in the United Kingdom
by MPG Books Ltd, Bodmin, Cornwall

For further information on
Blackwell Publishing, visit our website:
http://www.blackwellpublishing.com

Contents

NOTES ON CONTRIBUTORS

Fatima El-Tayeb is a historian and currently Scholar in Residence at the University of Tennessee. She has published a book, *Schwarze Deutsche. 'Rasse' und nationale Identität 1890–1933* (Frankfurt: Campus 2001), and a number of articles on blacks in German history. Her recent work is on transnational identity concepts among European ethnic minorities. She has also co-authored a movie and a novel, *Alles wird gut/Everything will be fine* (with Angelina Maccarone).

Rhonda D. Frederick, an Assistant Professor of English at Boston College, teaches Caribbean and African American literatures. She is also interested in American literatures, particularly twentieth-century women's popular fiction, and literatures of the African Diaspora. Her research interests are in Post-colonial Studies, Cultural Studies and narratives of migration. She is presently working on a manuscript that examines Caribbean literature's recurrent figure of the Panamá Canal worker.

Sandra Gunning is Associate Professor in the Program in American Culture, the Center for Afroamerican & African Studies, and the Department of English at the University of Michigan, Ann Arbor. Her current research addresses gender and location in the early African diaspora.

Tera W. Hunter is an Associate Professor of History at Carnegie Mellon University. She is the author of *To 'Joy My Freedom: Southern Black Women's Lives and Labors After the Civil War* (Cambridge, MA: Harvard University Press, 1997). She is currently working on the history of marriages among African Americans in the nineteenth century.

Anne S. Macpherson is Assistant Professor of Latin American and Caribbean History at SUNY College at Brockport. She co-edited *Race and Nation in Modern Latin America* (University of North Carolina Press, 2003) and authored 'Citizens v. Clients: Working Women and Colonial Reform in Puerto Rico and Belize, 1932–45', *Journal of Latin American Studies* 35 (2003). She is completing a book manuscript on gender and politics in twentieth-century Belize.

Patrick Manning is Professor of History and African-American Studies at Northeastern University, where he directs the World History Center. His work on the demography of slavery in Africa and the African diaspora, including *Slavery and African Life* (1990), emphasises the disproportions in sex ratios brought by the slave trade and the resulting transformations in gender relations throughout the regions affected by enslavement. He is author of *Navigating World History: Historians Create a Global Past* (2003).

J. Lorand Matory is Professor of Anthropology and of African and African-American Studies at Harvard University. He is the author of *Sex and the Empire that Is No More: Gender and the Politics of Metaphor in Ọ̀yọ́ Yorùbá Religion* (University of Minnesota Press, 1994; Berghahn, 2003) and of the forthcoming *Black Atlantic Religion: Tradition, Trans- nationalism and Matriarchy in the Afro-Brazilian Candomblé* (Princeton University Press).

His general interest is in the ongoing and mutually transformative dialogue between African and African-American cultures. His current research concerns the diversity of immigrant and indigenous ethnic groups of African descent in the United States.

Michele Mitchell is Assistant Professor in the Department of History and Center for Afroamerican & African Studies at the University of Michigan, Ann Arbor. Her research focuses upon the production and maintenance – biological, material, discursive, cultural – of "racial" collectives. She is the author of *Righteous Propagation: African Americans and the Politics of Racial Destiny after Reconstruction* (Chapel Hill: University of North Carolina Press, 2004).

Jenny Sharpe is professor of English and Comparative Literature at the University of California at Los Angeles. Her publications include a recent book, *Ghosts of Slavery: A Literary Archeology of Black Women's Lives* (Minneapolis: University of Minnesota Press, 2003). Her current research is on nation, gender and technology in diasporic cultures.

Martin Summers is an assistant professor of history at the University of Oregon. His writing includes '"This Immoral Practice": The Prehistory of Homophobia in Black Nationalist Thought', in Toni Lester, ed., *Gender Nonconformity, Race, and Sexuality* and *Manliness and Its Discontents: The Black Middle Class and the Transformation of Masculinity, 1900–1930* (Chapel Hill: University of North Carolina Press, 2004).

Sophie White received her PhD from the Courtauld Institute, University of London. Her research and publications investigate issues of gender, consumerism and the role of dress and appearance in managing gender, race, class and ethnic encounters in French Colonial Louisiana. She currently serves as Assistant Director of the Gender Studies Program at the University of Notre Dame.

1

Gender, Sexuality, and African Diasporas

Sandra Gunning, Tera W. Hunter and Michele Mitchell

The months before and after manumission must indeed have been a bittersweet time for Phillis Wheatley. In the summer of 1773 she debuted in London as the young slave poet from the American colonies, an object of both celebration and astonishment for British abolitionists. Recalled suddenly to Boston – her beloved mistress Susanna Wheatley was fatally ill – Phillis was by the end of the year emancipated by her owners. Phillis now dared to contemplate the unorthodox life as a self-supporting Negro poetess, but her white patrons had another plan, namely that she should return to Africa as the wife of a black missionary. In a letter written in October 1774, Wheatley's objections were polite but firm:

> Upon my arrival [in Africa], how like a Barbarian Should I look to the Natives; I can promise that my tongue shall be quiet for a strong reason indeed being an utter stranger to the Language of Anamaboe. Now to be Serious, This undertaking appears too hazardous, and not sufficiently Eligible, to go – and leave my British & American Friends – I am also unacquainted with those Missionaries in Person.[1]

As Marsha Watson has argued, though Phillis had been born in West Africa, she probably felt betrayed by such counsel, because she was by nurturance and cultural affiliation a child of the New World.[2] In choosing to remain in the colonies Phillis took her chances with both the possibilities of the American revolution and Boston's small black community, since by 1778 she had married John Peters, a free black much disliked by the white members of her former circle.

Taken as simply one figure connecting what Earl Lewis has defined as a series of 'overlapping diasporas', Phillis Wheatley's life simultaneously engages histories of trans-Atlantic slavery and abolition, of competing European and American imperialisms, of a particular kind of gendered mobility and stasis, of freedom and containment, of cultural reformation and cultural frustration.[3] At the same time her determination to carve out (albeit with a conflicted, Janus-faced attitude to Africa) a 'home' in the midst of New World homelessness references a vastly complex and barely containable field of human experience that is the mark and measure of the African Diaspora.

Centuries old, the dispersal of African-born peoples and their cultures has been an ongoing process. Indeed, forced, coerced or voluntary migration has produced a Phillis Wheatley in the eighteenth-century, but also countless economic and political refugees from post-colonial African nation states in the twenty-first century. Yet, as Tiffany Patterson and Robin Kelley have suggested, the concept of the African Diaspora is primarily a convenient construction for organising academic knowledge.[4] As a field African Diaspora studies emerged 'officially' in the mid-twentieth century as scholars such as St. Clair Drake and George Shepperson theorised the formation of New World black cultures, and the potential of Pan-Africanism as a movement for social change in the post-World War II era.[5] Earlier work on African retentions by anthropologists such as Melville Herskovits had already laid considerable groundwork.[6] By the 1980s and early 1990s scholarly interest grew at a steady pace, so that by the end of the twentieth- and the start of the twenty-first century, the field of African Diaspora studies has virtually exploded, blurring disciplinary boundaries and challenging our understanding of everything from working-class culture, to cultural technologies of empire, to globalisation.[7] At the same time, the transformative power of black hip hop on a world stage, as well as the creation of new sites of dispersal and contested agency made possible by the World Wide Web, are pressing the traditional limits of our scholarly analyses and research methods.[8] At the present moment perhaps the most famous 'cross-over' hit in academic terms has been sociologist Paul Gilroy's *The Black Atlantic* (1993), a study that has engaged a new generation of academics outside of history and anthropology; now virtually everybody has been forced to reframe contemporary black culture in Britain, the Caribbean and the United States beyond a one-way connection to Anglo-European traditions, and especially beyond the confines of the national.[9] Contemporary scholars are also now equally concerned now with the neglected impact of non-US based African diasporas as they have been with the more traditional focus on Atlantic communities.[10] And there has a growing recognition of the importance of viewing the African continent past and present as a site of multiple internal diasporas that have existed synchronically with black communities in the rest of the world.[11]

Still, the use of gender as a category of analysis remains something of a challenge for African Diaspora studies. There has been a steady stream of anthologies, monographs and articles by feminist scholars of both sexes, such as Adelaide M. Cromwell, Barbara Bush, Barbara Bair, Verene Shepherd,

Bridget Brereton, Beryl Satter, Hilary McD. Beckles, Rosalyn Terborg-Penn, Faith Smith and Jenny Sharpe.[12] However, too many studies past and present have addressed the experience of black masculinity as a collective identity, without a self-conscious assessment of the continual transformation of gender roles and sexuality within a black diasporic framework.

As has been the case in other bodies of historically informed scholarship, many of the first attempts to gender the history of African-descended peoples focused upon the past experiences and lived realities of women. In certain regards, a critical attempt to gender scholarship on African Diasporas began with publication of Filomena Chioma Steady's anthology, *The Black Woman Cross-Culturally,* in 1981. Steady – Sierra Leone-born and an anthropologist – contended that if women of African descent had 'been a subject of study long before women's liberation came into vogue', such scholarly attention had primarily been the provenance of function-alist anthropologists.[13] *The Black Woman Cross-Culturally* was preceded by the path-breaking *Women in Africa: Studies in Social and Economic Change* (1976) and would soon be followed by *Women in Africa and the African Diaspora* (1987). Indeed, scholars who either rejected or embraced Western second-wave feminism or who were committed to materialist analyses consistently produced provocative works that paved the way for recent scholarship on gender and sexuality in African and Afro-diasporic communities.[14] Since the mid-1980s, for example, Africanists and Latin Americanists have produced a number of critical monographs and articles.[15] Scholars whose analytical focus and intellectual preoccupations centre on the United States have generated a wealth of scholarship as well, on topics ranging from health and medicine to cultural expression and resistance.[16] If much scholarship – especially that produced within Europe and North America – has focused upon slavery and the after-shocks of abolition,[17] scholars interested in the past and present dispersal of African-descended women, men, and children have also mined familiar topics in any number of creative ways, including dynamic and provocative assessments of visual and material culture.[18]

The essays in this special issue provide a range of historically informed scholarship on the intersections of gender, sexuality and the African Diaspora. While they speak to many of the seminal concerns and questions in the larger body of work preceding it, they are distinctive in centralising the core themes and expanding the geographical boundaries of the forced and voluntary migrations of African peoples beyond the Atlantic World and urban life that has typified many other studies. These articles cover a broad chronological sweep as well, from pre-colonial and colonial times up to the present day.

The volume opens with three essays traveling the globe, from West Africa to Brazil, Jamaica and Germany. All three address questions of inclusion and exclusion and how gender and sexuality influence the politics of narration, performance and recognition.

The first essay, by anthropologist Lorand Matory, is a provocative critique of the symbiosis of academic scholarship and religious communities in the New World, particularly Candomblé. He argues that in the process of delimiting a historical narrative of the religion, scholars have played a role in shaping its internal hierarchies. Not only has the scholarship been read by priests and practitioners, there has been engaged dialogue between these groups in international conferences. If there is often doubt about the impact of seemingly esoteric intellectual work outside academe, Matory's article makes clear just how powerful it can be in canonising what is known or regarded as 'authentic'. New World religion (like Candomblé in Brazil) and its African predecessor (like Yorùbá òrìṣà-worship in West Africa) have been selectively constructed by some as an idyllic matriarchy or a genderless society untainted by foreign and 'Western' concepts of male dominance, female subordination and homosexuality. Matory debunks these views, exposing the secrets and the 'hidden transcripts' behind their formulation. Diasporas as 'imagined communities', he argues, can function like nation states with vested interests in concealing, denying, and explaining away ideas, individuals, and social practices that contradict the images they wish to safeguard and project.

Jenny Sharpe's essay comments on the limitations of exclusivity by challenging the conception of the Diasporan subject as male, urban and Western. She makes a case for the far-reaching implications of globalisation in rural Third World peripheries. According to Sharpe, traditional readings of diasporan musical cultures generated in major international cities such as London and New York obscure the existence of creativity and production in more localised centers. Sharpe explores post-colonialism and the gendered politics of a transnational recording industry through the music of Jamaican 'dub' poet Jean 'Binta' Breeze. Her reading of Breeze takes into account Breeze's biography as a cultural producer living back and forth between Britain and Jamaica and engages her political commitment to post-colonial critiques. Her essay examines the social consciousness within Breeze's 'dub' poetry, as it pertains to black female struggles for sexual and economic empowerment in Jamaica. Breeze and other working-class 'dancehall divas' and 'female DJs' demonstrate 'women claiming male-dominated territory through a technologically-driven female sexuality', asserting themselves in a world in which 'the agents of control increasingly exist elsewhere.' This essay is critical in that it makes visible black women (artists and consumers) in the music industry, the primary site that scholars like Paul Gilroy have theorised as constitutive of transatlantic black culture and increasingly others are using as a basis for 'a general theory of the African Diaspora'.

Fatima El-Tayeb's article shows how the boundaries of inclusion and exclusion in hip hop and popular culture have been policed along gender lines in ways that betray the feminist origins of the broader social movement from which it evolved in Germany. Given the uniqueness of Germany as a site of scholarly inquiry on African dispersal, El-Tayeb first establishes Afro-Germans' place within diasporic histories, identities and cultures. She begins by highlighting the contested nature of German identity by providing an overview of racial politics within both colony and metropole. She then suggests that if the simultaneous denial and reification of race in the Federal Republic after World War II prohibited the formation of identity-based activism among Afro-Germans, the 1980s witnessed the emergence of a movement due largely to the efforts of women, many of whom were lesbian. Feminists were the first to express a collective sense of Afro-German identity, inspired in part by black feminists in the USA. They brought to public view a narration of the long history of unacknowledged black presence within the country to strengthen their claims and organisation for justice, recognition and social change. Using the foundation and inspiration built by this movement, black youth in Germany transformed US models of political hip hop into a vehicle for multiracial, anti-racist activism in the 1990s. Though initially progressive on issues of gender and sexuality, hip hop relented to 'selling homophobia and sexism as authentic ghetto culture – not only in their songs but on their political agendas'. El-Tayeb exposes the irony of this turn in light of the feminist activism and vibrant intellectual networks within the African Diaspora from which hip hop in Germany was produced.

The next two essays interrogate issues of colour and class in the Caribbean and Central America. Rhonda Frederick's essay examines the autobiography of the Jamaican entrepreneur and 'doctress' Mary Jane Seacole, as one way into the complicated politics of class, colour, race and nationality in the Anglophone West Indies, following the end of slavery in the early nineteenth century. For Frederick, Seacole represents a particular kind of mixed-race identity that challenges the fixed binaries of 'black' and 'white', of colonial subject and Englishman, in order to reformulate an emergent 'Caribbean' subjectivity. But Seacole's goal, according to this essay, is not the total subversion of colonial categories. Rather, Seacole engages in a highly selective recuperation of 'otherness' in ways that will shore up her identity as a respectable but independent 'colored lady,' despite her penchant for travelling to the ends of the earth in the company of gold miners in New Grenada and soldiers in the Crimea. Seacole 'asserts her creoleness by highlighting those behaviours that affirm her desired social position, in spite of her ambiguously raced and stereotypically gendered physical appearance and the meanings attached to them'. Frederick argues that through the autobiography, Seacole achieves an idealised persona by way of a rhetorical performance that forces her audience to call into question traditional assumptions about the gendered, raced bodies of empires.

Anne Macpherson's essay links gender, colour and class issues to twentieth-century Creole descendants of the Seacoles in the New World. Whereas the mother figured prominently in Seacole's effort to wrestle with the conception of her identity, motherhood was a weapon and political tool for middle-class women in Belize in quite different ways. Macpherson broadens our understanding of how social movements can have multiple – and often conflicting – constituencies by focusing upon a vital aspect of Garveyism within the English-speaking Caribbean. Macpherson contributes significantly to literature on gender, race, reform and empire. Her focus on a Caribbean-based Universal Negro Improvement Association provides a rich, compelling example of how and why women of colour adopted maternalist strategies within colonial settings. Macpherson boldly contends that whereas Belize's Black Cross Nurses had unusual access to the state in comparison to black club women in the United States, the Nurses' inability to forge alliances across class lines ultimately buttressed hierarchies that collaborated with colonial rule. Their political mobilisations were not founded upon a discourse of sisterhood and can be described as 'nonfeminist women's activism'; although 'the same women could dispute male domination while placing class-race hierarchy above equal women's rights'. She builds upon important feminist scholarship on one of the most significant black mass movements, continuing to complicate our understanding of intra-racial dynamics within diasporan communities – not unlike Matory's interjections.

The last set of essays shares in common considerations of masculinity, their relationship to femininity, race, class and the Diaspora. Sophie White looks at the construction of masculinity and ethnicity through signs of dress. While this is the only article devoted to clothing, the issue is raised in several other pieces, if only tangentially. In Matory's essay, male Ọ̀yọ́-Yorùbá possession priests in West Africa cross-dress in female clothing, but the culturally specific reading of this symbolism is that they are wives of the gods – not necessarily a sign of homosexuality, but perhaps interpreted as such when translated by Candomblé devotees in Brazil. In Sharpe's examination of dancehall music, working-class women use flashy, glittery, fringed and synthetic outfits and hairdos to articulate their sexuality. In Frederick's article, dress is one of several yardsticks by which the itinerant Seacole measures her womanhood and distinguishes herself from others of a similar anatomy. In all of these situations the meaning of dress augments Sophie White's argument that it serves more than the potential it contains as material goods or cover for the body.

Masculinity and dress intersect in Sophie White's article, especially through the criminal case of Francisque a self-styled 'Englishman from Philadelphia' by way of Havana, who created a stir in the slave and free black community of colonial New Orleans when he attended dances, paying too much for music and courting the ladies. The other men present resented the intrusion on their turf and the expressions of ostentation, as well as his theft of items from a fellow black. Yet Francisque had seemingly made overtures to conform to what he perceived to be the deployment of emblems of an African-derived identity – 'three or four handkerchiefs around his collar and elsewhere about him'. Here again, tensions within diaspora communities emerge, this time between Creoles and Africans. Clothing served as an important mediator and source of conflict, not just between blacks and whites, but also among blacks. Clothing (all be they European manufactured garments) represented signs of belonging, exclusion, ways of helping to initiate and maintain sexual and non-sexual relationships, gift-giving and debt.

Martin Summers' article looks at the appropriation of fraternal orders – other kinds of Western forms – among Africans and African descended people in the United States. Summers offers a striking analysis of how diasporic identities are gendered as well as classed through an exploration of an early twentieth-century transatlantic epistolary relationship between two fraters, D. K. Abadu Bentsi from the Gold Coast and Harry A. Williamson from the United States. This article is distinctive in studying freemasonry outside of Western contexts and across national boundaries. Summers persuasively argues that the rhetoric and rituals of freemasonry grounded in producer values and bourgeois morality enabled black men to 'lay claim to a middle-class subjectivity' that depended as much upon men's homosocial networks with one another as it did models of 'masculine provider-hood' within households. In equating masculinity with production, freemasons also connected femininity with domesticity. They were able to construct a 'specifically racialised masculinity' while also distancing themselves from white middle-class men, including many fellow masons who shunned them. Economic depression and racial proscription might have frustrated the material realisation of middle-class status for black men, yet dialogue between the two men about their respective experiences with racism and colonisation allowed both men to articulate common belonging to a community of diasporic citizens. In toto, this article potently suggests that diasporic identities not only involve gender and class as well as exchange and process, but those imaginings of belonging invoke both exclusion and inclusion.

And finally, the issue ends with an essay by Patrick Manning on how to locate electronic research materials on gender and the Diaspora. In the interest of encouraging further research, Manning's article highlights many new and innovative resources for scholars across many disciplines interested in the topics. Manning draws our attention to the 'digital divide' as he underscores the significance of 'language of presentation' in the very dissemination of electronically stored information, research and primary documents.[19] While much of the research materials are still located in archives, increasingly, the World Wide Web is opening up new possibilities that will undoubtedly contribute tremendously to the growth and development of the field. Manning's essay is therefore a fitting conclusion to this particular volume, one that highlights the vivacity, complexity, interdisciplinarity and growth of scholarship on African-descended peoples as it underscores myriad ways in which the nexus of gender and sexuality has shaped – and continues to impact on – diasporic histories and communities.

Notes

The authors extend special thanks to editorial administrator Kristin McGuire and to all of the reviewers who read essays for this volume.

1. Letter to John Thornton, 29, March 1774, reprinted in *Phillis Wheatley: Collected Writings*, ed. Vincent Carretta (Penguin, 2001), p. 156. In the same volume see also Wheatley's letter to the Rev. Samuel Hopkins, 9 February 1774, *Collected Writings*, pp. 151–2.
2. Marsha Watson, 'A Classic Case: Phillis Wheatley and her Poetry', *Early American Literature* 31 (1996), pp. 103–32.
3. Earl Lewis, 'To Turn as on a Pivot: Writing African Americans into a History of Overlapping Diasporas', *American Historical Review* 100 (1995), pp. 765–87.
4. Tiffany Ruby Patterson and Robin Kelley, 'Unfinished Migrations: Reflections on the African Diaspora and the Making of the Modern World', *African Studies Review* 43 (2000), pp. 13–14. See also Deborah Gray White, '"Yes," There is a Black Atlantic', *Itinerario* 23 (1999), pp. 127–40; Karen J. Winkler, 'Historians Explore Questions of How People and Cultures Disperse Across the Globe', *Chronicle of Higher Education*, 22 January 1999, pp. A11–12; Brent Hayes Edwards, 'The Uses of *Diaspora*', *Social Text* 66 (2001), pp. 45–73; Kristin Mann, 'Shifting Paradigms in the Study of the African Diaspora and of Atlantic History and Culture', *Slavery & Abolition* 22 (2001), pp. 3–21; Jana Evans Braziel and Anita Mannur (eds), *Theorizing Diaspora: A Reader* (Oxford: Blackwell Publishing, 2003); and Khalid Koser (ed.), *New African Diasporas* (London: Routledge, 2003). A fascinating take on migration and dispersal may be found in Donna R. Gabaccia, 'Is Everywhere Nowhere?: Nomads, Nations, and The Immigrant Paradigm of United States History', *Journal of American History* 86 (3), pp. 1115–34.
5. For example see St. Clair Drake, 'Negro American and the Africa Interest', in *The American Negro Reference Book*, ed. John P. Davis (Englewood Cliffs, NJ: Prentice Hall, 1966), pp. 662–705 and 'Diaspora Studies and Pan-Africanism', in *Global Dimensions of the African Diaspora*, ed. Joseph E. Harris (Washington, DC: Howard University Press, 1982), pp. 451–514; George Shepperson, 'Notes on Negro American Influences on the Emergence of African Nationalism', *Journal of African History* 1 (1960), pp. 299–312, and 'African Diaspora: Concept and Context', in *Global Dimensions of the African Diaspora*, pp. 41–9.
6. Melville Herskovits, *The Myth of the Negro Past* (Beacon Press, 1941).
7. While this is not the place for an exhaustive bibliography, here are a few key texts: Margaret Washington Creel, *A Peculiar People: Slave Religion and Community Culture Among the Gullahs* (New York University Press, 1988); Joseph E. Holloway (ed.), *Africanisms in American Culture* (Indiana University Press, 1990); Gwendolyn Midlo Hall, *Africans in Colonial Louisiana: The Development of Afro-Creole Society in the Eighteenth Century* (Louisiana State University Press, 1992); Michael Mullin, *Africa in America: Slave*

Acculturation and Resistance in the American South and the British Caribbean, 1736–1831 (University of Illinois Press, 1992); Mavis Campbell, *Back To Africa: George Ross and the Maroons: From Nova Scotia to Sierra Leone* (Africa World Press, 1992); Sidney J. Lemelle and Robin D. G. Kelley (eds), *Imagining Home: Class, Culture and Nationalism in the African Diaspora* (Verso, 1994); Mary Turner (ed.), *From Chattel Slaves to Wage Slaves: The Dynamics of Labour Bargaining in the Americas* (James Curry, 1995); Darlene Clark Hine and David Barry Gaspar (eds), *More than Chattel: Black Women and Slavery in the Americas* (Indiana University Press, 1996); Darlene Clarke Hine and Jacqueline McLeod (eds), *Crossing Boundaries: Comparative History of Black People in Diaspora* (Indiana University Press, 1999); Lamin Sanneh, *Abolitionists Abroad: American Blacks and the Making of Modern West Africa* (Harvard University Press, 1999); Joanna Brooks and John Saillant (eds), *'Face Zion Forward': First Writers of the Black Atlantic, 1785–1798* (Northeastern University Press, 2002).

8. The following texts are but a few examples: Gina Dent, *Black Popular Culture*, A Project by Michele Wallace (Bay Press, 1992); Tricia Rose, *Black Noise: Rap Music and Black Culture in Contemporary America* (Wesleyan University Press, 1994); The Black Public Sphere Collective, *The Black Public Sphere: A Public Culture Book* (University of Chicago Press, 1995); Penny Von Eschen, *Race Against Empire: Black Americans and Anticolonialism, 1937–1957* (Cornell University Press, 1997); Michael Gomez, *Exchanging Our Country Marks: The Transformation of African Identities in the Colonial and Antebellum South* (University of North Carolina, 1998); Shane White and Graham White, *Stylin': African American Expressive Culture from Its Beginnings to the Zoot Suit* (Cornell University Press, 1998); and Monique Guillory and Richard C. Green (eds), *Soul: Black Power, Politics, and Pleasure* (New York University Press, 1998). Note as well the number of special journal issues, for example 'Transcending Traditions', special issue of *Black Scholar* 30 (2000); 'Africa's Diaspora', special issue of *African Studies Review* 43 (2000); 'Transnational Black Studies and Beyond', special issue of *Radical History Review* 87 (2003).

9. Paul Gilroy, *The Black Atlantic: Modernity and Double Consciousness* (Harvard University Press, 1993). Key examples of transnational scholarship include: Michael Confino, 'Servage Russe, Esclavage Américain (Note Critique)', *Annales: Économies, Sociétés, Civilisations* 45 (1990), pp. 1119–41; James Clifford, 'Diasporas', *Routes: Travel and Translation in the Late Twentieth Century* (Harvard University Press, 1997), pp. 244–77; Michel S. Laguerre, *Diasporic Citizenship: Haitian Americans in Transnational America* (St. Martin's Press, 1998); Lisa Brock and Digna Castaneda Fuertes (eds), *Between Race and Empire: African-Americans and Cubans before the Cuban Revolution* (Temple University Press, 1998); Winston James, *Holding Aloft the Banner of Ethiopia: Caribbean Radicalism in Early Twentieth-Century America* (Verso, 1998); Peter Linebaugh and Marcus Rediker, *The Many-Headed Hydra: Sailors, Slaves, Commoners, and the Hidden History of the Revolutionary Atlantic* (Beacon Press, 2000); Douglas B. Chambers, 'Ethnicity in the Diaspora: The Slave-Trade and the Creation of African "Nations" in the Americas', *Slavery & Abolition* 22 (2001), pp. 25–39; Brent Hayes Edwards, *The Practice of Diaspora: Literature, Translation, and the Rise of Black Internationalism* (Harvard University Press, 2003); Kim D. Butler, 'Africa in the Reinvention of Nineteenth-Century Afro-Bahian Identity', *Slavery & Abolition* 22 (2001), pp. 135–154.

10. For example, see Joseph Harris, *The African Presence in Asia: Consequences of the East African Slave Trade* (Northwestern University Press, 1971); Denise Helly, *Idéologie et ethnicité: Les Chinois Macao à Cuba, 1847–1886* (Les Presses de l'Université de Montréal, 1979) Allison Blakely, *Russia and the Negro: Blacks in Russian History and Thought* (Howard University Press, 1986), and also his *Blacks in the Dutch World: The Evolution of Racial Imagery in A Modern Society* (Indiana University Press, 1993); José Baltar Rodríguez, *Los Chinos de Cuba: Apuntes etnográphicos* (Fundacíon Fernando Ortiz, 1997); Madhavi Kale, *Fragments of Empire: Capital, Slavery, and Indian Indentured Labor Migration in the British Caribbean* (University of Pennsylvania Press, 1998); John O. Hunwick, 'Black Slaves in the Mediterranean World: Introduction to a Neglected Aspect of the African Diaspora', *Slavery & Abolition* 22 (2001), pp. 25–39; Eric Louw and Gary Mersham, 'Packing for Perth: The

Growth of a Southern African Diaspora', *Asian & Pacific Migration Journal* 10 (2001), pp. 303–33; Eve Troutt Powell and John O. Hunwick (eds), *The African Diaspora in the Mediterranean Lands of Islam* (Markus Wiener Publishers, 2002); Tina Campt, 'The Crowded Space of Diaspora: Intercultural Address and the Tensions of Diasporic Relations', *Radical History Review* 83 (2002), pp. 94–113; Herman L. Bennett, *Africans in Colonial Mexico: Absolutism, Christianity, and Afro-Creole Consciousness, 1570–1640* (Indiana University Press, 2003).

11. For a useful meditation see Richard Roberts, 'The Construction of Cultures in Diaspora: African and African New World Experiences', *South Atlantic Quarterly* 98 (1999), pp. 177–90. See also Linda Heywood (ed.), *Central Africans and Cultural Transformations in the American Diaspora* (Cambridge University Press, 2001).

12. Adelaide M. Cromwell, *An African Victorian Feminist: The Life and Times of Adelaide Smith Casely Hayford, 1868–1960* (Howard University Press, 1992); Barbara Bush, *Slave Women in Caribbean Society, 1650–1838* (Indiana University Press, 1990); Barbara Bair, 'Pan-Africanism as Process: Adelaide Casely Hayford, Garveyism, and the Cultural Roots of Nationalism' in *Imagining Home: Class, Culture and Nationalism*, ed. Lemelle and Kelley, pp. 121–44; Verene Shepherd, Bridget Brereton and Barbara Bailey (eds), *Engendering History: Caribbean Women in Historical Perspective* (St. Martin's Press, 1995); Beryl Satter, 'Marcus Garvey, Father Divine and the Gender Politics of Race Difference and Race Neutrality', *American Quarterly* 48 (1996), pp. 43–76; Hilary McD. Beckles, *Centering Woman: Gender Discourses in Caribbean Slave Society* (1999); Rosalyn Terborg Penn, 'Free Women Entrepreneurs form the 1820s to the 1850s: The Cases of Nancy Prince and Mary Seacole', *Crossing Boundaries*, ed. Cline and McLeod, pp. 159–75; Faith Smith, *Creole Recitations: John Jacob Thomas and Colonial Formation in the Late Nineteenth-Century Caribbean* (University of Virginia Press, 2002); Jenny Sharpe, *Ghosts of Slavery: A Literary Archaeology of Black Women's Lives* (University of Minnesota Press, 2003).

13. Filomina Chioma Steady (ed.), *The Black Woman Cross-Culturally* (Schenkman Publishing Company, Inc., 1981), 1. For revealing analysis of different schools within anthropology, see Micaela di Leonardo, 'Gender, Culture, and Political Economy: Feminist Anthropology in Historical Perspective', in di Leonardo (ed.) *Gender at the Crossroads of Knowledge: Feminist Anthropology in the Postmodern Era* (University of California Press, c. 1991), pp. 1–48. A classic early ethnography of an African woman is Mary F. Smith's *Baba of Karo* (Philosophical Library, 1955. Reprint. New Haven: Yale University Press, 1981).

14. Again, this is but a sampling of key texts: Nancy J. Hafkin and Edna G. Bay (eds), *Women in Africa: Studies in Social and Economic Change* (Stanford University Press, 1976); Margaret Strobel, *Muslim Women in Mombasa: 1890–1975* (Yale University Press, 1979); Christine Obbo, *African Women: Their Struggle for Economic Independence* (Zed Press, 1980); Christine Oppong (ed.), *Female and Male in West Africa* (Allen & Unwin, 1983); Karen Sacks, 'An Overview of Women and Power in Africa', *Perspectives on Power: Women in Africa, Asia, and Latin America*, ed. Jean O'Barr (Duke University Center for International Studies, 1982); Margaret Jean Hay and Sharon Stichter (eds), *African Women South of the Sahara* (Longman, 1984); Muthoni Likamani, *Passbook Number F.47927: Women and Mau Mau in Kenya* (Macmillan, c. 1985); Claire Robertson and Iris Berger (eds), *Women and Class in Africa* (Africana Publishing Company, 1986); Rosalyn Terborg-Penn, Sharon Harley and Andrea Benton Rushing (eds), *Women in Africa and the African Diaspora* (Howard University Press, 1987).

15. Cherryl Walker, *Women and Resistance in South Africa* (Onyx Press, 1982); Tabitha Kanogo, 'Kikuyu Women and the Politics of Protest: Mau Mau', in *Images of Women in Peace and War: Cross-Cultural and Historical Perspectives*, ed. Sharon MacDonald, Pat Holden and Shirley Ardener (Houndmills: Macmillan, 1987), pp. 78–99; Patricia W. Romero (ed.), *Life Histories of African Women* (The Ashfield Press, Ltd., 1988); Nancy Rose Hunt, 'Placing African Women's History and Locating Gender', *Social History* 14 (1989), pp. 359–79; Shula Marks, 'Patriotism, Patriarchy, and Purity: Natal and the Politics of Zulu Ethnic Consciousness', in *The Creation of Tribalism in Southern Africa*, ed. Leroy Vail (Berkeley:

University of California Press, 1989), pp. 215–40; Cherryl Walker (ed.), *Women and Gender in Southern Africa to 1945* (D. Philip, 1990); Luise White, *The Comforts of Home: Prostitution in Colonial Nairobi* (University of Chicago Press, 1990); Belinda Bozzoli with Mmantho Nkotsoe, *Women of Phokeng: Consciousness, Life Strategy, and Migrancy in South Africa, 1900–1983* (Heinemann, 1991); Verena Stolcke, *Coffee Planters, Workers and Wives: Class Conflict and Gender Relations on São Paulo Plantations, 1850–1980* (Macmillan Press in association with St. Antony's College, Oxford, 1988); Kenda Mutongi, '"Dear Dolly's" Advice: Representations of Youth, Courtship, and Sexualities in Africa, 1960–1980', *International Journal of African Historical Studies* 33 (2000), pp. 1–23; Mieko Nishida, *Slavery & Identity: Ethnicity, Gender, & Race in Salvador, Brazil, 1808–1888* (Indiana University Press, 2003) and Martha Abreu, *O império do divino: Festas religiosas e cultura popular no Rio de Janeiro, 1830–1900* (Nova Fronteira, 1999); Critical anthologies and special journal issues include: Robert Morrell (ed.), 'Masculinities in Southern Africa', special issue of *Journal of Southern African Studies* 24 (1998); Jean Allman, Susan Geiger, and Nakanyike Musisi (eds), *Women in African Colonial Histories* (Indiana University Press, 2002); Lisa A. Lindsay and Stephan F. Miescher (eds), *Men and Masculinities in Modern Africa* (Portsmouth, NH: Heinemann, 2003); Daniel Balderston and Donna J. Guy (eds), *Sex and Sexuality in Latin America* (New York University Press, 1997); and Gilbert M. Joseph (ed.), 'Gender and Sexuality in Latin America', special issue of *Hispanic American Historical Review* 81 (2001).

Work that explores the reproduction of nations and nationalism includes: Ada Ferrer, 'Rustic Men, Civilized Nation: Race, Culture, and Contention on the Eve of Cuban Independence', *Hispanic American Historical Review* 78 (1998), pp. 663–86; Eileen Suárez Findlay, *Imposing Decency: Race & Sexuality in Puerto Rico, 1870–1920* (Duke University Press, 1999); Alejandro de la Fuente, *A Nation for All: Race, Inequality, & Politics in Twentieth-Century Cuba* (University of North Carolina Press, 2001); Fernando Martínez Heredia (trans. Lara Putnam), 'Nationalism, Races, and Classes in the Revolution of 1895 and the Cuban First Republic', *Cuban Studies* 33 (2002), pp. 95–123; Nancy P. Appelbaum, Anne S. Macpherson, and Karin Alejandra Rosemblatt (eds), *Race & Nation in Modern Latin America* (University of North Carolina Press, 2003).

Analyses of diasporan communities and law may be found in the following: Margaret Jean Hay and Marcia Wright, eds., *African Women and the Law: Historical Perspectives* (Boston University African Studies Center, 1982); Takyiwaa Manuh, 'The Asantehemaa's Court and its Jurisdiction over Women: A Study in Legal Pluralism', *Research Review* 4 (1988); Keila Grinberg, *Liberata: a lei da ambigüidade. As ações de liberdade da Corte de Apelação do Rio de Janeiro, século XIX* (Relume-Dumará, 1994); Sueann Caulfield, *In Defense of Honor: Sexual Morality, Modernity and Nation in Early-Twentieth-Century Brazil* (Duke University Press, 2000).

16. Important examples include: Gertrude Jacinta Fraser, *African American Midwifery in the South: Dialogues of Birth, Race, and Memory* (Harvard University Press, 1998); Sharla M. Fett, *Working Cures: Healing, Health, and Power on Southern Slave Plantations* (University of North Carolina Press, 2002); Tera W. Hunter, '"Work that Body": African-American Women, Work, and Leisure in Atlanta and the New South', in Eric Arnesen, Julie Green and Bruce Laurie (eds), *Labor Histories: Class, Politics and the Working-Class Experience* (University of Illinois Press, 1998), pp. 153–74; Stephanie M. H. Camp, 'The Pleasures of Resistance: Enslaved Women and Body Politics in the Plantation South, 1830–1861', *Journal of Southern History* 67 (2002), pp. 533–72; see also Lilia Moritz Schwarcz, *O espetáculo das raças: Cientistas, instituções e questão racial no Brasil, 1870–1930* (Companhia das Letras, 1993); Sidney Chaloub, *Cidade febril: Cortiços e epidemias na Corte imperial* (Companhia das Letras, 1996).

Scholarship on resistance outside of North America includes: John Dumoulin, *Azúcar y lucha de clases: 1917* (Editorial de Ciencias Sociales, 1980); Mário José Maestri Filho, 'A Propos du "Quilombo": Esclavage et Luttes Sociales au Brésil', *Genève-Afrique* 22 (1984), pp. 7–31; Tomás Fernández Robaina, *El negro en Cuba, 1902–1958. Apuntes para la historia de la lucha contra la discriminación racial en la neocolonia* (Editorial de Ciencias

Sociales, 1990); Jocélio Teles dos Santos, 'Nação Mestiça: Discoursos e Praticas Oficias sobre os Afro-Brasileiros', *Luso-Brazilian Review* 36 (1999), pp. 19–31; João José Reis, 'Candomblé in Nineteenth-Century Bahia: Priests, Followers, Clients', *Slavery & Abolition* 22 (2001), pp. 116–34; Maya Talmon Chvalcer, 'The Criminalization of Capoeira in Nineteenth-Century Brazil', *Hispanic American Historical Review* 82 (2002), pp. 525–47. For a different take on the interaction between institutions of religion and slavery, see Philippe Delisle, 'Église et Esclavage dans les Vieilles Colonies Françaises au XIX Siècle', *Revue d'Histoire de l'Église de France* 84 (1998), pp. 55–70.

17. An invaluable source on post-emancipation societies (with exception of the Francophone Caribbean) is Rebecca J. Scott, Thomas C. Holt, Frederick Cooper, and Aims McGuinness (eds) *Societies after Slavery: A Select Annotated Bibliography of Printed Sources on Cuba, Brazil, British Colonial Africa, South Africa, and the British West Indies* (University of Pittsburgh Press, 2002).

18. Stuart Hall, 'Cultural Identity and Cinematic Representation' (1989), reprinted in *Black Cultural Studies: A Reader*, ed. Houston A. Baker, Jr., Manthia Diawara and Ruth H. Lindeborg (University of Chicago Press, 1996), pp. 210–22; Valerie Smith (ed.), *Representing Blackness: Issues in Film and Video* (Rutgers University Press, 1997); Tommy L. Lott, *The Invention of Race: Black Culture and the Politics of Representation* (Blackwell, 1999); Nicholas Mirzoeff, ed., *Diaspora and Visual Culture: Representing Africans and Jews* (Routledge, 2000); and Marcus Wood, *Blind Memory: Visual Representations of Slavery in England and America, 1780–1865* (Routledge, 2000). For discussion of a range of media within visual anthropology, see Leslie Devereaux and Roger Hillman (eds) *Fields of Vision: Essays in Film Studies, Visual Anthropology, and Photography* (University of California Press, 1995).

19. A decidedly different take on technology, 'future texts', and African diasporas is Alondra Nelson's 'Introduction: Future Texts', *Social Text* 20 (2002), special issue on 'Afrofuturism', pp. 1–15.

2

Gendered Agendas:
The Secrets Scholars Keep
about Yorùbá-Atlantic Religion

J. Lorand Matory

The secret makes the sacred in the religions of the Yorùbá Atlantic. Writes Karin Barber,

> It is by being made into a 'secret' [*awo*] that a spirit being gets its authority. It has been said, '... if we put a stone in a gourd and make a couple of taboos to stop people from looking into it, it's become an *awo* ...' Human collusion to keep the 'secret' endows the object with spiritual power: perhaps what the secret really comes down to in the end is the open secret that gods are made by men'.[1]

This essay concerns the role of scholars in making the secrets of the sacred, and, indeed, in remaking the boundaries and the internal hierarchies of the communities fashioned to guard those secrets.

Nation states too create boundaries and hierarchies around secrets. I am speaking not of national security secrets but of the everyday acts of dissimulation by which imagined communities energise their boundaries with popular emotional support. Nation states selectively identify certain practices and symbols of the national community as normative and define certain other commonplace behaviours and symbols as non-existent, for fear that they might reduce the nation in the eyes of powerful foreign observers.[2] Thus Michael Herzfeld describes what he calls 'cultural intimacy' – a sensibility that encourages state élites to propagate official visions of the nation state that exclude embarrassing aspects of national cultural life, even though these aspects of life are the focus of family feeling within the nation and the focus of many people's emotional loyalty to the national community and its state representatives.[3] In other words, the spokespersons of the nation state have an image to protect in the court of international public opinion and ideological priorities at odds with both popular consciousness and the inevitable cultural heterogeneity of the nation. Thus, I might add, 'cultural intimacy' sets up a *hierarchy* within the group con-stituted by the secret: some members' practices are normalised, while other members' practices are branded abnormal, shameful and best kept invisible. The bearers of normalised practices assert the right to speak for the group, while everyone else is reduced to silence.

The West African tradition of *òrìṣà*-worship is one among multiple religions around the Atlantic perimeter that share historical roots among the eighteenth-century ancestors of the Yorùbá. Cuban Ocha, Trindidadian Shango and the Brazilian religions of Umbanda, Xangô and Candomblé came about through the nineteenth-century dispersion of enslaved Òyọ́, Ègbá, Ijèṣà and Ègbádò people and others from West Africa, as well as the ongoing circuit of commerce, pilgrimage, books and scholarly debate that have, since then, continuously linked West Africa with its sons and daughters in the Americas.[4] In particular, Candomblé is a religion of divination, blood sacrifice, spirit possession and healing that came about chiefly in the Brazilian state of Bahia. Believers attribute miraculous powers and exemplary flaws to gods known as *orixás*, *voduns*, *inquices* and *caboclos*, depending upon the Candomblé denomination. The adventures, person-alities and kinship relations of these beings are described in an extensive mythology and body of oracular wisdom, which also serve to explain the personalities and fates of their worshipers, as well as the worldly relations among those worshipers. Through blood sacrifice and lavish ceremonies of spirit possession, the gods are persuaded to intervene beneficently in the lives of their worshipers and to keep the foes of those worshipers at bay. The priests and practitioners, no less than the social scientists and politicians who seek to speak for them, tend to emphasise the ancientness of Candomblé and its constituent 'traditions'.

In this essay, however, I document a series of international dialogues – involving Afro-Brazilian priests alongside state officials and an international community of scholars – in the absence of which the massive changes in the gendered leadership of this religion over the course of the twentieth century would have been difficult to explain. Indeed, I will argue that the Candomblé religion owes not only much of its international fame but also the internal transformation of its leadership to Ruth Landes's 1947 *City of Women*, in which she offers Candomblé as a living and time-honoured example of matriarchy, available to inspire the opponents of sexism in her own native society, the United States. Yet Landes's international exposé was so influential precisely because Candomblé has been a convenient template for other scholarly and political agendas as well, ranging from Gilberto Freyre and Édison Carneiro's 'Regionalist' nationalism to Melville J. Herskovits' effort to redeem African Americans from the myth that they are cultureless and therefore inferior to whites and Oyeronkẹ Oyewumi's diasporic Yorùbá nationalism. This international array of scholarly agendas has shifted not only the reputation but also the practice of *orișa* worship in the diaspora. Since the 1930s, a series of scholarly conferences uniting scholars and priests has made it increasingly important for us to acknowledge the role of scholars' interventions and cover-ups in the ongoing transformation of the Yorùbá-Atlantic religions.

Not only scholars but also political leaders of local or international standing have presented Candomblé as a metonym of the imagined communities they would invoke and lead.[5] Yet the realities of Candomblé in some respects resist the agendas and normative dispositions of these imagined communities, especially those of the nation state and of those who fear its judgement. For example, a silent touchstone in the trans-national debates over the meaning of Candomblé and the communities it authenticates is a cultural persona who is as normal in the Candomblé priesthood as he is anathema to the normative vision of the nation state – the *adé*, or 'passive homosexual'.

The *adé* priest, like his counterparts in the African-inspired religions of Cuba and Haiti, is regarded as normal and eminently respectable by most devotees but has, since the 1930s, been summarily dismissed by an alliance of nationalist and feminist scholars as either 'untraditional' or non-existent. Yet this essay is not intended simply to correct what I believe is a wrongheaded scholarship but to observe the role of national and international scholars in canonising and, consequently, in biasing the reproduction of what are widely regarded as unchanging 'traditional' religions.

'The City of Women'

Ruth Landes became a great foremother of feminist anthropology by underlining the unique status accorded to women in Candomblé. Landes's feminism was transnational. She stands in a long line of twentieth-century travellers – including Margaret Mead and Simone de Beauvoir – who either found hope in international dialogue and cooperation among women or found in the women of other societies ideal models (and anti-types) of their own oppressed compatriots' liberation. Landes's 1947 title, *The City of Women*, advanced the opinion that, by tradition, women were uniquely suited to serve the Yorùbá, or Nagô, gods of Brazil. Besides the 'Nagô nation' (which is nowadays also called the 'Quêto' nation, or denomination), there were other nations in the Candomblé of Landes's day, and they endure into the present – for example, the Fon-inspired 'Jeje nation,' the 'Angola nation,' and the ever-expanding body of clergy worshiping the Indian, or *caboclo*, spirits. Landes added her voice to an ongoing tradition of privileging the Quêto/Nagô nation in particular, on the grounds of its alleged African purity and, therefore, its unique authenticity. Landes added the claim that the Quêto/Nagô nation accorded priestly leadership exclusively to women. Thus, for Landes and her many North American fans, the Quêto/Nagô Candomblé of Salvador, Bahia, has inspired great hope as a shining example of female dominance in the real world. For this reason, she named Candomblé and its major host city 'the City of Women'.

However, Landes's research embarrassed Euro-Brazilian nationalists for two reasons – race and sexuality. First, in a country ambivalent about its demographic and cultural blackness, she studied Candomblé. Yet, as a student of anthropologist and cultural relativist Franz Boas, she studied Afro-Brazilian religion not as a racial flaw to be hidden but as proof of the richness of a transnational African legacy and, more importantly, of the potential for women's equality elsewhere in the world. The final two paragraphs of the book summarise how Landes saw her own relationship to the guardians of Brazil's international reputation:

> When I left Rio for the United States, Brazilian friends escorted me to the boat, and one of them said, half teasing but with a certain defiant patriotism, 'Now you can tell them that no tigers walk in our streets.'

> I nodded, and added: 'I'll tell them also about the women … Will Americans believe that there is a country where women like men, feel secure and at ease with them, and do not fear them?'.[6]

In her study of Candomblé in Brazil, a country that she knew to be highly sexist, she felt that she had found evidence of what she called a 'cult matriarchate,' in which women ruled in the religious affairs, and therefore the most important affairs, of blacks in the Brazilian state of Bahia.[7] Arguably, however, Landes had tampered with the evidence and assumed that her audience was too far away to inspect it. Indeed, argues Healey, she had constructed a primitivist cliché.[8] In her search for the antipodes, for a primordial alternative to the lamented condition of her home audience and herself, she had created an other-worldly Bahia, of which she declared, 'I know by now that women are [in Bahia] the chosen sex … I take it for granted just as I know in our world that men are the chosen sex'.[9] Yet, like Margaret Mead in Samoa, Landes had silenced or distorted a great deal of the evidence at her disposal.[10] For example, in order to account for the significant number of men leading Candomblé temples at the time of her visit, she claimed that, no matter how numerous they might be, they did not count, because they were violating 'African tradition' due to their own personal psychological problems and due to the ritual laxity of the women who had, according to Landes, only recently begun to initiate them.

Landes associated this alleged laxity chiefly with a variant of the Nagô religion in which Indian spirits, or *caboclos*, were also worshiped prominently. But given the fact that a priestess of the Nagô nation is credited with having founded the *caboclo* cult,[11] that the Nagô *orixás* remained pre-eminent even in the *caboclo*-worshiping houses,[12] and that virtually every Nagô temple also worshiped the *caboclos*,[13] the categorical separation that Landes drew between the female-dominated 'Nagô' temples and the male-dominated '*caboclo*' temples seems suspiciously *a priori* and inconsistent with the self-declarations of the temple leaders.[14]

In fact, across all nations, including the supposedly traditionalist Nagô and Jeje nations, male leadership in the Candomblé had been an old phenomenon. Throughout the nineteenth century, men significantly outnumbered women in the Bahian Candomblé priesthood generally, and men were common in the priesthood of the supposedly all-female priesthood of the Nagô and Jeje nations as well. Indeed, the increase in *female* leadership was the more recent phenomenon.[15] Butler believes that a tradition of exclusively female temple leadership began in the Casa Branca, or the Ilê Iyá Nassô, temple, in the mid-nineteenth century (which, one might add, is relatively late in the documented history of Jeje and Nagô religious activity in Brazil) and that the tradition spread due to the fast-growing prestige of that particular temple among scholars and bourgeois élite sponsors.[16] Yet, as we shall see, the evidence of an exclusively female leadership – statistically or in principle – is ambiguous even in Casa Branca and its scions before 1930s.

In the 1930s, male priests still significantly outnumbered female priests.[17] Nonetheless, since the publication of Landes's work,[18] the scholarly advocates of Jeje and Nagô superiority have come to speak with one voice on the matter: in the Candomblé priesthood generally, 'women are the chosen sex'. Fortunately for subsequent students of Candomblé, she and her companion Édison Carneiro recorded, albeit dismissively, copious evidence against their own interpretive models. Yet Landes's interpretive model clearly changed the minds and conduct of Candomblé's leading bourgeois advocates and, consequently, the conditions of that religion's reproduction in Brazilian society.

Grounds for dismissal: the nation state against the *adé*

Besides truth, the greatest casualty in this struggle for the possession of the sign was the *adé* – anti-hero to the territorial nation and to Landes's 'cult matriarchy' alike.[19] In the just cause of women's liberation, Landes played with the facts and canonised the view that women were accorded a unique status in this religion. The credibility of Landes's novel assertion that Candomblé is a matriarchy, despite demographic and historical facts to the contrary, relied on the vilification of the *adé*.

Landes's argument of images harmonised with the transnationally exported logics of North American and European nationalisms. As George

Mosse shows, homophobia is a common adjunct of nationalism.[20] In Landes's appeal to a counterfactual nostalgia equally typical of national-isms, she dismissed the male presence as the result of a recent corruption. As if to confirm that the male presence was recent and non-normative, Landes reported the widespread view that all male possession priests were *adés*, or, in Landes's medico-pathological parlance, 'passive homosexuals' – that is, men who are penetrated during sexual intercourse. Thus, without reference to any indigenous discourse, Landes inaugurated the scholarly tradition of diagnosing male Candomblé priests as diseased and therefore alien to any legitimate cultural tradition.[21] However, as Landes herself reported, the *adés' sexual* identity seems not to have troubled the other priests or adherents of Candomblé. As priests, these men were, observed Landes, 'supported and even adored by those normal men of whom they were before the butt and object of derision'.[22]

Landes's revelation of these sexual matters particularly discomfited her Brazilian scholarly colleagues, even those who would have been perfectly happy for her to write about the demographic and cultural importance of black people in Brazil. These colleagues were clearly more attuned to transnational standards of national respectability and more concerned to guard the open secrets of the Brazilian nation than were the priests and subjects of Candomblé's sacred nations. Sometime Brazilian state functionary and culture-broker extraordinaire Arthur Ramos flatly denied Landes's claims about a 'cult matriarchate' and about a significant homosexual presence, and, in retaliation for Landes's divulgence, he cooperated with Melville J. Herskovits in foreclosing future professional opportunities to Landes. Landes blamed Ramos' anger over her specific revelation of 'homosexuality' for a significant part of her professional undoing.[23]

Though Carneiro had started out as Landes's guide, his attitudes, or at least his public discourse, about the male Candomblé possession priest changed remarkably over the course of his dialogue with Landes. In 1936, before Landes's sojourn in Bahia, Carneiro wrote of the possession priests:

> In Bahia, those priestesses are called daughters-in-saint. In the olden days (and even still today), the men could be sons-in-saint too. It is noteworthy that they had to dance, during the grand festivals, wearing women's clothing.[24]

Throughout his 1936 publication, he casually describes male and female possession priests engaged in the same ritual duties, doing so with equal legitimacy and with equal deference from the public.

In the midst of his professional and personal relationship with Landes, he is at first quoted expressing a subtly different range of ideas and feelings, which appear to entitle 'abnormal' men to a respected and beautiful role in the possession priesthood. Yet, apparently embarrassed by the pathologising gaze of this powerful transnational visitor, Carneiro would, within a few years correct his earlier position and end all equivocation.

We cannot say with certainty whether his was a true change of heart or a façade thrown up against a critical foreign gaze, but the fact that he presents his first full about-face in the Anglo-American *Journal of American Folk-Lore*, and an article paired with one by Ruth Landes leaves little doubt about the motive and the origin of this change. Over the course of their acquaintance, Landes seems to have changed Carneiro's mind, or at least made him answer to a homophobic transnational culture of national respectability. Having declared in 1936 to a Brazilian reading public that the male possession priesthood had originated in 'the olden days' and even continued today, Carneiro chose later to tell the US reading public,

> It seems that formerly the *candomblé* was a woman's business ... The ascendancy of women dates from the introduction of the *candomblés* in Bahia, with the establishment of the Nagô house of [Casa Branca do] Engenho Velho about 1830 ... As against so many 'mothers,' we know of the existence of only a few 'fathers,' like Bambuxê and 'Uncle' Joaquim ... Despite the superior importance of women in *candomblé*, today the number of 'fathers' and 'mothers' is equal.[25]

Thus Carneiro had literally reversed the course of history. This English-language publication is also the first in which Carneiro systematically lambastes the male possession priests, condemning them for 'giving themselves up to homosexuality, where they take the passive role, dropping into the small gossip typical of lower-class women'. Of Bahian public opinion toward the 'homosexual' priests, Carneiro tells the USA, 'criticism is always more venomous about "fathers" than about "mothers", labelling them insincere, dishonest, and evil'.[26] His condemnation even exceeds that of Landes, who, as we have seen, acknowledges the support and admiration that 'passive' male possession priests receive from 'normal men'.[27]

To summarise, in 1936, Carneiro wrote of male priests as normal. In their early dialogue during the late 1930s, Landes quoted Carneiro voicing admiration for the beauty of the 'abnormal' male homosexual priests and the liveliness of *caboclo*-worship. It was first in 1940, before a US audience, that Carneiro would excommunicate these men from the authentic regional and national folklore. By 1948, in a publication for the Museum of the State of Bahia, he was prepared to denounce the male priesthood before the Brazilian national public.

He did so in *Candomblés da Bahia* (1948), a decade after their collaboration had begun and after Landes's two major publications on the subject, in 1940 and 1947. With his region and his religious friends under the spotlight of international scrutiny, Carneiro moved to rescue the reputation of the supposedly *authentic* Candomblé with the unsubstantiated claim that the Candomblé priesthood had once been exclusively female. Following Landes, he established the canonical view in Brazilian and Brazilianist folklore studies, and even in the historical consciousness of many priestly élites, that male priests are uniquely disreputable, that their numerical predominance is recent, and, therefore, that they are unrepresentative of the authentic folklore of the Northeastern region and of the Brazilian nation. Carneiro added that these allegedly new male priests belonged to what he considered the least representative and respectable of Candomblé nations – the Angola, Congo and Caboclo nations.[28]

Carneiro had a special stake in dignifying the West African Nagô and Jeje nations and in guarding them from derogation by the national and transnational public. Carneiro was affiliated with the Northeastern Region-alists, who sought to rescue their region from its reputation as inferior on account of its relative poverty and of its black and mulatto majority. At the turn of the century, state officials inspired by eugenics had invested enormous resources in recruiting European immigrants to whiten the population of the Centre-South state of São Paulo, which had also industrialised itself with the profits of its lucrative and initially slave-based coffee plantations. Advocates of the superseded and underdeveloped Northeast argued that, though their region was poorer and blacker, its blacks and mulattoes were superior (on account of their disproportionately West African Nagô and Jeje origins) to those of the Centre-South (whose origins were mainly West-Central African – e.g. Congo and Angola). A Northeastern mulatto himself, Carneiro had a personal and political stake in doing whatever it took to preserve the dignity of the Nagô and Jeje nations and to make theirs the standard by which the typical folk religion of his region was judged. Thus, nostalgia for the Jeje-Nagô-centered, putatively matriarchal and innocent pre-history of Candomblé came to unite the spokespersons of two imagined communities – Northeastern Regionalist Édison Carneiro and transnational feminist Ruth Landes.

Yet the copious detail in his 1948 volume frequently undermines his own tendentious argument that the Nagô nation is exclusively or in principle matriarchal. For example, Carneiro credits the nineteenth-century African-born priest Bambuxê (Bamgbose) with initiating Aninha, the future chief priestess of the prestigious Ilê Axé Opô Afonjá temple. Aninha's disappoint-ment that another man, Joaquim Vieira, did not succeed the recently deceased chief-priestess of Casa Branca, the mother church of Bahia's pre-eminent family of Quêto/Nagô temples, is given as the reason for Aninha's secession from the Casa Branca temple in the first place and for her role in the founding of Opô Afonjá. Finally, even though the histories recounted nowadays at Opô Afonjá seem to leave no doubt that Aninha founded that temple and was its first chief priest, Carneiro actually reports that the male priest Pai Joaquim had been that temple's first 'chief'.[29] Carneiro documented the esteemed leadership of the Yorùbá/Nagô babalawo diviners Martiniano do Bonfim and Felisberto Sowzer, who are not possession priests. But he also mentions in passing numerous eminent male possession priests of the Jeje and Nagô nations who were alive during his time, such as Eduardo Mangabeira, Procópio, Manuel Falefá, Manuel Menez, Cosme, Antônio Bonfim and Otacílio.[30] Despite all the contrary evidence that he himself recorded, Carneiro's synoptic statements about the 'tradition' seem aimed to satisfy the same partisan notions of respectability that Landes invoked. Not even the most gymnastic and speculative argument was barred in the effort to dismiss the male priests and thereby guarantee the international respectability of an 'authentic' tradition left by their absence.

Landes's transnational feminism and Carneiro's efforts in the Regionalist project thus conspired to keep a secret. Yet Carneiro had not thought of Candomblé's 'passive homosexuals' as much of a secret before 1938. The *adés* first became a secret amid the conflict between North American Ruth Landes and Brazilian academic gatekeeper Arthur Ramos. A close observer of Bahia and a close friend of Landes's, Carneiro could not deny the newly embarrassing reality, as Ramos had done, but he was in a position to marginalise that reality authoritatively. A half-century after the publication of *The City of Women* (1947) and *Candomblés da Bahia* (1948), women have, in fact, now become the majority of the chief priests in this religion.[31]

The cultural logic of 'passivity'

First in 1988 and then at a Yorùbá conference in 1999, I publicly proposed an explanation for the locally perceived normalcy of 'passive homosexuals,' or *adés*, as possession priests and therefore as the heads of Candomblé temples.[32] The debate it engendered demonstrates that Regionalist, nationalist and international feminist communities are not the only ones that are continually transformed, in a cosmopolitan context, by the gaze of other imagined communities and by the nationalist silencing of certain home-grown realities. The African Diaspora too is constituted by certain open secrets, and can be reconstituted by re-selections and re-readings of what secrets need to be defended.

There are no reliable statistics on how many Candomblé priests engage in what Landes called 'passive homosexuality'. Nor does my thesis concern their actual numbers. Rather, I have sought to understand why so many members and cognoscenti of Candomblé assume – with or without statistical accuracy – that male initiates in the possession priesthood are normally *adés*, why many Afro-Brazilian men who love men feel at home in Candomblé, and why Candomblé-inspired terminology dominates the argot of gays all over urban Brazil.

Today there are numerous explanations of *adés'* alleged prominence among Candomblé possession priests. But before we can understand them, we must identify the set of semantic contrasts of which the 'passive homosexual' is a part in Brazil. On the one hand, English-speaking North Americans tend to distinguish sharply between those men who engage in sex with other men ('homosexuals') and those who do not ('heterosexuals'). On the other hand, Brazilians are far more likely to distinguish men who penetrate others during sexual intercourse (*homens*, or '[real] men') from those who are penetrated (*bichas, viados* or, in Candomblé language, *adés*).[33] Brazilians share the basics of this pattern of classification with many peoples around the Mediterranean, as well as much of pre-nineteenth-century Europe, Native America and most of the rest of the world.[34] Contemporary European and Anglo-American prison populations and sailors seem no exception.[35] Even when the Bahians I know use the term 'homosexual', most are referring only to the party in sexual intercourse who is assumed to be habitually penetrated, or 'passive.' Of course, the real behaviour of both *homens* and *bichas*, or *adés*, is regularly more varied than what is stereotypically attributed to them, and the normative assumption that the 'active' party is dominant in the sexual act and in the non-sexual dimensions of the social relationship is often more fantasy than material reality.[36] However, local *ideological* assumptions and expectations tend to link habitual male 'passivity' in sexual intercourse with transvestism, feminine gestures, feminine occupations and the social subordination of the penetrated party.[37]

So why do many Brazilians think there is a connection between the possession priesthood and so-called 'sexual passives'?[38] Peter Fry suggests that the shared classification of male 'passives' and possession cults as 'deviant' makes the priesthood an appropriate niche for homosexuals. Following Victor Turner and Mary Douglas, Fry argues that the homosexuals' *liminal* status in Brazilian national society suits them symbolically, in the Brazilian popular imagination, to professions dealing with 'magical power.'[39] Lima moves in the direction of acknowledging what is *normal* about homosexuality in Candomblé ideology: both Afro-Brazilian religions and Brazilian Kardecist Spiritism, he argues, have shown themselves more generally *tolerant* than the Roman Catholic church.[40] More to the point, Birman reports that men whose heads are governed by female divinities and sex-changing gods – like Iançã, Oxum, Oxumaré and Logunedé – are expected to share in the female dispositions and desires of those gods.[41] Thus, according to Candomblé's indigenous personality theory, the homosexuality of male priests is in their 'natures' (*naturezas*), is derived from 'nature' (*natureza*), and is authorised by the sacred – hence their attraction to and acceptance in Candomblé.

Fry also notes the advantageous flexibility enjoyed by *bichas*, or 'passives,' in the performance of social roles normally reserved, in the wider society, primarily for one sex or the other. That is, they can acceptably do the cooking and embroidering necessary for the temple and yet, in a similar religion in Belém do Pará (where Fry conducted his research), retain the social advantages of men in transactions with the 'world of men' – of police, judges, doctors, lawyers and politicians, 'whose services they themselves may use or broker to clients for their own advantage'.[42] In the Bahian case, men's advantages over the great Nagô mothers in this regard are not so evident. What is more evident, and is observed by Leão Teixeira, is that homosexual men bring to the Candomblé three other advantages over women: (1) the higher average earnings of men and (2) their ritual licence as men to perform all the *ritual* duties normally *restricted* to men, such as the sacrifice of four-legged animals, and the care of the all-important Exú (god of sex, mischief and communication), Ossaim (god of herbal medicine), and the Eguns (ancestral spirits); and (3) men's immunity to the restrictions placed upon menstruating women, such as the prohibition against their entering the shrine rooms.[43] A woman consecrated to a male god is eligible to receive a further initiation (*mão de faca*) that entitles her to sacrifice birds, but, while menstruating, she cannot even do that.[44]

My point is that what Landes called Candomblé's 'cult matriarchate' is not a fact given simply by 'tradition'; nor is it simply a lie. It is a plausible but *interested* and *contested construction* of 'tradition' based upon a cosmopolitan repertoire of precedents and interpretive logics. It is also the product of various imagined communities' fear of outside judgment or pursuit of an ideal model of community for themselves. And despite the pronounced homophobia of many contemporary Third-World bourgeois nationalists (including a number of prominent Anglophone African élites[45]), one would be hard-pressed to locate the pre-colonial, 'traditional' Yorùbá precedents for the homophobia that Landes, Ribeiro and Bastide have presented as psychoanalytic proof of male priests' inferiority. The homophobia that de-normalises *adés*, or 'passives,' in the Candomblé priesthood has its origins not in an aboriginal Africa but in nationalisms and a particular brand of transnational feminism of the mid-twentieth century.

A word of caution before proceeding to the second point: this argument must not be mistaken for the plainly false claim that all transnational feminists or all Brazilian nationalists are homophobic. Such a misreading would misconstrue the nature of imagined communities and their leadership. Demagogues are the most extreme example of leaders who, by making bold, vivid and distinctive pronouncements, capture the imagination of large populations and thereby rearrange people's sense of where the boundaries of the community lie, how its internal hierarchies are arrayed, and what the shared purpose of the community is. However, not even the most capable demagogues win the unanimous agreement or consent of their target populations. Rather, demagogues become centres of gravity in target populations that often have multiple centres of gravity. Gilberto Freyre, Arthur Ramos, Édison Carneiro and Ruth Landes are hardly demagogues, but Freyre, Ramos and Carneiro are important centres of gravity in the Regionalist imagination of the Brazilian national community, just as Landes is an important centre of gravity in the transnational feminist imagination of community. While her homophobia is accidental to the entirely rightful feminist aspiration to gender equality (and, once detected, anathema to the principles of most feminists I know), her particular discursive strategy and the Regionalists' fear of the transnational gaze have deeply compromised the status of the *adé* priest in Northeastern Brazil.

The proliferation of latter-day explanations of the prominence of *adés* in the Brazilian Candomblé, Cuban Ocha and Haitian Vodou priesthoods, and the well-documented history of Candomblé adherents' comfort with *adés* in this role, appear to share a common root. That root is evident between the lines of Landes's informants' testimony in the 1930s and most clearly implied by my own comparative field research between Brazilian Candomblé and its West African 'homeland'. I will argue here, as I have argued elsewhere, that a West African logic of 'mounting' and its attendant transvestism converged in Brazil with a Brazilian logic of sexuality and social hierarchy, thereby helping us to understand why, *in Brazil*, male Candomblé possession priests are widely believed to be *bichas*, *adés* or 'passive homosexuals'.[46] Thus, mine is an argument about the local 'reinterpretation', to borrow Herskovits' term, of cultural forms that appear in diverse but historically connected places.[47] It is, in short, a case study of syncretism, in which the transnational community of scholars is one of the stakeholders in the reinterpretation (and agents in the transformation) of local cultures.

Mounted men: what Nigerian male ẹlẹ́gùn and New-World 'passive' priests do and do not have in common[48]

Ọ̀yọ́-Yorùbá people formed not only a plurality of the African captives taken to Bahia in the nineteenth century but also the founding priests and priestesses of Bahia's most influential temples – including Casa Branca. No African ethnic group has influenced Candomblé more than this Yorùbá subgroup.

In West Africa, Ọ̀yọ́-Yorùbá worshipers employ multiple metaphors to evoke the nature of people's relationships to the gods. Like Brazilian Candomblé adherents, West African Yorùbá worshipers of the òrìṣà gods might call any devotee of a god the 'child' (*ọmọ* [Yorùbá]; *filho* [Portuguese]) of that god. In both traditions, motherhood and fatherhood are used as metaphors of leadership in the worship and activation of the gods. For example, a senior male West African Yorùbá priest of, say, Ṣàngó might be addressed as *Bàbá Oníṣàngó* ('Father [or Senior Male] Owner-of-Ṣàngó'); a senior priestess would be addressed as *Ìyá Oniṣango* ('Mother [or Senior Female] Owner-of-Ṣàngó'). In Brazil, the male head of a Candomblé temple is called a *pai-de-santo* ('father-of-divinity'), while a chief priestess is called a *mãe-de-santo* ('mother-of-divinity').

Yet the Yorùbá terms that mark out the priest's competency to embody the god through possession-trance and to act as the god's worldly delegate rely, above all, upon allied metaphors of marriage and sexuality. According to Édison Carneiro, as we shall see, these metaphors were very much alive in the Brazilian Candomblé of the 1930s, and they were consciously present in local understandings of both male and female participation in the priesthood. In the speech of many twenty-first century Brazilian *orixá*-worshipers these metaphors are now dead or dying. Yet the 'death' of a metaphor seldom means that it has lost its effectiveness in communicative acts; instead, its implications have often become naturalised, implicit and pervasive rather than poetic, novel and conscious. In present-day Brazilian Candomblé, metaphors of marriage and sexuality stand powerfully alongside metaphors of parenthood and birth in the often-contested representation and reproduction of the priesthood.

Most Òyó-Yorùbá possession priests in West Africa are women. The numerous male possession priests, on the other hand, cross-dress. But their cross-dressing requires a culture-specific reading. They dress not as 'women' but as 'wives' or 'brides' (*ìyàwó*) – a term that otherwise refers only to the women married to worldly men. Novices to the priesthood – whether male or female – are designated metaphorically as *ìyàwó*, meaning 'brides' or 'wives'.[49] The degree to which Bahians understand the word *iaô* to mean 'wife' or 'bride' has declined since the 1930s, but the implications of its Yorùbá meaning upon the logic of priestly recruitment have echoed into the third millennium.

For months after the initiation, male and female novices among the West African Òyó-Yorùbá wear women's clothes: *ìró* (wrap skirts), *bùbá* (blouses), and *òjá* (baby-carrying slings); on ceremonial occasions, they also wear *tiro* (antimony eyeliner), *làálì* (henna for the hands and feet), delicate bracelets, earrings and so forth. As mature priests, or *eléégùn*, women and men braid their hair, and follow the latest styles in women's coiffures. But, on ceremonial occasions, they *also* continue to don *tìróò* eyeliner, henna and delicate jewellery. Many uninitiated Yorùbá *women* do these things but, male possession priests are virtually the only men who do so. In the Òyó-Yorùbá town where I conducted my principal West African field research, Ìgbòho, both the strip-weaving of cloth and bar-keeping are considered female professions. So, almost predictably, the only male strip-weaver and the only male bar-keeper in the town are Ṣàngó possession priests. Thus, West African Ṣàngó priests present themselves ritually, sartorially and verbally not as women *per se* but as wives of the gods, *by analogy to the female wives of earthly husbands*. This extended metaphor includes a further important term.

Indeed, the most pervasive and dramatic gendered symbol in this metaphoric representation of the possession priests' relationship to the gods – from the initiation onward – is the complex web of metaphors implicit in the Yorùbá verb *gùn* – meaning 'to mount.' Indeed, the term for 'possession priest' (*ẹlégùn*) means 'the mounted one'. *Gùn* refers to what a *rider does to a horse* (hence, possession priests are sometimes called 'horses of the gods' [*ẹṣin òrìṣà*]). The term *gùn* also refers to what an animal or a brutal man does sexually to his female partner (and possession by Ṣàngó is often spoken of as a brutal act).[50] The term *gùn* also refers to what a god – especially Ṣàngó – does to his possession priests. And Ṣàngó's is the most influential possession priesthood not only on the Bight of Benin but also, to an even greater extent, among the *orixá*-worshipers of Brazil, Cuba, Trinidad and the United States. However we translate the verb *gùn* into English, the term *montar* in Caribbean Spanish and Brazilian Portuguese and the Haitian Kweyòl term *monte* (all cognates of the English verb 'to mount'), encode the same three referents – sexual penetration, horsemanship and spirit possession – and have a long history of usage by worshipers in Cuba, Brazil and Haiti.

Let me illustrate how Afro-Latin Americans – such as the priests and cognoscenti of the Bahian Candomblé – consciously construed these West African Yorùbá metaphors in the 1930s, at the time of Landes's research in Bahia. These are the words of journalist and long-term Candomblé affiliate Édison Carneiro early in his acquaintance with Ruth Landes:

> Sometimes they call a priestess the *wife* of a god, and sometimes she is his *horse*. The god gives advice and places demands, but often he just *mounts* and plays.

> So you can see why the priestesses develop great influence among the people. They are the pathway to the gods. But no *upright* man will allow himself to be *ridden* by a god, unless he does not care about *losing his manhood* …

> Now here's the loophole. Some men do *let themselves be ridden*, and they become priests with the women; but they are known to be *homosexuals*. In the temple they *put on skirts and mannerisms of the women* … Sometimes *they are much better-looking than the women* (Landes 1947: 37).

This parlance is highly consistent with the West African, Ọ̀yọ́-Yorùbá symbolism of spirit possession I observed among Nigerian Ṣàngó priests of both sexes in the 1980s, save one important detail: the reluctance of 'real men' to be possessed in the Brazilian Candomblé.

Sex was not an infrequent topic of conversation among male friends of my age group in Ìgbòho, and, no matter what their age, the Ṣàngó priests in the town were vocal and ribald in their humour about the matter. Yet I never became aware of any commonly used vocabulary in Ọ̀yọ́-Yorùbá language to distinguish 'upright men' from a category of men who are 'homosexual' or somehow like women. I have never heard any West African *òrìṣà* priest speak of himself or his fellow priests as anything like a 'homosexual' or as engaging in same-sex intercourse. I argue simply that the Afro-Brazilians have *re-interpreted* West African metaphors of spirit possession in the light of Brazilian gender categories. For many Brazilians in the 1930s and now, submission to a god's agency has seemed analogous to sexual 'passivity,' or the experience of being penetrated during sexual intercourse. In other words, a physically mountable man seems highly qualified, in a symbolic sense, to be mounted spiritually. The metaphor-ridden *'loophole'* by which Édison Carneiro and his priestly friends understood men to have recently entered the Yorùbá/Quêto/Nagô possession priesthood in the 1930s was virtually identical – in both its terms and its emphases – to the *dominant* logic of the Ọ̀yọ́-Yorùbá Ṣàngó priesthood that I observed in the 1980s and others had observed since as long as that West African priesthood has been written about.[51]

Were it not for the increasingly vocal homophobia of Anglophone African bourgeoisies and the hot-button nature of sex as an object of cultural intimacy among nationalists, my argument would be not only better substantiated but also little more controversial than Herskovits' view that 'shouting' in black North American churches is a 'reinterpretation' of African spirit possession.[52] It would be little more controversial than explaining how the *ìdòbálẹ̀* and the *ìyíkàà* salutes in Cuba and Brazil reinterpret similar gestures in West Africa. That is, among the West African Yorùbá, *men* prostrate themselves flat on the ground, while the *ìyíkàà* (lying first on one side and then on the other) is the more appropriate gesture for *women* in sacred contexts. In Cuban Ocha and Brazilian Candomblé, by contrast, it is the gender of one's divinity, or 'saint', that determines the appropriate style of self-prostration. Whether male or female, a person governed by a male saint salutes elders and altars with the *ìdòbálẹ̀*, whereas a male or female person governed by a female saint performs the *ìyíkàà*.

I have never said or believed that the West African transvestite priests were or are in any sense homosexual.[53] While many have embraced my argument as logical and empirically sound, some others have found it easy to misinterpret, either as (1) proof that homosexuality is as widespread and natural in Africa as it is in the West, or as (2) a defamation of authentic, 'traditional' Yorùbá culture.[54] The first proposition is beyond the scope of my argument and of the evidence that I present here.[55] The second misinterpretation is the subject of the next section. But, first, a parenthesis.

At the time of my research in Ìgbòho, I had never heard of a named or symbolically marked category of men who are penetrated *sexually* by other men, but, in sum, I could see that those who are regularly penetrated *spiritually* by the gods have a great deal in common (sartorially, professionally and symbolically) with the Brazilian *bicha* or *adé* category. Imagine my surprise when I made the acquaintance of a highly respected Yorùbá art historian from Òyó, whose extended family included many Ṣàngó priests in that West African cultural capital. During his time among *oricha*-worshippers in the United States, this scholar too became aware of the importance of men who love men in the New-World priesthoods. Without having read my work, he had concluded that male-male sexual conduct among New World priests was a *continuation* rather than a mere reinterpretation of West African religious traditions. He told me that, on two occasions between 1968 and 1973, he witnessed possessed male Ṣàngó priests anally penetrating unpossessed male priests in an Òyó shrine. He does not know, however, if this practice was widespread or whether it represented a tradition or norm. Nor do I. As yet, I would extend my case no further based upon this unique testimony, which the original observer has shared with me privately but has himself – with a sense of 'cultural intimacy' – hesitated to publish.

The controversy

Dozens of Yorùbá scholars have written with sharpness and clarity about gender and gender relations in Yorùbá religion and culture generally.[56] However, these discussions have acquired new dimensions and new content as the number of Yorùbá scholars in the diaspora, and the occasions for their interaction with New-World priests of the Cuban *orichas*, Brazilian *orixás* and African-American orishas have increased. In this context, my argument has recently sparked controversy in a new, diasporic community – that of Yorùbá scholars and New-World priestesses of Yorùbá religion in the USA. It also seems to have provoked new questions about who legitimately belongs to the imagined community of this 'world religion' and who does not, who should speak for it and who is silenced, which practices are canonised and which ones are branded abnormal, shameful and best kept invisible.

One Yorùbá scholar in the United States, sociologist Oyeronkẹ Oyewumi, read my argument and then, in print, accused me of describing the West African possession priests as 'drag queens' and 'actual if not symbolic homosexuals'.[57] Oyewumi is clearly less interested in summarising my argument than in expressing her deep offence and her own preference to classify 'homosexuals' as anathema to this new Yorùbá diasporic nationalism.

This caricature of my argument was but one link in Oyewumi's argument that there is no gender whatsoever in authentic Yorùbá culture. Writes Oyewumi, 'Yorùbá is a non-gender-specific language'[58] which she takes as evidence that 'gender was not an organizing principle in Yorùbá society prior to colonization by the West'[59] and that 'Yorùbá society did not make gender distinctions and instead made age distinctions'.[60] People's anatomical sex 'did not privilege them to any social positions and similarly did not jeopardize their access'.[61] The physical differences between men and women mattered, 'only in regard to procreation, where they must'.[62]

Oyewumi's language-based inferences about the Yorùbá people's distant past slip, without explanation, into counterfactually present-tense assertions about 'the Yorùbá frame of reference',[63] as though the alleged precolonial genderlessness of the Yorùbá's ancestors represents the under-lying core and essence of a cultural system that has only recently, and at its margins, become sexist due to foreign influence.[64] In fact, once Oyewumi has defined a social ideal that she senses must have prevailed during a period before there were written records to prove or disprove it, she defines all of the numerous exceptions, past and present, as the products of Western contamination.[65]

Oyewumi argues, in sum, that colonisation by the West is the origin of all the sexism and, indeed, of all the gender conceptions that exist in Yorùbáland today, and that, because English language continuously marks the gender of its human referents, conventional scholarly discourse in English consistently misrepresents the gender-free culture of the Yorùbá. Ungendered features of the Yorùbá language are taken as proof that the culture in general was once and still is, in its essence, both non-sexist and free of any form of gender differentiation. Therefore, argues Oyewumi, Yorùbá and non-Yorùbá scholars who see gender in Yorùbá cultural history do so simply because they have falsely translated the gender-neutral terms of Yorùbá language into the gender-specific terms of the English language. Oyewumi therefore regards such scholars as thus both victims and agents of Western imperialism.[66]

Oyewumi's argument is passionate and persuasive to some New World priests and to many scholars – hence the extensive attention it merits in this article. Yet much of its persuasiveness lies in its misrepresentation of the existing scholarship on gender and on Yorùbá society, which, at least since the 1970s, has highlighted the differences between Western and Yorùbá gender roles. As I will show in this section, Oyewumi's attention to linguistic and ethnographic evidence is selective to the point of misrepresent-ing Yorùbá cultural history. More importantly, for the sake of this historical analysis of scholarship and society, the reader will see that her rhetorical strategy – including the silences it keeps – shares structural similarities with nationalist discourses the world over.

Like Brazilian nationalist Gilberto Freyre, Oyewumi turns the tables on North American and Western European cultural and racial chauvinism. She does so, however, not through the Freyrean style vivid storytelling but by constructing an antipodean difference between 'the West' and 'the Yorùbá conception'. In 'the West', argues Oyewumi, everything about a person's social status is determined by his or her visible biology (in which Oyewumi includes a person's genotype) – that is, according to Oyewumi, by a person's race and sex. Oyewumi then defines 'gender' as the allegedly 'Western' notion that every aspect of an anatomical female's life is determined by her anatomy, that no cross-cutting identity or category of social belonging (such as kinship, age or marital status) shapes any anatomical female's social role or status, that every anatomical female is always socially inferior to every anatomical male, that an anatomical female may perform no roles that anatomical males also perform, that the gender categories are determined entirely by the referent's visible or chromosomal biology. Moreover, despite her citation of several scholarly works that discuss third genders or relational gender, she argues that the analytic term 'gender' always imposes a binary or dichotomy upon its referents.[67]

On the basis of this unusual definition of 'gender' and a somewhat unempirical assessment of 'Western' social life, Oyewumi asserts that 'gender' prevails in the West, but not in Yorùbá society. Only one's age relative to other people and the family to which one belongs, the author concludes, determine anything about one's social status and relationships in authentically Yorùbá society.

In evidence, the author cites the extensive gender coding of pronouns, names, kinship terms, and occupational terms in English, as well as numerous Yorùbá pronouns, kinship terms, and occupational terms that, in her opinion, do not encode gender – such as òun ('s/he'), omo ('child'), ègbón ('senior sibling or cousin'), oba ('monarch'), Ìyá Olóńjẹ ('Food Vendor' [lit., 'Senior-Female Owner-of-Food']), and Bàbá Aláṣo ('clothier' or 'weaver' [lit., 'Senior-Male Owner-of-Cloth']). Oyewumi spends much of her argument explaining away or concealing the gender coding that actually does appear in these and other Yorùbá terms and social practice. For example, there are clearly words in Yorùbá for 'male' (ako), 'female' (abo), 'man' (okùnrin), and 'woman' (obìnrin). The terms of address and reference for parents, senior relatives, senior strangers, and people of almost every occupation indicate the referent's gender – as in Bàbá Ayò (the teknonymic 'Father of Ayò'), Bàbá Eléran ('butcher'), and Ìyáà mi ('Mommy'). Most professions in Yorùbáland have and have long had vastly more of one sex than another practising them, and virtually all social clubs (egbé) are segregated according to sex. Certain Yorùbá religious and political titles are strongly gender-marked, despite their infrequent adoption by a person of the other sex, such as babaláwo (a type of divination priest [lit., 'senior-male-who-owns-the-mystery']), *baalè* (non-royal quarter or town chief [lit., 'father of the land']), and *baálé* (head of residential compound [lit., 'father of the house']). But as far as I know, a man can never be an *ìyálé* (eldest wife of the house [lit., 'mother of the house']). It should be noted that these last two terms – *baálé* and *ìyálé* – are *etymologically* distinguished from each other *only* by the gender of the referent. Yet *in real social life* the persons described as 'fathers of the house' rank far higher in the house than do the people called 'mothers of the house'.

On the other hand, one of the most important chieftaincies of the nineteenth-century was that of the *Ìyálóde* (the Chief of the Market [lit., 'Mother-Who-Owns-the-Outside']), and, as far as I know, this title has never been held by a man. Oyewumi argues that the *ìyálóde* title originated in the nineteenth century and was a product of influence by Ìbàdàn, an ethnically Òyó-Yorùbá military republic.[68] She does not demonstrate, however, the sense in which its gender-specificity results from foreign or Western influence or is foreign to 'the Yorùbá conception'. She also argues that, because not all women fell under the authority of the *ìyálóde* and the *ìyálóde* governed affairs beyond the affairs of women, the title is not gendered. I fail to see how this evidence proves that a title reserved for women escapes analysis in terms of gender.

Moreover, the fact that there are a few female *baálè*, or 'village chiefs', near Oyewumi's hometown should not allow us to overlook the male gendering of authority that the term implies, especially if Oyewumi intends to be true to her hypothesis that vocabulary reveals the culture-specific ideology underlying statistics of otherwise unclear implications. In this case, contrary to her general argument, Oyewumi chooses to privilege the statistic of the exception over the linguistically implicit ideology of male dominance.[69]

This is a society in which men and women have long worn markedly different styles of clothing, a wife is regularly expected to supply her husband with cooked food (and not vice-versa), almost all professional cooks (except in European-style establishments) are women, and the social norms of legitimate reproduction differentially affect the experience of anatomical males and females throughout the life-cycle, in ways ranging from infant clitoridectomy to earlier marriage for women than for men, bridewealth, polygyny (and the unthinkability of polyandry), viri-patrilocal postmarital residence, the levirate and the normatively different roles of mothers and fathers in childcare. Oyewumi even makes the credible claim that motherhood is the most honoured of Yorùbá institutions, but, given her peculiar definition of 'gender,' this observation is taken to illustrate the absence of gender in Yorùbá society.[70] The author also claims that polygyny is frequently initiated by the existing wife, that male interests are not supreme in polygynous marriages, that married women's sexual dalliances are tacitly accepted, and that husbands have no rights over the wife's labour. These indications of wifely 'agency,' alongside Oyewumi's argument that polygyny entails male self-discipline and deprivation, are taken to prove that polygyny is 'ungendered'.[71] Most of Oyewumi's claims are inconsistent with my observations in Ọ̀yọ́ North, Ibadan and Lagos during the 1980s and 1990s, and with others' observations during the past two centuries. Even if they were true, however, the claim that they prove an absence of gender in Yorùbá culture follows more from Oyewumi's idiosyncratic definition of gender than from a careful assessment of the empirical data on Yorùbá marriage. They also fail to reflect the full complexity of the scholarship on 'gender' in Western marriage and social life.

The levirate (or 'widow-inheritance') is no longer commonly practiced in Yorùbáland, but the archival records of the Customary Courts during the early colonial period demonstrate, contrary to Oyewumi's claim, that it was often practised without the widow's consent.[72] Records from just before the colonial period indicate that adultery was often severely punished by indigenous authorities, and women were sometimes forced, on threat of violence, to remain in marriages that they wished to leave.[73] Oyewumi fails to produce any documentation of her claims that Yorùbá marriage does not and did not, throughout its documented history, entail systematically different social experiences for the male and female partners. The statistical and ideological norm that a wife moves to her husband's natal household and enters as a subordinate to every person previously born to or married into that household is a structural disadvantage that affects most women in this society *because* they are women and not men. These facts cannot easily be dismissed.

Oyewumi focuses great attention upon linguistic evidence because any claim that present-day Yorùbá culture and society fail to distinguish men from women, or offer them equal access and privileges to important social options, is manifestly false. Hence, Oyewumi claims that her analysis reconstructs the *real* Yorùbá culture, which preceded colonisation and/or the slave trade, a period to which we have hardly any documentary access. The earliest document the author consults is dated 1829, long after the slave trade had begun to affect the Ọ̀yọ́-Yorùbá, and the author elides all historical periods that preceded the slave trade and colonisation (including several unmentioned centuries of Islamic influence) into a single 'authentic' prototype, which she believes remains evident and alive only in those aspects of present-day Yorùbá parlance that do not mark gender.

When evidently old gender-marked aspects of Yorùbá language are addressed at all, they are excused by various arguments that would obviously be absurd if applied to languages and cultures more familiar to the reader. For example, *bàbá* ('father' or 'senior man') and *ìyá* ('mother' or 'senior woman') are said to indicate not only sex but *also* adulthood; therefore they are not gendered, argues Oyewumi. Does it follow, then, that the terms 'father' and 'mother' in English are not gendered?

Oyewumi argues that the term for 'bride' or 'wife' (*iyawo*) is ungendered because it refers to both the female brides of worldly husbands and possession priests regardless of sex. Does the fact that the church is called the 'bride of Christ' in English then imply that the English term 'bride' is also ungendered? Is the church not made up of males and females?

The fact that a fruitful year is called a 'female year' (*abo òdun*) is said not to indicate any Yorùbá conception of gender because, Oyewumi reports falsely, no one speaks of its opposite as a 'male year' (*ako òdun*).[74] Even if the statement were true, its logic would imply that the term 'phallic symbol' in English is ungendered because there is no commonplace word for its feminine opposite.

In English, as in Yorùbá, one could recite an endless list of gender-free references to people without ever proving that the language or the culture is gender-free. Could one reliably infer from the gender-neutral English terms 'I', 'you', 'we', 'they', 'parent', 'cousin', 'sibling', 'child' and 'president' that Anglo-Saxon or Western language and culture are in their essence or once were free of gender and of gender hierarchy? I think not. But this is the logic of Oyewumi's linguistic argument that Yorùbá culture, in its deep past and in its present essence, is completely without gender.

Oyewumi's linguistic argument simply does not stand up to sustained ethnographic investigation, as the work of important Yorùbá scholars demonstrates. For example, Wande Abimbọla offers an overview of the images of women in the ancient Ifá literary corpus, the carefully preserved basis of the Ifá oracular system and, arguably, the centrepiece of Yorùbá 'traditional' culture as most Yorùbá people understand it. These texts have existed for centuries and, though they are not static, they undoubtedly preserve a great deal of social history from pre-nineteenth-century times, which would hardly disappear from an overview by a scholar and *babaláwo* of Abimbola's competency and standing. He is the official spokesman (*Àwíṣẹ*) of the Ifá priesthood headquartered at Ilé-Ifẹ̀. Indeed, Abimbola's assessment both relies on stronger evidence of the Yorùbá past and strongly contradicts Oyewumi's argument that Yorùbá culture in no way represents anatomical men and anatomical women as socially or morally different. For example, according to Abimbola, a world-renowned Ọ̀yọ́-Yorùbá *babaláwo*, Ifá represents only women as capable of being an *àjé*, which he defines as 'a blood-sucking, wicked, dreadful cannibal who transforms herself into a bird at night and flies to distant places, to hold nocturnal meetings with her fellow witches who belong to a society that excludes all men'.[75] On the one hand, Ifá credits women uniquely with the marvellous capacity to bear children and to be loyal wives. On the other hand, it represents women as deceitful. The Ifá verse called Oyeku Meji says:

Obinrin leke
Obinrin lọdalẹ
Women are deceitful
Women are liars[76]

Abimbọla summarises, 'These few examples of women in the Ifá literary corpus clearly demonstrate the ambivalent attitudes of Yorùbá men to women and the powers women possess. There is a love-hate relationship in the attitude of Yorùbá men to women'.[77] Contrary to Oyewumi's understanding of Yorùbá culture, it seems highly doubtful that the gendered elements of the Ifá literary corpus were imposed recently on Yorùbá culture by 'the West'. On the other hand, the motives to pursue such an explanation, I will argue, are foreign to neither Yorùbá culture nor 'the West'.

For example, Oyewumi's argument neatly parallels the claim that Brazil is a 'racial democracy' (opposite in character to the USA and the rest of the Euro-Atlantic world) and that foreigners' analyses of race and racism in Brazil result from the imposition of an imperialist North American logic.[78] Both Oyewumi's argument and Freyre's dramatically remind us of the cross-cultural variation in the interpretation of human phenotypes (a point that may have been surprising to the Brazilian general public in the 1930s but is hardly news to the scholars who studied gender in the 1990s).[79] However, the work of Oyewumi and Freyre also alerts us to a genre of nationalistic allegory that is common in a transnational world, where scholars and other workers in the diaspora articulate some of the most emotionally powerful and politically persuasive images in the national imaginaries of the homeland. The Brazilian Freyre too formulated his influential socio-moral allegory during and following his sojourn in the United States. Both arguments rely on the construction of an idyllic past time in the homeland that is beyond immediate scrutiny. They equally invoke a sense of national honour – or 'cultural intimacy' – around the conspiracy to conceal contrary facts that every insider knows.

No careful and knowledgeable student of Brazil could, in my opinion, claim that racism works the same in Brazil as it does in the United States, but 'race' and 'racism' are useful categories by which to compare and contrast, analyse and re-think the ways in which discrimination based upon presumed or visible ancestry works in each of the two countries. Likewise, Oyewumi's redefinition of 'gender' does little to clarify or improve upon existing discussions under that rubric, many of which subtly analyse much the same empirical turf that Oyewumi considers: the diversity of female roles and powers in Yorùbá society, the ways in which they overlap with men's powers, the way these differ from the arrangements of roles and powers in other societies, and the ways in which male-female difference and interrelatedness are projected metaphorically onto other social and symbolic relationships. Oyewumi's redefinition of gender does little more than flatten both 'the Yorùbá conception' and 'the West' into opposite stereotypes.

A (culturally) intimate gathering of priests and scholars

Since Gilberto Freyre organised the First Afro-Brazilian Congress in 1934, dozens of such conferences have brought together priests and scholars intent on re-thinking and reorganising *orişa* religion, and reflecting on its significance for the imagined communities of the region, the nation and the African Diaspora as well. Several such conferences have had momentous effects, largely because they have helped to establish which priests' practices are normal, which are best silenced, and who legitimately speaks for the group.[80] For example, the 1937 Congress organised by Édison Carneiro in Bahia culminated in the organisation of the Union of Afro-Brazilian Sects, the first organisation to regulate priestly conduct and to unite the Bahian temples and their supporters against police repression. In 1983, Wande Abimbọla and Marta Moreno Vega organised at the University of Ifẹ, Nigeria, the first World Conference of Orisha Tradition and Culture. Thus, for the first time in history, a conference brought together scholars and priests of *orişa* religion from Brazil, Cuba, Puerto Rico, Trinidad, the United States and Nigeria. A dozen such conferences have followed, albeit under an increasingly factionalised leadership. As the leader of one series of conferences, Abimbola is now regarded by some priests as the paramount leader of the global *orişa*-worshipping community. Such an understanding of Abimbola's role is clearly con-tested. However, until now, no one else has to my knowledge ever even been credited with such authority. This is cultural history in the making.

It is against this backdrop that events at the 1999 conference at Florida International University acquire their historical significance. Titled 'Òrìşà Devotion as a World Religion: the Globalization of Yorùbá Religious Culture', this conference brought together dozens of US-based Nigerian, Cuban, Puerto Rican, native US American and Brazilian scholars with priests of equally diverse geographical and national origins. On and off the dais, priests and scholars debated over whether whites and Westernised-looking Yorùbás could legitimately speak for Yorùbá tradition, whether Yorùbá was the only language in which Yorùbá religious concepts could be discussed, whether 'each group [i.e., Cuban and Cuban-inspired *santeros*, Brazilian *Candomblécistas*, Nigerian Yorùbá people, Trinidadian Shango practitioners, etc.] should speak for itself',[81] and whether certain scholarly

disagreements should be settled publicly or privately. University conferences are not simply forums where truth is worked out through debate;
they are also stages where *social* priorities are debated and dramatised.
Officially authorised speakers have diverse priorities, and so do audiences.

Oyewumi's *ex tempore* presentation at this conference urged caution
in translating Yorùbá concepts into English terms. She gave examples of
bad translations, such as glossing *ọba* as 'king' (when, in truth, it means
'monarch') and insisted that the term *iyawo* ('bride') was ungendered
since it describes not only married women but also junior *òrìṣà* possession
priests of either sex. Based upon this evidence, she reaffirmed her
conclusion that Yorùbá language, and therefore Yorùbá culture, is devoid
of gender.

The talk's logical and empirical inadequacies notwithstanding, two
Trinidadian priestesses and an African-American priestess in attendance
stood up to applaud it. Oyewumi's nostalgic reconstruction of an ideal
Yorùbá past and essence held great appeal for New-World priestesses
who would resist the patent sexism of American societies (including the
forms of gender inequality strongly evident in New-World traditions of
òrìṣà-worship), for diasporic Yorùbá people anxious to subvert North
Americans' tendency to regard Africa and its cultures as inferior, and
particularly, according to Mọlara Ogundipẹ, for Yorùbá men happy to be
exonerated of sexism.[82] The African-American priestess who applauded
told me years later that she liked Oyewumi's presentation because of
Oyewumi's assertiveness, because the scholar delivered it *ex tempore*, and
because she seemed to know what she was talking about. The priestess
said, however, that she harboured some doubts on account of the fact that
Oyewumi wore trousers and cut her hair short – conduct that the priestess
did not regard as traditional. What is most striking is that she remembered
little of Oyewumi's argument.

In an apparent effort to support Oyewumi's argument, several senior
male Yorùbá scholars in the audience offered further examples of Yorùbá
gender configurations that might surprise most Americans, such as the
Yorùbá practice, in certain contexts, of calling one's patrilateral relatives
of either sex *bàbá* (normally meaning 'father' or 'senior man') and matri-
lateral relatives of either sex *ìyá* (normally meaning 'mother' or 'senior
woman'). Whether they agreed with Oyewumi's overall proposition that
there is no gender in Yorùbá culture is unclear. It seems to me that people
who address their mother's and their father's relatives by opposite terms,
and regard the two families' normative roles in their lives are indeed
employing a gendered distinction that Anglo-Americans simply do not
typically make. An unsubtle analysis could thus conclude that Yorùbá culture
is even more gender-bound than US culture, rather than differently gender
bound.

Others among the senior Yorùbá scholars in attendance restricted their comments to private conversations. For example, one male Yorùbá philosophy professor at first agreed enthusiastically with Oyewumi but stopped short when I asked him to consider the implications of viri-patrilocal post-marital residence, whereby a Yorùbá woman is normally expected to spend most of her life in a household where she automatically becomes the junior to everyone else in the house. There, she will always owe deference and a measure of servility to those male and female in-laws born before her marriage into the house and to the earlier-married wives, and her rights to land and chieftaincy titles will, in most regions of Yorùbáland, always be secondary to those of anyone born in the house.

Another Yorùbá male scholar told me that Oyewumi's argument was not significant enough to challenge, though this same scholar apparently advocated for the book to receive the prestigious Herskovits Prize of the African Studies Association. Others told me that criticising a junior scholar in public would be considered distasteful in Yorùbá culture. Many of these scholars have already contributed significantly to the academic study of gender in Yorùbá culture and have chosen other venues to express their opinions. Hence, my observations are intended not to impugn the quality of these scholars' work but to illustrate the social dynamics by which community is dramatised at university conferences and certain images of community come to be projected as scholarly truths.

Nor are large North American professional organisations exempt from such dynamics. For example, without consulting any Africanists, much less Yorùbánists, the Sex and Gender Section of the American Sociological Association awarded Oyewumi's *Invention of Women* its 1998 Distinguished Book Award.[83] Thus, a new form of nostalgia and silencing has united the Sex and Gender Section of the ASA in common cause with both Yorùbá long-distance nationalism and with New-World priestesses who are not only aware of the gender bias that has long been a part of their New-World orisha traditions but are ready to do something about it. This nostalgia is new in some details but is logically similar to the reasoning that united Brazilian Regionalism and nationalism with Landes's brand of transnational feminism. It is not clear how fast, how commonly or how deeply this new alliance of ideological forces will affect the practice of òrìṣà-worship, but every subsequent conference of scholars and priests is likely to add authority to these motivated representations of (and silence about) the shared past. These motivated representations, in turn, acquire the credibility to structure new communities and hierarchies in the present, just as the historical revisions of Landes and Carneiro did in Brazil after the 1930s.

It is by now old news that the priests and followers of the Yorùbá-Atlantic traditions frequently own and read books about those traditions written by university-trained scholars – such as Juana Elbein dos Santos' *Os Nàgô e a Morte* (1976) and Pierre Verger's *Orixás* (1981) in Brazil, Lydia Cabrera's *El Monte* (1954) among Cuban-inspired adherents of Ocha, and Robert Farris Thompson's *Flash of the Spirit* (1983) among North American Orisha devotees.[84] The degree to which these books become catechisms or procedural guides is variable, but it is clear that many priests use the information that scholars bring, particularly when those scholars possess a credible claim to information from the African 'motherland'.[85] Thus, the opinions of even West African and West Africanist scholars with no priestly credentials can be enormously influential in the transformative projects of New-World priests and priestesses. Our analyses are often employed as models of African 'tradition', which can be used to include and elevate particular segments of New-World religious communities. Therefore, our analyses can also be used to marginalise other segments of those communities and to de-legitimise existing practices. Our influence can be powerful, whether we are committed to studying our field sites honestly, or we are committed to misrepresenting them as allegories of some ideal that we are recommending to an audience unable to check our facts. Thus, African, Africanist and Afro-Latin Americanist scholars can be influential not only in priestly projects but also in the political projects of First-World scholarly communities with little knowledge of Africa and little intrinsic interest in Africa's complex truths.

Conclusion

In sum, neither the Candomblé 'cult matriarchate' of Landes nor the 'genderless' Yorùbá society of Oyewumi is a neutral, or completely truthful, report of cultural history. They are inventions in the service of overlapping imagined communities. Yet they also do a disservice both to Yorùbá cultural history and to the thousands of male priests who have built institutions, housed the poor, and healed the sick in the Brazilian Candomblé. Nonetheless, one cannot avoid the fact that these inventions move people and change history. The debates and transformations that I have detailed here reveal not only the pitfalls of tendentious scholarship but also the fact that long-distance, transnational dialogues have continually re-shaped even 'traditional' cultures and religions like Candomblé.

And there is a further point. Transnational social movements and diasporas, like nation states, propagate secrets and defend the intimate zones that are created around those secrets. The facts that the leaders of imagined communities choose to make secret can be surprising – such as the facts of gender and racial inequality in Brazil and gender inequality in Yorùbáland, not to mention the open secret of intergenerational class inequality in the United States; it is difficult to fathom how an outsider could *fail* to see them. However, any fact that a community can be persuaded to discuss privately and to silence in the company of outsiders can serve the same community-defining function – a function that Herzfeld calls 'cultural intimacy'.[86] Indeed, old imagined communities can be reinforced and new communities imagined into being by the forceful assertion that some fact of its life needs to be hidden from a larger encompassing group or forbidden for outsiders to speak of.

Notes

1. Karin Barber, 'How Man Makes God in West Africa: Yorùbá Attitudes toward the Orìṣa', *Africa* 51 (1981), p. 739–40; also p. 744 footnote 31.
2. Consider also Scott's concept of the 'hidden transcript', matters that members of the same status group will verbalise among themselves but not with their social superiors or inferiors. See James C. Scott, *Weapons of the Weak: Everyday Forms of Peasant Resistance* (Yale University Press, 1990).
3. Michael Herzfeld, *Cultural Intimacy: The Social Poetics of the Nation-State* (New York and London: Routledge, 1997), pp. 1–36.
4. J. Lorand Matory, *Black Atlantic Religion: Tradition, Transnationalism, and Matriarchy in the Afro-Brazilian Candomblé* (Princeton NJ: Princeton University Press, forthcoming); J. Lorand Matory, 'The English Professors of Brazil: On the Diasporic Roots of the Yorùbá Nation, *Comparative Studies in Society and History* 41 (1999), pp. 72–103; J. Lorand Matory, 'Jeje: Repensando Nações e Transnacionalismo', *Mana* 5 (1999), pp. 57–80.
5. See Benedict Anderson, *Imagined Communities*, revised edition (London and New York: Verso, 1991[first edition London and New York: Verso, 1983]). I broaden Anderson's concept of 'imagined communities' by suggesting that nation states are not the only communities so united by machine-reproduced texts and that the rituals shared by dispersed populations (including those recommended by texts that are distributed fast or over long distances) enable powerful 'imaginations' of communally shared experience among unacquainted parties.
6. Ruth Landes, *The City of Women* (Albuquerque: University of New Mexico Press, 1994 [repr. New York: Macmillan, 1947]), p. 248.
7. Ruth Landes, 'A Cult Matriarchate and Male Homosexuality', *Journal of Abnormal and Social Psychology* 35(1940), pp. 386–97.
8. Mark Alan Healey, '"The Sweet Matriarchy of Bahia": Ruth Landes' Ethnography of Race and Gender', *Disposition* 23 (1998 [2000]), pp. 87–116.
9. Landes, *The City*, p. 202.
10. Derek Freeman, *Margaret Mead and Samoa: the Making and Unmaking of an Anthropological Myth* (Cambridge MA: Harvard University Press, 1983); Margaret Mead, *Coming of Age in Samoa* (Boston: Beacon, 1928).
11. Landes, 'A Cult Matriarchate', pp. 386–97, 391.
12. Landes, 'A Cult Matriarchate', pp. 391–92.
13. Édison Carneiro, *Os Candomblés da Bahia*, 7th edn (Rio de Janeiro: Civilização Brasileira, 1986 [repr. Salvador da Bahia: Museu do Estado da Bahia, 1948]), p. 54.
14. Compare Landes, 'A Cult Matriarchate', p. 393; and Carneiro, *Os Candomblés*, p. 52.
15. Rachel E. Harding, *A Refuge in Thunder: Candomblé and Alternative Spaces of Blackness* (Bloomington and Indianapolis: University of Indiana Press, 2000), pp. 71–4; Carneiro, *Os Candomblés*, pp. 57, 104–9; Kim D. Butler, *Freedoms Given, Freedoms Won: Afro-Brazilians in Post-Abolition São Paulo and Salvador* (New Brunswick NJ and London: Rutgers University Press, 1998), pp. 193, 195; Fayette Wimberly, 'The Expansion of Afro-Bahian Religious Practices in Nineteenth-Century Cachoeira', *Afro-Brazilian Culture and Politics: Bahia, 1790s to 1990s*, ed. Hendrik Kraay (Armonk NY: M.E. Sharpe, 1998), pp. 82–5.

16. Butler, *Freedoms Given*, pp. 193–209; private conversation, 3 December 2002.
17. Mariza Corrêa, 'O Mistério dos Orixás e das Bonecas: Raça e Gênero na Antropologia Brasileira', *Etnográfica* 4 (2000), p. 245; Carneiro, *Os Candomblés*, p. 104.
18. Landes, *The City*; Landes, 'A Cult Matriarchate', pp. 386–97.
19. On the term 'struggle for the possession of the sign', see Dick Hebdige, *Subculture: the Meaning of Style* (London and New York: Methuen, 1979).
20. George Mosse, *Nationalism and Sexuality* (Madison: University of Wisconsin Press, 1985).
21. See Corrêa, 'O Mistério', pp. 246–8, esp. 246 footnotes 24 and 25; Healey, 'The Sweet Matriarchy', p. 88; Roger Bastide, *O Candomblé da Bahia* (São Paulo: Editora Nacional, 1961), p. 309; René Ribeiro, 'Personality and the Psychosexual Adjustment of Afro-Brazilian Cult Members, *Journal de la Société des Américanistes* 58 (1969), p. 122.
22. Landes, *The City*, p. 37; Landes, 'A Cult Matriarchate', p. 393.
23. Corrêa, 'O Mistério', pp. 241–51, esp. 251; Healey, 'The Sweet Matriarchy', pp. 97–8.
24. Édison Carneiro, *Religiões Negras e Negros Bantos* (Civilização Brasileira, 1991 [repr. *Religiões Negras*, Rio: Civilização Brasileira, 1936, and *Negros Bantos*, Rio: Civilização Brasileira, 1937]), pp. 58, 60, 91.
25. Édison Carneiro, 'The Structure of African Cults in Bahia', *Journal of American Folk-Lore*, 53 (1940), p. 272.
26. Carneiro, 'The Structure of African', p. 273.
27. Landes, *The City*, p. 37; Landes, 'A Cult Matriarchate', p. 393.
28. Carneiro, *Os Candomblés*, pp. 103–9.
29. Carneiro, *Os Candomblés*, p. 57; also Butler, *Freedoms Given*, p. 195.
30. Carneiro, *Os Candomblés*, pp. 106, 119–23.
31. Jocélio Teles dos Santos, *O Dono da Terra: o Caboclo nos Candomblés da Bahia* (Salvador, Brazil: SarahLetras, 1995), p. 19.
32. J. Lorand Matory, 'Homens Montados: Homossexualidade e Simbolismo da Possessão nas Religiões Afro-Brasileiras', *Escravidão e Invenção da Liberdade*, ed. João José Reis (São Paulo: Brasiliense, 1988), pp. 215–31.
33. Peter Fry, 'Male Homosexuality and Spirit Possession in Brazil', *Journal of Homosexuality* 11 (1986), pp. 137–53.
34. Richard C. Trexler, *Sex and Conquest: Gendered Violence, Political Order, and the European Conquest of the Americas* (Ithaca NY: Cornell University Press, 1995).
35. The contrast between penetrators and penetrated is not the only idiom of sexual classification available in Brazil, but this particular idiom of sexuality and power remains central to most working-class Brazilians' vocabulary of social classification, and to Brazilian men's and boys' daily negotiation of respect. See Peter A. Jackson, 'Reading Rio from Bangkok: An Asianist Perspective on Brazil's Male Homosexual Cultures' (review article), *American Ethnologist* 27 (2000), pp. 950–60; Don Kulick, *Travestí: Sex, Gender and Culture among Brazilian Transgendered Prostitutes* (Chicago: University of Chicago Press, 1998); Richard G. Parker, *Beneath the Equator: Cultures of Desire, Male Homosexuality, and Emerging Gay Communities in Brazil* (New York: Routledge, 1998); Richard G. Parker, *Bodies, Pleasures, and Passions: Sexual Culture in Contemporary Brazil* (Boston: Beacon Press, 1991); James N. Green, *Beyond Carnival: Male Homosexuality in Twentieth-Century Brazil* (Chicago and London: University of Chicago Press, 1999).
36. For example see Kulick, *Travestí*.
37. The reader should not misinterpret 'transvestism', which means 'cross-dressing', as a euphemism for or type of 'homosexuality.'
38. Many Cuban and Puerto Rican adherents of similar traditions think so too. See Lydia Cabrera, *El Monte*, 5th edn (Miami: Colección del Chicherekú, 1983 [repr. Havana: Ediciones CR, 1954]), p. 56; Rómulo Lachatañeré, *El Sistema Religioso de los Afrocubanos* (Editorial de Ciencias Sociales, 1992), pp. 223–4.
39. Fry, 'Male Homosexuality' p. 138. Note that Fry does not pathologise the *adé*, as do Landes, Carneiro and their successors, such as Bastide (*O Candomblé*, p. 309) and Ribeiro ('Personality', pp. 109–20).

40. Délcio Monteiro de Lima, *Os Homoeróticos* (Rio de Janeiro: F. Alves, 1983), pp. 167ff.

41. Patricia Birman, 'Identidade social e homossexualismo no Candomblé', *Religião e Sociedade* 12 (1985), pp. 2–21; also Maria Lina Leão Teixeira, 'Lorogun – Identidades sexuais e poder no candomblé', *Candomblé: Desvendando Identidades*, ed. Carlos Eugênio Marcondes de Moura (São Paulo: EMW Editores, 1987), p. 48; and Landes, 'A Cult Matriarchate', p. 395.

42. Fry, 'Male Homosexuality', pp. 147–9.

43. For the argument that men of any given social race earn more on average than the women of that social race see George Reid Andrews, 'Racial Inequality in Brazil and the United States: A Statistical Comparison', *Journal of Social History* 26 (1992), p. 252. In the contexts where light-skinned gay men successfully conceal their sexuality, they possess considerable economic and political advantages over women as a group and blacks as a group, see *Veja* Magazine, 12 May 1993, pp. 52–9. For an explanation of the term 'social race', see Charles Wagley, Introduction, *Race and Class in Rural Brazil*, ed. Charles Wagley (New York: UNESCO/International Documents Service, Columbia University Press, 1963), p. 14; Carl N. Degler, *Neither Black Nor White: Slavery and Race Relations in Brazil and the United States* (Madison: University of Wisconsin Press, 1971), p. 105.

44. Teixeira, 'Lorogun', pp. 44–5; also Maria Stella de Azevedo Santos, *Meu Tempo É Agora* (São Paulo: Editora Oduduwa, 1993), pp. 52–4 on the servile status of women consecrated to female *orixás*.

45. For example, James H. Sweet, 'Male Homosexuality and Spiritism in the African Diaspora: The Legacies of a Link', *Journal of the History of Sexuality* 7 (1996), pp. 184–202.

46. J. Lorand Matory, *Sex and the Empire That Is No More: Gender and the Politics of Metaphor in Ọ̀yọ́ Yorùbá Religion* (Minneapolis: University of Minnesota, 1994); J. Lorand Matory, *Sex and the Empire That Is No More: A Ritual History of Women's Power among the Ọ̀yọ́-Yorùbá*, Ph.D dissertation, Department of Anthropology, University of Chicago, 1991; Matory, 'Homens Montados'.

47. Melville Herskovits, *The Myth of the Negro Past* (Boston: Beacon, 1958) p. 214; Melville Herskovits, *The New World Negro*, ed. Frances S. Herskovits (Bloomington: Indiana University Press, 1969), pp. 13–16, 35–8, 57–8, 79.

48. See Matory, *Gender and the Politics of Metaphor*; Matory, *A Ritual History*; Matory, 'Homens Montados'.

49. Matory, *A Ritual History*; Matory, *Gender and the Politics of Metaphor*.

50. In a contrast case equally revealing of the sexual implications of the verb, the term *mágùn* (lit. 'don't mount') refers to a 'medicine', or magical application, that kills the paramour of a married woman at the moment that he attempts to penetrate her.

51. Matory, *Gender and the Politics of Metaphor*, p. 171. This priestly cross-dressing has been documented at least since 1910, and there is no reason to believe that it was new at that time.

52. Herskovits, *Myth*, pp. 211–16.

53. Matory, *Gender and the Politics of Metaphor*, p. 208; Matory, *A Ritual History*, pp. 22, 520–1, 538; pace Oyeronkẹ Oyewumi, *The Invention of Women: Making an African Sense of Western Gender Discourses* (Minneapolis and London: University of Minnesota Press, 1997), p. 117.

54. Stephen O. Murray, 'Overview [West Africa]', in *Boy-Wives and Female Husbands*, eds. Stephen O. Murray and Will Roscoe (New York: St. Martins Press, 1998), p. 100; personal communication, 1996). Oyewumi, *The Invention of Women*, p. 117.

55. While African nationalists are often wont to dismiss homosexuality as a 'white man's disease', there is evidence of its practice in contemporary and pre-colonial Africa. There is nothing 'un-African' about homosexuality. See J. Lorand Matory, *Sex and the Empire That Is No More: Gender and the Politics of Metaphor Ọ̀yọ́ Yorùbá Religion* (Minneapolis: University of Minnesota, 1994), p. 2 for additional citations on same-sex sexual practices in the recent and distant past of sub-Saharan Africa. See also James H. Sweet, 'Male Homosexuality and Spiritism in the African Diaspora: The Legacies of a Link', *Journal of the History of Sexuality* 7 (1996).

56. For example, Rowland Abiọdun, 'Women in Yorùbá Religious Images.' *African Languages and Cultures* 2 (1989), pp. 1–18; Bọlanlẹ Awẹ, 'The Iyalode in the Traditional Yorùbá Political System', *Sexual Stratification*, ed. Alice Schlegel (New York: Columbia University Press, 1997); Bọlanlẹ Awẹ, 'The Economic Role of Women in Traditional African Society: the Yorùbá Example', *La Civilisation de la Femme dans la Tradition Africaine*, Proceedings of a Colloquium in Abidjan, Ivory Coast, 3–8 July 1972; N. A. Fadipe, *The Sociology of the Yorùbá* (Ibàdàn: Ibàdàn University Press, 1970); O. O. Okediji and F. O. Okediji, 'Marital Stability and Social Structure in an African City', *The Nigerian Journal of Economic and Social Studies* 8 (1966); Mọlara Ogundipe-Leslie, 'Women in Nigeria', *Women in Nigeria Today*, ed. S. Bappa, J. Ibrahim, A. M. Imam, F. J. A. Kamara, H. Mahdi, M. A. Modibbo, A. S. Mohammed, H. Mohammed, A. R. Mustapha, N. Perchonock, and R. I. Pittin (London: Zed Books, 1985); Jacob K. Olupọna, 'Women's Rituals, Kingship and Power among the Ondo-Yorùbá of Nigeria', *Queens, Queen Mothers, Priestesses, and Power*, ed. Flora E. S. Kaplan (New York Academy of Sciences, 1997); Wande Abimbọla, 'Images of Women in the Ifa Literary Corpus', *Queens, Queen Mothers, Priestesses, and Power*, ed. Flora E. S. Kaplan (New York: New York Academy of Sciences, 1997).
57. Oyewumi, *The Invention of Women*, p. 117.
58. Oyewumi, *The Invention of Women*, p. 158.
59. Oyewumi, *The Invention of Women*, p. 31.
60. Oyewumi, *The Invention of Women*, p. 157.
61. Oyewumi, *The Invention of Women*, p. 78.
62. Oyewumi, *The Invention of Women*, p. 12.
63. Oyewumi, *The Invention of Women*, p. 78.
64. Oyewumi, *The Invention of Women*, pp. 13, 29, 42, 47, 61, 160, 163, 166, 169.
65. Oyewumi, *The Invention of* Women, for example, pp. x, xi, xiv, xv, 162–3. Among the numerous ironies of this argument is that there was no Yorùbá language or ethnic identity per se before Western-educated, Christian Ọ̀yọ́ people constructed that hybrid language in the mid-19th century as a means of proselytizing the Ọ̀yọ́, the Èkìtì, the Ègbà, the Òǹdó and other linguistically related peoples who had been scattered by the slave trade and resettled in Freetown, Sierra Leone. Oyewumi's 'Yorùbá conception' is more certainly a product of Western colonisation than most of the gendered phenomena that she describes. See Matory, 'The English Professors of Brazil'.
66. Oyewumi, *The Invention of Women*, p. 16.
67. Oyewumi, *The Invention of Women*, pp. ix–xxi, 1–17; see also Ifi Amadiume, *Male Daughters, Female Husbands: Gender and Sex in an African Society* (London: Zed Books, 1987) and Matory, *Gender and the Politics of Metaphor*; Matory, *A Ritual History* for non-dichotomous treatments of gender relations in southern Nigerian cultures.
68. See Oyewumi, *The Invention of Women*, p. 108.
69. Oyewumi, *The Invention of Women*, pp. 41, 49, 75, 77.
70. Oyewumi, *The Invention of Women*, p. 75.
71. Oyewumi, *The Invention of Women*, pp. 61–2.
72. Oyewumi, *The Invention of Women*, pp. 45, 53, 62.
73. Matory, *Gender and the Politics of Metaphor*, pp. 28–44.
74. Oyewumi, *The Invention of Women*, p. 33. Consider also the Yorùbá proverb *Pèlé lábo; pèlé láko* ('Even in expressing sympathy, there's a nice [lit. 'female'] way and a mean, ornery [lit. 'male'] way'). In both verbal expressions, the contrast between male and female has a moral valence easily recognised by most Yorùbá people.
75. Wande Abimbọla, 'Images of Women in the Ifa Literary Corpus', *Queens, Queen Mothers, Priestesses, and Power*, ed. Flora E. S. Kaplan (New York: New York Academy of Sciences, 1997), p. 403.
76. Abimbọla, 'Images of Women', pp. 408–9.
77. Abimbọla, 'Images of Women', p. 411.
78. See Gilberto Freyre, *The Masters and the Slaves*, translated by Samuel Putnam, 2nd English-language edition, (Berkeley: University of California Press, 1986), [originally published as

Casa-Grande e Senzala]; J. Michael Turner, 'Brown into Black', *Race, Class and Power in Brazil*, ed. Pierre-Michel Fontaine (Los Angeles: Center for Afro-American Studies, UCLA, 1985), pp. 78–9; Thomas E. Skidmore, 'Race and Class in Brazil: Historical Perspectives', in *Race, Class and Power in Brazil*, ed. Pierre-Michel Fontaine (Los Angeles: Center for Afro-American Studies, UCLA, 1985); Thales de Azevedo, *Democracia racial* (Pétropolis, Rio de Janeiro: Vozes, 1975).

79. For an excellent overview of the anthropological literature on gender in sub-Saharan Africa (and one greatly at odds with Oyewumi's presentation of 'Western' views of gender in Africa and elsewhere), see Betty Potash, 'Gender Relations in Sub-Saharan Africa', *Gender and Anthropology*, ed. Sandra Morgen (Washington DC: American Anthropological Association, 1989) and Flora E. S. Kaplan (ed.) *Queens, Queen Mothers, Priestesses, and Power: Case Studies in African Gender* (New York: New York Academy of Sciences, 1997). Cross-cultural variation in the construction of gender roles has been a central theme in anthropology since the 1920s, for example, Margaret Mead, *Sex and Temperament in Three Primitive Societies* (New York: Morrow Quill, 1963); Mead, *Coming of Age*.

80. On the importance of similar conferences, linking scholars and nationalist laypeople, in the overseas propagation of Greek nationalism see Loring M. Danforth, *The Macedonian Conflict: Ethnic Nationalism in a Transnational World* (Princeton NJ: Princeton University Press, 1995), pp. 90, 92, 95.

81. The author of the position that each group should speak for itself did not appear to be advocating the truth of Oyewumi's argument but was instead defending the autonomy of each national tradition within the Yorùbá-Atlantic world. This person was, from the beginning, an important leader of the movement to re-unite the international community of *orişa*-worshipers but came to resist the emergent principle of West African Yorùbá supremacy and the apparent male supremacy that she encountered among West African collaborators in the project.

82. Molara Ogundipẹ-Leslie at 'Roundtable: The Invention of Woman: Theorizing African Women and Gender Now and into the Future', African Studies Association, Washington, D.C., 6 December 2002.

83. Anonymous selection committee member, private conversation, 19 November 2001.

84. Juana Elbein dos Santos, *Os Nàgô e a Morte* (Pétropolis, Brazil: Vozes, 1976); Pierre Verger, *Orixás* (São Paulo: Corrupio, 1981); Lydia Cabrera, *El Monte*, 5th ed. (Colección del Chicherekú, 1983); Robert Farris Thompson, *Flash of the Spirit* (New York: Random House, 1983).

85. For example, see Mikelle Smith Omari, 'From the Inside to the Outside: the Art and Ritual of Bahian Candomblé', Monograph Series #24 (Los Angeles: Museum of Cultural History, U.C.L.A., 1984), p. 54 footnotes 50, 55 and 64.

86. Michael Herzfeld, *Cultural Intimacy: The Social Poetics of the Nation-State* (New York and London: Routledge, 1997).

3

Cartographies of Globalisation, Technologies of Gendered Subjectivities: The Dub Poetry of Jean 'Binta' Breeze

Jenny Sharpe

It is generally recognised that an academic use of 'African Diaspora' grew out of the civil rights movement, anti-colonial struggles and the building of pan-African movements.[1] What is less acknowledged, perhaps, is how the current usage of 'diaspora' as a category of analysis is implicated in today's global cultures. Globalisation, in its simplest terms, refers to the transnational mobility of capital, labour, technology, consumer goods, art forms and media images. As a cultural phenomenon, the term refers to the labour diasporas that straddle national borders, existing in a state of 'cultural flux'.[2] It also denotes a decentering that allows for new hybrid cultures to emerge through an 'indigenisation' of metropolitan culture.[3] As a sociological phenomenon, it means that remote events can have an effect on local ways of life despite the distances separating geographically removed locations.[4] Marshall McLuhan coined the term 'global village' to describe a world in which new media, advanced telecommunications and rapid transportation shrunk distances between continents and nations. Yet, as Arjun Appadurai observes, McLuhan's metaphor is conceptually inadequate to a world that has become more 'rhizomic' in the sense that identities are no longer rooted in a single geographical place.[5]

The paradigm shift of 'African Diaspora' from signifying cultural survivals, commonalities and continuities to denoting cultural hybridities, difference and discontinuities reflects the new conditions of globalisation. One of the studies that has been instrumental in this conceptual shift is Paul Gilroy's *Black Atlantic: Modernity and Double Consciousness* (1993). Guided by a discourse of travel rather than an ideology of return, the book seeks to demonstrate the 'rhizomorphic, fractal structure of the transcultural,

international formation' that is the black Atlantic.[6] Gilroy suggests multiple
centres and points of migration that can account for the mutations and
hybridities of black culture on both sides of the Atlantic. And, it is primarily
through black popular music that he makes his case. Ronald Judy is
correct to identify the third chapter, '"Jewels Brought from Bondage":
Black Music and the Politics of Authenticity', as central to the book's
argument.[7] The value Gilroy ascribes to music as an expressive form has
to do with its marginalisation in Western systems of knowledge, a history
in which slaves' access to literacy was denied or restricted, and its anti-
phonal (call and response) form that decentres 'Africa' as a fixed point of
reference for the disapora.[8] As he explains, 'the circulation and mutation
of music across the black Atlantic explodes the dualistic structure which
puts Africa, authenticity, purity and origin in crude opposition to the
Americas, hybridity, creolisation, and rootlessness'.[9] The transatlantic circulation of black popular music, however, is inseparable from a corporate
industry responsibility for its marketing as a cultural commodity. And,
although a globalisation of the recording industry means that Anglo-
American corporate control has been replaced with transnational corporations that are not headquartered in any one nation, all of these
corporations operate out of 'wealthy, developed nations'.[10] It is not accidental, then, that most of the recording artists Gilroy discusses are located
in First World city centres.[11]

   The Black Atlantic has received criticism for its narrow definition of the
black Atlantic, one that excludes Africa, the Caribbean and Latin America.[12]
An absence of the Caribbean as a space of intellectual and cultural
production is particularly conspicuous because of the centrality of Afro-
Caribbean culture to Gilroy's rethinking of modernity. Although he
admits to having 'said virtually nothing about the lives, theories, and
political activities of Frantz Fanon and C.L.R. James, the two best-known
black Atlantic thinkers', he is less aware of how his examples of transatlantic cultural practices are rooted in global city centres.[13] The Soul II
Soul song, 'Keep on Moving,' that serves as an icon for the restlessness of
the black Atlantic world he wants to chart is an indication of how the
Caribbean that is everywhere in the book is also nowhere to be found.
The song appeals to Gilroy as an instance of 'transnational black Atlantic
creativity' because it was recorded by the British-born descendents of
Caribbean settlers in north London and re-mixed in a dub format in New
York by an African-American DJ, who sampled from American and
Jamaican records.[14] Although there is a distinctive Jamaican sound or
style to the song, Jamaica does not exist as a geographical location but
only in its British diasporic form or as 'raw materials' for American DJs
to sample. 'Keep on Moving' was produced in London and remixed in
New York because these are centres of the music industry. In this regard,

the global village – as a metaphor derived from an agrarian way of life – is no village at all but a series of interconnected urban centres.

To consider London and New York as global city centres is to recognise the degree to which Gilroy's mapping of the black Atlantic follows a cartography of corporate globalisation. As a dialogic engagement with African-American intellectuals, the book is a transatlantic exchange between Britain and the United States that passes through the Caribbean. In this regard, the absence of Africa, the Caribbean, and Latin America in the black Atlantic is better understood as an effect of the centre and periphery structures that are maintained by corporate globalisation, despite new transnational cultures that make such structures appear obsolete. On the one hand, globalisation breaks down centre-periphery relations through a two-way traffic that cannot be explained simply as cultural imperialism and which allows independent artists and cultural producers access to an international market. On the other hand, neo-colonial relations are maintained through the uneven distribution of resources in the global market place, the unlevel playing field established by the World Trade Organisation (WTO), International Monetary Fund (IMF) and World Bank, and a global assembly line that draw primarily on cheaper Third World female labour.[15] In addition, the tendency to regard globalisation as a trans-urban phenomenon elides its effect on rural economies. The growth of agrobusiness and biotechnology, accompanied by the need for expanding agricultural markets, has destroyed small farms and their related industries throughout the Third World.[16] Any theory of diaspora that follows a cartography of corporate globalisation risks reproducing its structures of power and knowledge.

The transatlantic travel of black popular music in Gilroy's study not only takes place between First World city centres; the unacknowledged subject of black modernity is also Western, urban and male. Alluding to Toni Morrison's observation that 'modern life begins with slavery', Gilroy argues for black modernity as a thoroughly diasporic, transcultural and creolised experience.[17] And, it is through black popular music that he establishes his definition of modernity.[18] His interest in black music as a modern diasporic cultural form lies in its constitutive role in the formation of a black British subjectivity. At the end of the third chapter, he describes his own experience of growing up in a London where 'the Caribbean, Africa, Latin America, and above all black America contributed to our lived sense of a racial self'.[19] To be fair to Gilroy, he states at the outset that his primary interest in a black Atlantic world lies in defining the cultural politics of Britain's black citizens. However, since his model of a transatlantic black culture is becoming institutionalised as a general theory of the African Diaspora, it is necessary to recognise its limitations.

Feminist scholars have shown how the chronotope of mobility in Gilroy's transatlantic model is male-gendered.[20] A similar argument could be made about his discussion of black music as a transatlantic phenomenon. Gilroy considers the consumption of music to be an activity that plays a central role in the formation of a black identity. And, he describes this identity as gendered because so many songs are about 'the conflict between men and women'.[21] Yet nowhere does he explain what the music means for black women or how their listening pleasures might differ from men's. Nor does he explain how female performers have contributed to the diasporic music he describes. Rather, his discussion centres on distinguishing male musicians who give a 'respectful and egalitarian representation of women' from their more misogynistic brothers.[22] And, he relies on 'dubbing, scratching, and mixing' as technological innovations that 'joined production and consumption together' for decentering the musician as artist.[23] The 'cutting and mixing techniques through digital sampling' that are so characteristic of contemporary black music hold a particular appeal for Gilroy as creative acts that are both modern (because technologically-driven) and syncretic (because they sample from global cultures).[24] By 'sampling' a few notes or lines from a recording and remixing it with the beats of synthesised drum machines, the musician plays the role of technician rather than creator. Although digital sampling undermines traditional notions of originality and authorship, the artistic creativity of the musician is reconstituted around technological innovations associated with masculinity.[25] It is not just that the musical innovations emerged from the 'electronic wizardry' of male DJs who built and repaired sound systems. Music critics and producers also promote the creativity of these musicians as a form of 'mastery'. The celebration of a 'cut-and-mix style' for its blurring of the boundaries between production and consumption nonetheless recentres black popular music around the disc jockey as producer.

To theorise the black Atlantic in terms of the decentering that Gilroy so admirably proposes, one would have to consider it as the site of multiple and heterogeneously-produced subjectivities. A theory of modern black subjectivities that are Third World, rural, domestic and female is available in the work of a diasporic Jamaican female performer, Jean 'Binta' Breeze, who employs reggae music and radio technology for staging Jamaican women's cultural identities. Reggae, and its offsprings of dub and dancehall, have spread throughout the African Disapora – there are even Nigerian and South African reggae bands. In its Jamaican birthplace, however, reggae is not simply one among several black musical styles but it is also the one that predominates. Its rhythm, from its early roots to its most recent incarnation as dancehall music, can be heard booming from large storefront sound systems, ghetto blasters and the radios that people listen to in their homes, cars, at work and on the streets. If, as Gilroy claims, music is

Figure 1: Jean 'Binta' Breeze, photo courtesy of 57 Productions.

central to a black sense of self, then one can make an even stronger case for the constitutive power of music in Jamaica – more records per capita are produced there than in any other part of the globe.[26] By invoking the mediation of the music through the radio and rhythm box, Breeze decentres the DJ as artist through Jamaican women's consumption of music rather than a cut-and-mix style that consigns them to a more passive role.

Jean 'Binta' Breeze grew up in Patty Hill, a small village in the rural hills of Hanover on the northwestern side of the island, before moving to Kingston in 1978 to study at the Jamaica School of Drama, where she met the dub poets Oku Onuora, Mikey Smith and Mutabaruka.[27] 'Dub' is a term used for the B-side or instrumental version of records over which DJs 'toast' their rhymes.[28] Dub poetry, however, fuses reggae beats with the spoken word so that the voice itself is an instrument. Incorporating a Rastafarian style of testimony and prophecy, dub poets merge their voices with those of the people through their use of oral speech patterns or patois and popular sayings to protest imperialism, racism, bourgeois norms and political corruption. Breeze first performed onstage in 1981 with Mutabaruka in Montego Bay and went on to record a number of songs that received airplay on Jamaica's popular reggae stations. She soon became recognised as the first woman dub poet in a male-dominated field.[29] Linton Kwesi Johnson, Britain's leading dub poet, heard her perform and brought her to London, where she has lived since 1985, although she spends a few months each year in Sandy Bay, a coastal town in Hanover, to be with her children. She is part of the transnational economic migration responsible for the popular saying that 'anywhere in the world you go, you find Jamaicans'.

Breeze's early poems, written while she still lived in Jamaica, were strident political messages that condemned the severe austerity measures imposed after Prime Minister Michael Manley signed with the IMF in 1978. 'Aid Travels With A Bomb' shows the 'structural adjustments' made to encourage foreign investments to be yet another form of colonisation. The designation of factories as export-free zones meant that the government received no compensation for providing cheap labour and could not prevent them from relocating to more cost-effective locations:

> They love your country
> They want to invest
> But your country don't get
> When it come to the test
> Dem gone home wid all de profit
> Your government left
> Upholding a racket[30]

In 'To Plant', Breeze is critical of the IMF recommendation that agriculture be shifted from produce for local consumption to cash crops for export. She sings about how these recommendations have contributed to world hunger:

> For de hungry getting rampant
> An de food is growing scarce
> De prices getting steeper
> De lan space jus kean waste[31]

These early poems are spoken out of a national pride that positions itself against the complicity of the national bourgeoisie and nation state with the forces of neo-colonialism. But the national voice is also female-gendered. In 'To Plant', Breeze assumes the traditional role of the woman as food provider in order to criticise the government for following the IMF recommendations that it shift agricultural production to cash crops and import food for local consumption. She is also critical of the dumping of surplus food and destruction of the land used to store nuclear waste in 'Aid Travels With A Bomb'. The neo-colonial relations that Breeze exposes in her early poems have not disappeared but only deepened with globalisation.

The effect that an integrated economy has had on a small Caribbean nation like Jamaica is further marginalisation through its inability to compete in a world market place even though, by virtue of its enormous debt, it must. Manley aptly describes the problem as going 'up the down escalator'.[32] Although Jamaica has increased its production of cash crops, it has been unable to compete in a market overseen by the WTO, which favours global giants. In 1997, the Jamaican government found itself facing a lawsuit led by the Clinton administration on behalf of Chiquita and Dole that challenged the special preferences European nations gave to Caribbean bananas, which was a holdover from their colonial interests in the region.[33] The US insistence on a free market policy meant that, in the absence of such preferences, Jamaican bananas were too expensive to produce, despite agricultural workers receiving the same wages as those in Haiti, the lowest paid workers in the Western hemisphere.[34] Jamaica now faces the problem of having to import produce for local consumption while being unable to export its cash crops. Jamaican women have traditionally been employed sewing inexpensive underwear and t-shirts at garment factories in export-free zones in Kingston and Montego Bay. Although they have constituted a larger percentage of the workforce than women in other undeveloped countries, as a result of the international stock exchange, civil unrest, and the ease with which manufacturers can move to more cost-effective regions, there has been a 40% decline in employment since 1988.[35] The globalisation of labour not only hurts women as wage earners; the scarcity of goods and soaring consumer prices that are a direct result of IMF policies also undermine their ability to manage households.[36]

Breeze's *Riddym Ravings* – which was published in 1988 and several poems of which were included on her 1989 LKJ Records release *Tracks* – stages the financial, emotional and psychological difficulties that working-class Jamaican women experience.[37] Her own diasporic existence between London and Sandy Bay is perhaps what gives this collection its keen sense of how global cultures are woven into the fabric of everyday life in Jamaica. In sharp contrast to her earlier work, in which a female-gendered voice was embedded into the public voice of the nation, the poems in this collection include dramatic monologues that express Jamaican women's thoughts and experiences that are distinct from a larger discourse of nation. *Riddym Ravings* denotes Breeze's break with dub poetry both in terms of its reggae rhythm and testimonial delivery style. As she explains, 'I lost the need to teach or preach, especially to audiences already converted, and found the courage to tell'.[38] But the poems do not only stage the economic and social marginalisation of Jamaican women; they also produce a black female subjectivity out of reggae's dancehall culture.

Dancehall, which is the new synthesised and electronic music that emerged from reggae in the eighties, is often characterised as a black Atlantic sound linking Kingston, New York and London.[39] But, at the local level, the term refers to the mobile sound systems travelling throughout

Jamaica bringing an urban sound to remote rural areas.[40] Anyone who crosses the border zone between city and country will quickly notice that the culture of pre-literate (i.e. oral-based) societies is also technologically-driven, even if it is not the cyber technology of post-literate societies like our own. Crews load up enormous speakers, multiple turntables and high-decibel amplifiers into open-air trucks and travel on dirt roads to the far reaches of the island to set up their sound systems on street corners and school yards for Saturday night parties. The observation of one music critic is an indication of the important linkage to the city that dancehall offers rural districts: 'The border crossing where St. Andrew parish gives way to St. Mary – where city cedes to country – is marked not by guards or even a sign but by jerry-built sound boxes blasting reggae at eardrum-splitting volume'.[41] The travelling sound systems were popular in rural parishes, where people could not afford the steep prices of live perform-ances, as far back as the early 1950s. A dancehall session consisted of a 'selector' or DJ spinning discs, while the 'toaster' or MC spoke from within a ghetto experience about unemployment, inflation and the 'dirty tricks' of politicians. Today, with the growth of the recording industry's promotion of stars, the DJ is no longer a technician but singer, songwriter and performer.[42]

Despite dancehall music's anti-authority stand and rootedness in ghetto culture, its politics are generally considered the antithesis of those espoused by dub poets.[43] Since the music has increasingly been taken over by gun talk and 'slackness' – the propensity of DJs to make sexual puns and wordplay, particularly ones that are demeaning to women – it is associated with the consumerism and free market liberalism promoted by Edward Seaga, who became Jamaica's prime minister after the violent 1980 general election.[44] Gilroy contrasts dancehall as the music of the pro-Reaganomics Seaga régime to dub poetry and roots reggae, which expressed the utopian vision of Michael Manley's socialist government.[45] And, the authors of *Reggae: A Rough Guide* characterise dancehall as a 'conservative and inward-looking' reaction to the deepening of the class gap that resulted from the free market policies of the new government.[46] These critical views from Britain are confirmed by Jamaica's leading dub poet, Mutabaruka, who has his own show on the popular IRIE-FM reggae station:

> Some people have said that dancehall music is anti-establishment; this is not true. The dancehall music is the most pro-establishment culture ever come inna Jamaica. It is dealing with exactly what the society is dealing with. The lewdness, the down-grading of women, the slackness, materialism, gun violence. The establishment is not against any of these things that dancehall personifies. I personally don't give any credence to dancehall culture. I think it is the worst thing that ever happen to Jamaica culture.[47]

Breeze does not share Mutabaruka's sentiments, and this difference is
also the sign of a gender difference in the subjects of her poems. Although
she castigates DJ slackness in the poem, 'Get Back', saying 'we tired of
degradation', she also credits dancehall music with breaking down the
middle-class mores that reinforced double standards for men and women.
'The DJs were saying jump and spread out, jump and chuck out', she
explains, 'and women broke out in the dancehall'.[48] Although most dancehall sessions take place in the Kingston metropolitan area, the mobile
sound systems also bring its synthesised rhythm and ghetto culture to
rural Jamaica.

The (mostly working-class) women don electric-coloured synthetic wigs
or extensions, large false eyelashes, glittery sequined, fringed or plastic
outfits consisting of not much more than g-strings and push-up bras to
step out at night in the dancehall. 'It does not matter if the women are fat',
explain Paulette McDonald and Carolyn Cooper. 'Fat is hot'.[49] Cooper
characterises dancehall women as 'disdainful, inaccessible sexual beings'
who revel in the 'DJ's "bigging up" of her person as desired and desiring
subject – not mere sex object'.[50] Despite the reduction of women to their
body parts in songs like Shabba Rank's 'Love Punaany Bad', women are
greater fans of these songs than are men.[51] The appeal slack lyrics have for
women has to do with their being sung by DJs (like Shabba Rank) who
have a lover-man reputation. But slackness also expresses ambivalence
about female sexuality that allows women to assume sexual agency within
dancehall culture. Since the singer expresses his sexual prowess through
his ability to satisfy women, he indirectly acknowledges women's need for
satisfaction.[52]

In two poems depicting the pleasure women derive from dancehall
culture, Breeze turns 'slackness' inside out by making it into a source of
female self-empowerment. 'Dubwise' presents the erotic gyrations of a
dancehall diva as a ritualised dance between the sexes for control of the
floor. The words of the poem snake across the page in imitation of the
female dancer's 'wining', which consists of pelvic rotations to the beat of
the music. The idea of the dance as a simulated sex act is made evident
through the poem's sexually explicit language:

'cool an
   deadly'
snake
   lady
writhing
   'roun
de worlie'
 wraps
  her sinews
 roun his

pulse
and grinds
his pleasure
and disgust
into a
one dance
stand[53]

The ambivalence the male dancer feels towards his partner's grinding of his pelvic region has to do with her sexual agressiveness that turns *him* into an object of desire:

to equalise
he grins
cockwise
at his bredrin
and rides
a 'horseman scabie'
or bubbles a
'water
bumpie'
into action.[54]

The male dancer's hypermasculine dance style is represented here as a defence mechanism, his effort to recuperate the control he has lost to his female partner, or which he perhaps did not have from the start. The dance – which is a ritualised enactment of the battle between the sexes in which pleasure is derived from the 'fight' – ends when the DJ 'smilingly / orders / "Cease"'.[55] The DJ occupies a godlike position, controlling the dance floor through the control he exercises over the music. As Gilroy explains, 'the DJ and the MC or toaster who introduces each disc or sequence of discs, emerge as the principal agents in dialogic rituals of active and celebratory consumption'.[56]

As much as women play a central – and flamboyantly visible– role in the dance hall, they are removed from the male-dominated technical fields of dubbing, mixing and versioning, and the verbal mastery of the MC. There appears to be a gendered division of labour, with women being associated with 'sexuality, the body, emotion and nature', while men are associated with 'culture, technology, and language'.[57] This gender division, however, is blurred through the skill with which the women manipulate and rotate their bodies on the dance floor – an activity that mirrors the selector's technical expertise and MC's verbal dexterity. One cannot help but marvel at the dancer's rhythmic interpretation of the music and skilful contortions of her body in such styles as 'head-top dancing', where she places both head and feet on the floor to emphasise her buttocks. Through the extension of male technical skills to dance and a hypersexualised female body, the women dancers assert an agency that articulates the technological innovations of the music.

Since Breeze's collection of poems first appeared, a number of women have emerged as DJs/singers, although the selectors who operate the sound systems are still men.[58] The most popular of the female DJs is Lady Saw, whose satirical wit, compelling stage presence and mike skills have earned her the title of First Lady of Dancehall. Behind the story of her achieving international fame in dancehalls from London to New York is the story of how Jamaica's mobile sound systems enabled her to make the journey from the rural parish of St Mary to Kingston. Born Marion Hall, she grew up in Galina, a coastal town east of Ocho Rios, and got her start by taking a turn at the mike of touring sound systems:

> I was begging the selector, 'Gimme a talk on the mic, gimme a talk!' But he didn't pay me any attention, I think because I was dressed like a real country girl, in some ugly shoes, and some stockings and shorts. And they were thinking, 'What's she got?'[59]

The 'country girl' soon earned the reputation of having 'mashed up' three veteran DJs. She made her way to Kingston, where in 1994 she recorded her first international hit, 'Find a Good Man', which, as a prayer for the miracle of finding a good man, became the 'ladies anthem'.

Lady Saw soon discovered that the only way she could break into the male-dominated field of deejaying was through slack lyrics. 'In those early days, when I was busting out, I did X-rated songs [on records], but now I only do them onstage', she reports; 'I've shown people that I can succeed on my talent alone'.[60] She soon earned notoriety for outdoing the male performers in slackness. By using the same raw language to undermine the sexual boasting of men who claimed to be 'strong black stallions', she demanded that they work harder at pleasing the ladies: 'You can't grind good and you can't fuck straight. Stab out the meat! Stab out the meat!' Songs like 'Stab Out the Meat' and 'Good Wuk' exploit the humour and wordplay of slackness in order to reverse its signification. Lady Saw's appearance onstage in a push-up bra and g-string, and grabbing her crotch (as she reminds her detractors Michael Jackson did), similarly displays female sexuality in the act of parodying the hypermasculinity of male DJs. When the guardians of middle-class morality criticised her slack lyrics and scandalous performances, she responded with 'What is Slackness', which lambasted them for their double standards for men and women, and pointed to the government's own slackness in providing basic social services for Jamaican people.[61] As Cooper explains, 'Lady Saw's brilliant lyrics, reinforced by her compelling body language, articulate a potent message about sexuality, gender politics and the power struggle for the right to public space in Jamaica'.[62] The dancehall divas and female DJs constitute a more visible form of women claiming male-dominated territory through a technologically-driven female sexuality. But there are also less dramatic ways in which Jamaican women assert themselves in public space.

While the female DJ explicitly weds the eroticised female body to the mike, in 'eena mi corner' a companion poem to 'Dubwise', Breeze metaphorically transforms the female body into a technological device. The speaker appears to be a passive observer of the dancehall scene, standing on the sidelines moving in steady rhythm to the music, except that she has turned her body into a radio so she can tune into the sexual energy being generated. The bass sound and synthesised reggae rhythm that reverberates through the woman's body as a site of sexual energy is reproduced in the onomatopoeia of the Jamaican speech patterns in the poem:

im jus a
im jus a
a eh i oh oooh
im way troo
de mos complex part
a mi lunar system[63]

Hans Enzensberger, building on Frantz Fanon's writings on the radio as an instrument for advancing the Algerian revolution, saw the revolutionary potential of the radio to turn actors into authors. He explains, however, that as an instrument for change, the radio would have to be able to transmit as well as receive signals.[64] In her use of the radio as a metaphor for female sexual energy, Breeze imagines a woman who can turn her receiver into a transmitter through the mere flick of a switch:

an jus
flip a switch
tun mi receiva
to transmitta
checking anadda one
wanderin troo
de sonic boom of a bassline[65]

In contrast to the dancehall diva's explicit display of her sexuality, the woman standing quietly in the corner equalises gender relations by sending her sexual desire through the sound waves of the music. Breeze uses the cyborgian image of a woman whose body is inhabited by a radio for representing a black female subjectivity that is rooted in the vernacular of Jamaica's dancehall culture. This subjectivity is not to be equated with a consciousness, because the rhythm box is in the woman's body rather than her mind. The question is not whether dancehall produces a revolutionary consciousness but how Jamaican women insert themselves into a popular cultural form in order to assert themselves in a world over which they have little control.[66]

Breeze also fuses the female body with radio technology in 'riddym ravings (the mad woman's poem)', where the ravings of a pregnant country woman issue from a radio embedded in her head. The poem is delivered in the voice of one of those crazy women seen wandering the city streets, singing and talking to themselves. Breeze has remarked that it 'represents the whole dislocation of a rural agricultural community into an urban setting of mass unemployment'.[67] Dislocation is one aspect of modernity belonging to globalisation, and in 'riddym ravings' we see the effect that the IMF's 'structural adjustments' have had on the rural poor. The country woman in 'riddym ravings' has been evicted for failing to pay her rent and ends up on the streets with nothing but her 'Channel One riddym box'. That same night a DJ flies into her head and plays this song:

> Eh, Eh,
> no feel no way
> town is a place dat ah really kean stay
> dem kudda – ribbit mi han
> eh – ribbit mi toe
> mi waan go a country go look mango.[68]

'Ribbit' (rivet) is a DJ term for describing the state of being caught in a heavy dub beat. In the song the woman hears in her head, the term refers to her being caught in the city but nonetheless able mentally to escape to the country through music. For her, the city is not a place of meeting and mobilisation for 'the migrants, the minorities, the diasporic', which is how Homi Bhabha describes a global city like London.[69] In a Third World city like Kingston, an unemployed country woman has no claim to a home or even the public space of the streets. After her landlord evicts her, she is picked up and sent to Bellevue, which is both a poorhouse and a mental hospital.

The homeless woman's madness is the overt manifestation of her effort to avert her dehumanisation in the city through the memory of country life back home. In identifying slavery as the first modern experience, Morrison characterises madness as a strategy for survival: 'Certain kinds of madness, deliberately going mad … "in order not to lose your mind"'.[70] The idea of 'deliberately going mad' makes madness into the exercise of control over the mind in the face of an absence of control over one's own body:

> an a ongle one ting tap mi fram go stark raving mad
> a wen mi siddung eena Parade
> a tear up newspaper fi talk to
> sometime dem roll up
> an tun eena one a Uncle But sweet saaf
> yellow heart breadfruit
> wid piece a roas saalfish side a i.[71]

Although the woman appears to be controlling the song she hears, it is not clear whether it originates in her mind or in the outside world, as she hears the same song playing on the bus she attempts to take back home:

an sometime mi a try board de bus
an de canductor bwoy a halla out seh
'dutty gal, kum affa de bus'
an troo im no hear de riddym eena mi head
same as de tape weh de bus driva a play, seh

The constant clamour of music blasting from huge storefront speakers, boom boxes and tiny transistor radios makes it difficult to locate the country song in any one place. By virtue of its mediation through a technology of reproduction, it has no single origin.

When talking about the mobility of today's global cultures, it is important to distinguish between the movement of cultural forms and people. In 'riddym ravings', the homeless woman lacks the ease of mobility belonging to the music that travels from country to town and perhaps back again. As a social being rather than a cultural form, she suffers the consequences of dislocation. It is not simply the case that she is unemployed; she is also stranded in a large impersonal city like Kingston. Cut off from her extended family that allows her to 'make do' (which is the Jamaican term for women's ability to survive on little or no money), she is ignored, laughed at or run off for being dirty and ragged. She wants to go home, but she does not have the money for bus fare. When, faint from hunger, she attempts to pick up a piece of banana dropped by a girl, she is sent back to Bellevue where the doctor and landlord pull the radio plug out of her head. But as soon as she is back on the street, she pushes it back in so she can continue to hear the song.

The madwoman then decides to walk home, the same way her grandmother used to walk to town to sell food. Here, Breeze invokes the memory of country higglers or market women, who dominated the informal economy of selling locally-grown produce in the cities and providing people who lived in rural areas with news gossip, and goods from town.[72] However, the domestic network in which the madwoman's grandmother participated is no longer available to her. In a modern world of rapid transportation, the journey from town to country on foot signifies the inability to 'make it' in the city. Taking pride in her appearance, the madwoman strips naked to bathe herself in water running from an open pipe so that she can be clean when she arrives home. However, she is arrested for indecent exposure and returned to the mental hospital. This time the doctor and landlord remove the entire radio from her head, but when they are not looking, she grabs it and pushes it up in her belly for her baby to hear:

> fah even if mi nuh mek i
> me waan my baby know dis yah riddym yah
> fram before she bawn[73]

By moving the radio from her head to her belly, the woman, like her sister standing in the corner of the dancehall, turns her receiver into a transmitter so that her baby can hear the sounds of the country. Her action of relaying the song to her unborn child transmutes one of the most normative and naturalised significations of the female body – maternity – into a technologically-mediated relation.

The poem ends with the mad woman hearing the DJ scream – 'Murther / Pull up Missa Operator!' – the same moment the doctor and landlord send an electric shock through her body.[74] These words, also from dancehall culture, allude to a particularly good or 'murderous' track that an audience wants to hear again. In response to the crowd's enthusiasm, the DJ pulls up the needle and places it at the beginning of the song again. Breeze performs a word play on 'mother' and 'murder' and the DJ and doctor as 'operators' through which the attempt to kill the music on the operating table is transformed, through dancehall language, into an act in which the song ends abruptly only so that it might be repeated once again. No matter how many times the forces of law and order attempt to 'cure' the woman by killing the song in her head, they cannot destroy the memory of her home or prevent her from passing on that memory to the next generation.

Breeze draws on the language of deejaying for articulating the consciousness of an unemployed rural woman who is otherwise classified as 'mad'. Yet, she does not simply extend the DJ's voice to the woman. Rather, she reworks it in a manner that inauthenticates both the presupposed masculinity of his voice and the rural origins of the song. As Joan Dayan remarks about the poem, the voice the mad woman hears does not express the male bravado of toasting, which is the name for the slick rhymes the MC or DJ speaks over the music. The wistful expression of a desire to be in the country suggests that the woman 'inhabits the DJ voice' rather than the other way around.[75] The image of country life as one of looking for mangoes perhaps displays a romantic nostalgia for a pastoral way of life that no longer exists. But that would be far too literal a reading of the song. For, even as the woman inhabits the DJ voice, the song is inhabited by DJ language ('ribbit'), thus undermining its authenticity as an instance of folk culture. This 'inauthentic' – in the sense of James Clifford's explanation of being 'caught between cultures' – and mechanised – because mediated through the radio – song is the sound of the country caught in the web of globalisation.[76] The woman has made her way to the city in search of work because an integrated market has destroyed Jamaica's rural economies. At the same time, a global reggae culture connects her with the rural origins from which she is removed.

The radio not only provides a woman seeking employment in the city with a connection to her home; it also brings the rest of world into the domestic space of women who stay home. In 'ordinary morning', Breeze weaves the national and international news relayed through the radio into the daily struggle of one unemployed, unmarried mother to survive. The poem linguistically connects the life of an ordinary Jamaican woman to the news she hears on the radio about 'Israel still a bruk up / Palestine / an Botha still have de whole world han / twist back a dem'.[77] The woman knows that, as in the case of the problem of nation in Israel and South Africa, there is no way out of her daily struggle:

so it did hard fi understand
why de ordinary sight of
mi own frock
heng up pon line
wid some clothespin
should a stop mi from do nutten
but jus
bawl[78]

If the woman cries at the sight of her frock hanging on the clothesline, it is not because she lacks an understanding of her life. Rather, she knows all too well that the ordinariness of the morning means that the future looks much the same as the past. The woman reveals, in the course of her musings, the effect that Jamaica's debt crisis has had on working-class women, whether they are part of the workforce or not. The currency devaluation and austerity programmes imposed by the IMF are responsible for 'de price rise pon bus fare/an milk an sugar'[79] that has contributed to the burden of everyday life for an unmarried mother like herself. While 'Dubwise', 'eena mi corner' and 'riddym ravings' show women claiming public space, this poem weaves the outside world into domestic space. It reworks the personal/political opposition so as to illustrate how so private a world as a woman's domestic musings is shot through with the shards of global culture.

The women who appear in *Riddym Ravings* challenge the perception that rural populations somehow exist outside the cultures of globalisation, that their entry into modernity has been stalled. Modernity is not just a trans-urban, diasporic experience; it is also the experience of forced migration from rural to urban areas and the fact that few parts of the world remain untouched by today's global cultures. Breeze's poems disrupt the taken-for-grantedness of modernity being equated with cosmopolitanism and global city centres. They use radio technology for shifting the signification of black popular music from production to consumption, while making consumption into a two-way process through the idea of the radio as both a receiver and transmitter. They also extend the power of the DJ's voice to the female body in order to assert black women's ability to act upon a world in which the agents of control increasingly exist elsewhere. In short, they provide a theory of gendered subjectivities that is derived from the cultures and everyday experiences of ordinary Jamaican women.

An academic discourse on diaspora escapes the critique of being parochial precisely because its scope extends beyond the national level. But, unless we locate our theoretical models within the geopolitical dimensions of their production, we risk turning diaspora studies into a new universalism. By examining the cultures that are unique to particular societies rather than globalising our own, we can consider how heterogenously-produced subjectivities might be part of the new world system known as globalisation. Then we might begin to see that the shrinking world being mapped is just a little bit less global.

Notes

This essay grew out of workshops organised by the Multicampus Research Group on Transnational and Transcolonial Studies at UCLA. I am indebted to the critical input on early drafts I received from the group, as well as from the anonymous readers for *Gender and History* and my student, Sam Pinto.

1. Stuart Hall, 'Cultural Identity and Diaspora', *Identity: Community, Culture, Difference*, ed. J. Rutherford (London: Lawrence & Wishart, 1990), pp. 222–37; Paul Gilroy, *The Black Atlantic: Modernity and Double Consciousness* (Cambridge MA: Harvard University Press, 1993), pp. 111–45; Tiffany Ruby Patterson and Robin D. G. Kelly, 'Unfinished Migrations: Reflections on the African Diaspora and the Making of the Modern World', *African Studies Review* 43 (2000), p. 14; Brent Hayes Edwards, 'The Uses of *Diaspora*', *Social Text* 109 (2001), pp. 46–8.
2. Arjun Appadurai, *Modernity at Large: Cultural Dimensions of Globalization* (Minneapolis: University of Minnesota Press, 1996), p. 44.
3. Appadurai, *Modernity at Large*, p. 32.
4. Anthony Giddens, *The Consequences of Modernity* (Stanford CA: Stanford University Press, 1990), p. 64.
5. Appadurai, *Modernity at Large*, p. 29.
6. Gilroy, *The Black Atlantic*, p. 4.
7. Ronald A. T. Judy, 'Paul Gilroy's Black Atlantic and the Place(s) of English in the Global', *Critical Quarterly* 39 (1997), pp. 22–9.
8. Gilroy, *The Black Atlantic*, pp. 72–110.
9. Gilroy, *The Black Atlantic*, p. 199.
10. Celia Colista and Glenn Leshner, 'Traveling Music: Following the Path of Music Through the Global Market', *Critical Studies in Mass Communication* 15 (1998), p. 183.
11. Gilroy makes brief mention of Nigeria's Fela Ransome Kuti's integration of African American funk into Afro-beat, but it is only from the perspective of James Brown's characterisation of Fela as 'the African James Brown' (*The Black Atlantic*, p. 199).

12. Special Issue 'The "Black Atlantic",' ed. Simon Gikandi, *Research in African Literatures* 27 (1996); Special Issue 'Africa's Diaspora', ed. Judith Byfield, *African Studies Review* 43 (2000).
13. Gilroy, *The Black Atlantic*, p. xi.
14. Gilroy, *The Black Atlantic*, p. 16.
15. Sarah Anderson (ed.) *Views from the South: The Effects of Globalization and the WTO on Third World Countries* (Oakland CA: Food First Books, 2000).
16. Vandana Shiva, 'War Against Nature and the People of the South', *Views from the South*, pp. 91–125.
17. Cited in Gilroy, *The Black Atlantic*, p. 221.
18. 'Music', explains Judy, 'is the principal mode in which and through which a distinctly "black" modern subjectivity is constituted' ('Paul Gilroy's Black Atlantic', p. 25).
19. Gilroy, *The Black Atlantic*, p. 109.
20. Elizabeth DeLoughrey, 'Gendering the Oceanic Voyage: Trespassing the (Black) Atlantic and Caribbean', *Thamyris* 5 (1998), pp. 205–3; Sandra Gunning, 'Nancy Prince and the Politics of Mobility, Home and Diasporic (Mis)Identification', *American Quarterly* 53 (2001), pp. 32–69.
21. Gilroy, *The Black Atlantic*, pp. 201–2.
22. Gilroy, *The Black Atlantic*, p. 85.
23. Gilroy, *The Black Atlantic*, pp. 103–8.
24. Gilroy, *The Black Atlantic*, p. 103. 'Unlike synthesizers, which generate tones artificially', explains Robert Burnett, 'samplers record real sounds. Anything audible is eligible: pre-recorded music, drumbeats, human voices. Samplers transform these sounds into digital codes, which in turn can be manipulated to produce melodies, rhythm tracks and other sound patterns' (*The Global Jukebox: The International Music Industry*, New York: Routledge, 1996, p. 93).
25. Barbara Bradby, 'Sampling Sexuality: Gender, Technology, and the Body in Dance Music', *Popular Music* 12 (1993), pp. 155–76. My discussion of the gendering of technological innovations in popular music is indebted to Bradby's provocative essay.
26. Elena Oumano, 'Reggae Says No to "Politricks"', *Nation* (August 25 1997), p. 24.
27. Jean 'Binta' Breeze, 'Can a Dub Poet be a Woman?' *Women: A Cultural Review* 1 (1990), pp. 47–9.
28. A Jamaican record producer describes the dub version of a title track as 'just the bare bones … just a naked dance rhythm'. Cited in Dick Hebdige, *Cut 'N' Mix: Culture, Identity, and Caribbean Music* (London: Methuen, 1987), p. 83.
29. Breeze, 'Can a Dub Poet be a Woman?' p. 47. For a discussion of women dub poets in Jamaica and the diaspora, see Christian Habekost, *Verbal Riddim: The Politics and Aesthetics of African-Caribbean Dub Poetry* (Amsterdam: Rodopi, 1993), pp. 201–8.
30. Jean 'Binta' Breeze, *Answers* (Kingston: Masani, 1983), p. 14.
31. Breeze, *Answers*, p. 8.
32. Michael Manley, *Up the Down Escalator: Development and the International Economy: A Jamaican Case Study* (Washington DC: Howard University Press, 1987).
33. Paul Blustein, 'Caribbean Could Wonder Where the Yellow Went', *Washington Post* (March 19, 1997), p. C9. Stephanie Black's documentary film *Life and Debt* (Tuff Gong Picture Production, 2001) shows how the problem of globalisation is not simply that of Jamaican farmers being able to compete internationally but also locally. A range of agricultural sectors – dairy, bananas, produce for local consumption – have been destroyed through the marketing of less expensive (and perceived as superior) American imports.
34. Augusta Lynn Bolles, *Sister Jamaica: A Study of Women, Work, and Households in Kingston* (Lanham: University Press of America, 1996), p. 111.
35. Leith L. Dunn, *Women Organising for Change in Caribbean Free Zones: Strategies and Methods* (The Hague: Institute of Social Studies, 1991).
36. Lynn Bolles, 'Kitchens Hit by Priorities: Employed Working-Class Jamaican Women Confront the IMF', *Women, Men, and the International Division of Labor*, ed. June Nash and María Fernández-Kelly (Albany: State University of New York Press, 1983), pp. 138–60.

37. Jean 'Binta' Breeze, *Riddym Ravings and Other Poems*, ed. Mervyn Morris (London: Race Today Publications, 1988).
38. Breeze, 'Can a Dub Poet be a Woman?' p. 49.
39. Paul Gilroy, *'There Ain't No Black in the Union Jack': The Cultural Politics of Race and Nation* (London: Hutchinson, 1987), pp. 187–92; Louise Chude-Sokei, 'Postnationalist Geographies: Rasta, Ragga, and Reinventing Africa' in *Reggae, Rasta, Revolution: Jamaican Music from Ska to Dub*, ed. Chris Potash (New York: Schirmer Books, 1997), p. 219.
40. For a historical and ethnographic account of Jamaican dancehall, see Norman C. Stolzoff, *Wake the Town and Tell the People: Dancehall Culture in Jamaica* (Durham NC: Duke University Press, 2000).
41. Oumano, 'Reggae Says No to "Politricks"', p. 25.
42. Carolyn Cooper, *Noises in the Blood: Orality, Gender, and the 'Vulgar' Body of Jamaican Popular Culture* (Durham NC: Duke University Press, 1995), p. 138–9; Barrow et al., *Reggae: The Rough Guide*, p. 234; Jordan Levin, 'Dancehall DJs in the House', *Reggae, Rasta, Revolution*, pp. 228–30; Stolzoff, *Wake the Town and Tell the People*, pp. 97–9.
43. Musically, however, dub poetry and dancehall have a shared origin in reggae's sound systems.
44. Hebdige, *Cut 'N' Mix*, pp. 122–7.
45. Gilroy, *'There Ain't No Black in the Union Jack'*, p. 188.
46. Steve Barrow, Peter Dalton, and Jonathan Buckley, *Reggae: The Rough Guide*, 1st edition (London: Rough Guides, 1997), p. 231.
47. Imani Tafari Ama, 'Muta and Yasus Defend the Culture', *Sistren* 16 (1994), p. 8.
48. Jean 'Binta' Breeze, *Bad Language: The Delights of Improper Language* (London: ICA Video, 1993).
49. Paulette McDonald and Carolyn Cooper, 'Dancehall Revisted/Kingston', *Review: Latin American Literature and Arts* 50 (1995), p. 30.
50. Carolyn Cooper, *Noises in the Blood*, p. 166, Carolyn Cooper, 'Lady Saw Cuts Loose: Female Fertility Rituals in Jamaica Dancehall Culture', in *Dancing in the Millennium: An International Conference Proceedings*, ed. Juliette Willis and Janice D. LaPointe-Crump (Washington DC: Congress on Research on Dance, 2000), p. 79. Also see Andrew Ross, *Real Love: In Pursuit of Cultural Justice* (New York: New York University Press, 1998), pp. 65–7.
51. Barrow et al., *Reggae: The Rough Guide*, p. 295.
52. For a more detailed reading of the ambivalence male DJs have toward female sexuality, see Cooper, *Noises in the Blood*, pp. 136–73. In 'Masculinity and Dancehall', Jarret Brown reads slackness less optimistically than does Cooper, arguing that the imaginary violence enacted against women in these songs maintains them in a submissive position (*Caribbean Quarterly* 45 (1999), pp. 1–16).
53. Breeze, *Riddym Ravings and Other Poems*, p. 28.
54. Breeze, *Riddym Ravings and Other Poems*, p. 28.
55. Breeze, *Riddym Ravings and Other Poems*, p. 28.
56. Gilroy, *'There Ain't No Black in the Union Jack'*, p. 164.
57. Bradby, 'Sampling Sexuality', p. 157.
58. Stolzoff, *Wake the Town and Tell the People*, p. 117–18.
59. Lady Saw, cited in Baz Dreisinger, 'Dancehall Star's Key to Success', *The Miami Herald* (October 27, 2002).
60. Cited in Elena Oumano, 'V.P. to make known Lady Saw's "Passion"', *Billboard* 109 (June 28, 1997), p. 8.
61. Stolzoff gives an account of the Lady Saw controversy in *Wake the Town and Tell the People*, pp. 238–46.
62. Cooper, 'Lady Saw Cuts Loose', p. 83.
63. Breeze, *Riddym Ravings and Other Poems*, p. 26.
64. Hans Magus Enzensberger, *The Consciousness Industry: On Literature, Politics and the Media*, trans. Stuart Hood (New York: Seabury Press, 1974), pp. 97–8.

65. Breeze, *Riddym Ravings and Other Poems*, p. 27.

66. Although I am primarily interested in Jamaican women as consumers of dancehall music, there is an entire transnational trade in dancehall clothing connecting Kingston to Miami and New York, in which higglers or Informal Commercial Importers (which is their government-designated name) have managed to carve out a space of economic independence for themselves. For a gendered model of globalisation derived from the transnational practices of Barbadian pink-collar higglers, see Carla Freeman, 'Is Local: Global as Feminine: Masculine? Rethinking the Gender of Globalization', *Signs* 26 (2001), pp. 1007–37.

67. Jean 'Binta' Breeze, 'An Interview with Jean Breeze', *Commonwealth* 8 (1986), p. 57.

68. Breeze, *Riddym Ravings and Other Poems*, p. 58.

69. Homi K. Bhabha, *The Location of Culture* (London: Routledge, 1994), pp. 169.

70. Cited in Gilroy, *The Black Atlantic*, p. 221.

71. Breeze, *Riddym Ravings and Other Poems*, p. 59.

72. Victoria Durant-González, 'The Occupation of Higglering', *Jamaica Journal* 16 (1983), pp. 2–12; Elsie LeFranc, 'Higglering in Kingston: Entrepreneurs or Traditional Small-Scale Operators', *Caribbean Review* 16 (1988), pp. 15–17.

73. Breeze, *Riddym Ravings and Other Poems*, p. 60.

74. Breeze, *Riddym Ravings and Other Poems*, p. 61.

75. Joan Dayan, 'Caribbean Cannibals and Whores', *Raritan* 9 (1989), p. 60.

76. James Clifford, *The Predicament of Culture: Twentieth-Century Ethnography, Literature, and Art* (Cambridge MA: Harvard University Press, 1988), p. 11.

77. Breeze, *Riddym Ravings and Other Poems*, p. 48.

78. Breeze, *Riddym Ravings and Other Poems*, p. 49.

79. Breeze, *Riddym Ravings and Other Poems*, p. 49.

4

'If You Can't Pronounce My Name, You Can Just Call Me Pride': Afro-German Activism, Gender and Hip Hop

Fatima El-Tayeb

it's strength and positivity / that keep me alive / growing is never easy / but still – I do try / if you have problems with my name / well for you, I'll be pride / there are spirits who protect me / so you better worry / I'll surely stay alive.[1]

In the mid-1990s, amid a resurgence of racist violence in Germany and elsewhere and the continuous tightening of anti-immigration policies within the European Union, the German public rediscovered a new, exiting phenomenon: black Germans. Contrary to the brief but intense focus on 'coloured occupation children' in the 1950s, this time the media interest rested on Afro-Germans who had gained a high-profile status. This handful of black German actresses and actors, TV presenters and athletes, were taken as symbols of the new, 'colourful', multicultural Germany. Despite the obvious instrumentalisation, the focus on any German ethnic minority in the context of 'normality' and entertainment rather than perceived crisis – for example, the presence of (black) occupation forces in post-War Germany – already marked a turn in media representations of ethnic diversity in the Federal Republic. But although these representations were remarkable because of the new and celebratory image of Afro-Germans they conveyed, in-depth articles and features were still few and far between.[2] This changed in 2001, when fourteen well-known male Afro-German rappers united in the Hip-Hop project 'Brothers Keepers'. The group's first single 'Adriano/Letzte Warnung' (Final Call) received wide media attention and started a downright hype around Afro-Germans and Hip Hop.

The connection between blacks and music certainly is far from original, but in this case there are a number of unusual features: The young MCs, who were highly sought after for interviews, consistently defined themselves as 'Afro-Deutsch' (Afro-German), rejecting the usual terms ascribed to black Germans by the white majority (such as 'coloured', 'half-caste', 'African'). Thereby, they placed themselves within the context of a black German movement that had coined the term 'Afro-Deutsch' twenty years earlier. 'Afro-German' is the term used by the majority of black German activists when describing themselves and their community. It refers to persons of African ancestry identifying as German or having spent a significant part of their life in Germany – which is not necessarily the same as being German citizens. According to the *jus sanguinis* version of citizenship practised in Germany until 2000, persons of non-German descent were legal 'foreigners', even if born and raised in Germany.[3] Many, though not all, Afro-Germans have one (white) German parent, therefore possessing citizenship. But not all people thus described are happy with the term 'Afro-German'. Some prefer 'black German', some reject all ethnic categorisations, while many use Afro- and black German interchangeably. There is a significant difference between the terms though, a difference that points to an important divide between the Americas and continental Europe: the latter's black populations originate not in slavery but in colonialism. In this essay I practise a 'strategic essentialism,' using the terms 'Afro-German'/'black German' for those whose primary socialisation and cultural experience is German, who have no other national identity available to them, and whose social experience is largely shaped by being perceived as 'African' by a majority of Germans (who usually equate 'African' with 'black').

By claiming an Afro-German identity, 'Brothers Keepers' not only challenged dominant German concepts of ethnicity, but also the widespread notion of Hip Hop culture and 'black consciousness' as recent US imports without a meaningful German context. The hit song's title, 'Adriano', refers to Alberto Adriano, a thirty-nine year-old father of three, killed by a gang of white German youths solely because he was black. The song threatened violent retaliation, and with its accompanying video (directed by acclaimed Jewish Swiss filmmaker Dani Levy) addressed German racism in a manner unusual for the type of Hip Hop showcased within the field of vision of typical German teenagers on *MTV Germany* and *Viva*.[4] The average German feature-writer's purview was quite similar. Numerous media responses to 'Brothers Keepers' made it seem as if they were the first 'migrant' voice on the Hip Hop scene, which had been dominated by 'German', i.e. white, crews. Moreover, mainstream media responded as though 'Brothers Keepers' were the first generation of Afro-Germans ever entering the public sphere.[5]

After 1945, the Federal Republic attempted to establish itself as a 'colour blind society'. This might have been an understandable and well-intentioned reaction to the national socialist past, but such a society cannot be achieved by an act of will or a taboo on all discourses around race and racism. If a vexing aspect of the past is simply declared dead and buried without examination, it will likely rise again in unintended manners, as unfortunately was the case here: underneath the post-war silence around race, pseudo-scientific, biologist theories that originated in late nineteenth century lived on in Germany.[6] The nation cut itself off from post-colonial discourses, in which minorities became active agents and race was deconstructed as a 'natural category'. This refusal to deal with the German investment in racist concepts cemented dogmatic claims that Germany never had any 'race issues'. (Accordingly, anti-Semitism was completely separated from racism.) This denial of the relevance of race meant that the century-long black presence in Germany never found its way into the public consciousness: neither did the last two decades of Afro-German activism.

Nevertheless, there have been testimonials of a black German identity throughout the twentieth century, often in reaction to racist state policies, such as the introduction of 'Anti-miscegenation-laws' in the colonial period or the prosecution of blacks under National Socialism. But these were either individual responses or part of a black movement that was initiated and dominated by African migrants/'colonial subjects' in Germany, a group that showed a high level of organisation as early as the turn of the last century. It was almost a hundred years later, during the mid-1980s, that a movement emerged which both claimed an identity as black *and* German (a perfect example of an oxymoron to white Germans of that period) and as part of a larger African Diaspora.

The interactive relations between black communities worldwide are reflected in the profound influence that African decolonisation struggles and the US black liberation movement had on the development of an Afro-German sense of identity. Audre Lorde, African-American lesbian feminist activist and poet of Caribbean descent, coined the term 'Afro-German' after meeting black German women when teaching in Berlin in 1984. While this moment was not the birth of a black German consciousness, Lorde's coinage nevertheless symbolises the central role that US activism had for Afro-Germans. The interest was rather one-sided for a long time: although black Germans who struggled against the racism and isolation that they faced were acutely aware of larger struggles in Africa and even more so those in the United States, black populations elsewhere rarely questioned Germany's (self)representation as a white nation.[7] Lorde's reaching out to a black community that most African Americans assumed to be non-existent is indicative of the important role of women and feminist issues in the first decade of Afro-German activism.

The nascent Afro-German movement soon gained momentum. The 1980s saw the publication of a book that remains the key-text of black Germany, *Farbe bekennen* (*Showing Our Colours: Afro-German Women Speak Out*). This was the first publication to express a collective Afro-German identity and point out the long history of a black presence within the nation. The decade further witnessed the launching of several magazines and the founding of two national organisations, 'Initiative Schwarze Deutsche' (ISD), and a women's association, 'Afro-deutsche Frauen' (ADEFRA), the latter of which pushed the debate on racism within the German feminist movement. The first decade of black German activism was successful in generating a debate among Afro-Germans and creating organisational structures. It was a phase that was necessarily introspective and devoted to discovering and building a community; during this period, activists laid important foundations for later attempts to reach out to African migrant communities in Germany and black communities elsewhere. The movement did not succeed, however, in breaking or even lastingly shaking the German majority's resistance to admitting that 'German' does not equal 'white' (and 'Christian').

Today, ethnic concepts of national identity and the restrictive citizenship law lead to a Catch-22 for German minorities: whoever does not conform to a certain physical image of 'Germanness' is considered a 'foreigner'. 'Foreigners', in turn, are not regarded as potential citizens; migrants who were brought to Germany by the millions in the 1960s were officially termed 'guestworkers', implying that their stay in Germany would be a temporary one. To fully include temporary guests, so the rationale ends, in the nation's social, cultural, and political structure is unnecessary – if not impossible.[8] There are a number of problems with this line of thinking, mainly the fact that the 'guest'-status is stretched over generations, creating a disenfranchised 'foreign' population actually born in Germany.[9] Such an anti-assimilationist ideology, which considers 'foreignness' a hereditary trait rather than a temporary state, additionally creates naturalised and racialised definitions of Germanness, which put minorities on the defence whether they possess citizenship or not. Until proven otherwise, they are 'outsiders' who are expected to be very literally on their (natural) way *out* of a nation they cannot belong to. This attitude is strikingly reflected by the almost complete media and scholarly consensus that Germany might have a growing 'xenophobia problem', but no racism whatsoever, even though the victims of 'xenophobic' attacks are overwhelmingly people of colour (with or without a German passport). This is not due to an unfamiliarity with the meaning of the term; 'race' and 'racism' are freely used in connection with the UK, the USA or South Africa, but are proclaimed inappropriate for Germany, where all non-whites are also non-German. Therefore, German minorities not only need to fight for political influence but also for recognition as part of German society at all.

Building on the momentum of their success, 'Brothers Keepers' try to do both. In addition to promoting an 'Afro-German' identity, they have initiated a variety of anti-racist project aimed at empowering black youths, supporting refugees (who independently of their ethnic origin live under deplorable conditions in Germany) and exposing police brutality against African migrants, thus explicitly defining Hip Hop as a political force.[10] Their ability to use the group's publicity to create awareness campaigns is a result in good part of twenty years of Afro-German activism and networking. The possession of a historical consciousness (being aware of and paying respect to those who paved the way) is a central concept within Hip Hop culture. Afro-German rappers honour this concept by positioning themselves within the context of an Afro-German community built by those who came before them. Some traditions have been easier to adopt than others, however. In particular, the strong presence of women – articulate, feminist, often lesbian – in the first decades of the Afro-German struggle has been hard for young male MCs to stomach, given that they generally model themselves after images of black masculinity that are often deeply sexist and homophobic.

In this article, I contextualise current Afro-German Hip-Hop activism within the tradition of two decades of a black German political movement, and the 'pan-ethnic' community concept of Hip Hip's old school. I propose that while these dual origins create some yet unresolved tensions, particularly around issues of gender and sexuality, they also place the black German Hip Hop community in a unique position within current German (and European) identity debates. Issues of migration and ethnicity have acquired centre stage in a unifying Europe. Moving between multicultural utopia and 'clash of civilisations' scenarios, these issues are often projected onto gendered images of ethnic Others (and this is even more the case when minority youths are the focus of attention). This development is magnified in Germany, where national reunification – achieved more than a decade ago – has not yet resulted in a united nation. Rather, reunification complicated the already-troubled relationship of Germans towards their own national identity. While it is unclear what 'German' actually signifies, insecurities about this matter tend to be externalised by definitions of what is absolutely *not* German.[11] This results in exclusionary tendencies towards all those who are visibly different – including Afro-Germans, who are persistently identified as 'Africans' or 'Americans'.[12] The explicitly political focus of Afro-German Hip Hop, often revolving around issues of national and ethnic identity, can only be understood against this background and the larger tradition of Afro-German resistance. I will therefore first sketch a brief history of the black presence in Germany, followed by a closer look at the origins of the modern Afro-German movement. By doing so I shall provide the necessary background for the analysis undertaken in the second half of the article, which focuses on the process by which black Germans have adapted and transformed US models of political Hip Hop. Black Germans appropriate these models, make them applicable to their living conditions, and use them for a successful intervention into German discourses regarding national identity.

Black German History: An Overview

In the course of our research we met Afro-German women who had lived in Germany under the reign of Kaiser Wilhelm II, in the Weimar Republic and through National Socialism. Some were immediately willing to meet with us younger ones and recount their lives. Today – several years later – it is difficult to describe how moved and excited we were at these meetings. We suddenly discovered that our history had not begun in 1945.[13]

It is impossible to say how far back the history of blacks in Germany dates.[14] Living dispersed among their white compatriots, blacks in Germany were common enough in the seventeenth and eighteenth century to be repeatedly mentioned in scientific studies of race, literary texts or newspaper accounts.[15] This presence of a small black population notwithstanding, the topic of 'blacks as exotics' has long played a central role in German discourses on race. Beginning in the seventeenth century, exhibits of 'savages' became an increasingly successful mass entertainment in German (and other European) metropoles, reaching a peak with the colonial exhibit of 1896, which attracted an audience of two million. Starting in 1884, Germany's African possessions included 'Southwest Africa' (now Namibia), 'East Africa' (parts of today's Tanzania and Kenya), Togo and Cameroon, while its Pacific empire encompassed Samoa, part of Papua-New Guinea and the Solomon islands. Though this colonial period was over by the outbreak of the First World War, the consequences for both coloniser and colonised were deep and lasting. Resistance against German rule was widespread in all African colonies. The uprising of the Herero and Nama in Germany's largest and economically most important colony 'Süwestafrika' (Southwest Africa) from 1904 to 1907 generated much attention in Germany and the prolonged success of the rebellion was hotly debated. The 1907 elections, which were necessary after the parliament refused to approve a further increase in the colonial war budget (which had exceeded 600 million Reichsmark), were commonly referred to as the 'Hottentott elections', after their central subject.[16] After the revolt's brutal suppression – only one quarter of the Herero and not many more of the Nama survived the war – German authorities established a system of control and oppression with a completeness that was unique in the world, and which later became a model for the South African apartheid system.[17]

Of particular importance is the fact that within colonial Southwest Africa, German nationality was for the first time legally linked to race. Persons with any trace of 'native blood' were excluded from German citizenship, and significantly, this measure was primarily directed against children of German men married to African women. In this context, the Social Darwinist equation of body and society meant that individuals had relevance not as such but only as members of the race. White settlers in relationships with black women therefore were 'race traitors' guilty of producing 'mixed-race' offspring that had access to German nationality and could therefore irreversibly 'pollute the nation's white blood' – as well as threaten the social and economic apartheid practised in the colony. During the colonial war, the authorities had taken measures against 'miscegenation' and from 1905 onwards all marriages between whites and 'natives' were declared illegal (including those already in existence). German men married to or living with African women were excluded from all German institutions in the colony, and could not vote, buy land or receive financial support from the government. At the same time, bi-racial children were denied access to schools. Though legitimate children automatically inherited their fathers' citizenship according to the German legal system, in the colony 'race' superseded both family ties and German law, leaving these 'Afro-Germans' without any of the rights they would have been entitled to had they been (legally) white.[18]

Within Germany itself, race remained outside of legal definitions of nationality until 1933, although the category became increasingly important socially. The deep-seated connection between tropes of 'blood' and 'race' during the 1910s and 1920s made the German status of non-whites a very tentative one. The new nationality law introduced in 1913 eliminated all traces of *jus soli*, thus strengthening the link between 'blood' (that is, ethnicity and race), and Germanness.[19] The law granted legitimate children fathered by German men an automatic right to citizenship, including children with black mothers; however, the law's focus on descent reaffirmed the existing notion that persons of 'foreign blood' could not be proper Germans. Additionally, it was almost impossible for Africans from the colonies to enter Germany, and a parliamentary motion to grant citizenship to children of German women married to stateless men (aimed at Danes in Northern Germany) failed out of concern that it would have to include marriages between African men and German women.[20] For those Africans who were able to move from the colonies to Germany, their status was that of 'colonial subjects'; after Germany lost her colonies, they were handed 'foreigners' passports,' which left them – and their families – in effect without nationality.

Despite these restrictions, African migrants in Imperial Germany developed strong informal and formal networks, from the conservative *Deutscher Afrikanerbund* (German Union of Africans) to the radical *Liga zur Verteidigung der Negerrasse* (League for the Defence of the Negro Race).[21] These organisational ties proved to be even more necessary during the Weimar democracy, which followed the Empire's collapse at the end of World War I. The loss of the colonies did as little to improve the status of blacks as did the newly installed socialist government. On the contrary, the early years of the Weimar Republic saw a racist campaign that far exceeded the one against intermarriage in the colonies. For a Germany still in shock about the lost war, the presence of several thousand African soldiers among the French troops occupying the Rhineland became the symbol of a world turned upside down. Germans of all classes and political affiliations saw black troops as a tremendous provocation. The socialist government initiated a campaign against them, which was largely financed by heavy industry and soon rested on a broad public alliance of political parties (with the exception of the Communists), nationalist groups, professional organisations, women's groups and churches.[22] Numerous propaganda materials – multi-lingual pamphlets, posters, postcards, novels, plays and even two movies – indulged in detailed descriptions of alleged acts of sexual violence perpetrated by black soldiers against white German women, giving the campaign a distinct pornographic tinge.

The focus on this most powerful racist image succeeded in creating a racial solidarity that overcame deep national and political antagonisms. From an aggressor responsible for the first 'world war', Germany was turned into a helpless victim of black aggression, in need of international white solidarity.[23] Government propaganda excluded the subject of 'mongrelisation', since a survey among women who had borne children by African soldiers revealed that only one of them had been raped, a fact that seemed better left unpublished.[24] Nevertheless, non-government organisations within and outside Germany emphasised miscegenation from the beginning, exploiting stereotypes that had been successfully activated at least a decade before, and now found widespread resonance. For example, in 1920, the medical journal *Ärztliche Rundschau* declared: 'Shall we silently endure that in future days not the light songs of white, beautiful, well-built, intelligent, agile, healthy Germans will ring on the shores of the Rhine, but the croaking sounds of greyish, low-browed, broad-muzzled, plump, bestial, syphilitic mulattos?'[25]

Within the Social Darwinist system of logic, the mere existence of black Germans was a threat. They were invested with an enormous power: even though they were few, they could destroy the German nation by tainting its still 'pure blood'. This topic had already dominated the discourse around the colonial 'mongrel-race', but grew even more important now that the enemy within, 'the mongrel', had penetrated the heart of the national body and was about to poison it. The propaganda against the African troops in the Rhineland had made the image of the 'syphilitic mulatto' commonplace. In connection with the discourse on degeneration, s/he became the symbol for the conjunction of the 'inner and outer fight for survival' as well as for the menace that inner and outer 'race enemies' posed to the German people.

This perception of black Germans as the vanguard of the deadly threat that the nation faced in the constant onslaught of 'inferior races' on its pure blood explains why the tiny group of an estimated 800 Afro-German children in the Rhineland was seen as a serious danger to a population of 80 million. There is no doubt that the danger was indeed perceived as real. In 1923, the Weimar government began a list of all Afro-German children in the Rhineland, and not only those fathered by soldiers; while it was not clear what should be done with these children, government officials did not doubt that a 'solution' had to be found. Several possibilities were discussed and rejected as impracticable, among them the plans to send all the children to Africa or to sterilise them so that they could not further 'poison the German nation'. In the end, though, no measures beyond registration were taken.

While the national and international accountability of the Weimar democracy had protected the black children in the Rhineland, the situation changed radically with National Socialist accession. The 'mongrelisation of the German nation', a stable topic for decades, now became one of the 'Third Reich's racial problems'. The forced and secret sterilisation of Afro-Germans registered on the Weimar-era list began in 1937. Apart from this measure, which explicitly singled out black Germans, they were affected by a number of laws aimed at 'Jews and other foreign elements', such as expatriation or reduction to a limited status of citizenship. Nazi racist policies generally focused on Jews and Gypsies (the Sinti and Roma); blacks were left relatively unharmed in some areas of the country. In other regions, however, blacks were not only excluded from schools, public spaces and most professions, but also sent to concentration camps.[26]

Black Germans have never been officially recognised as victims of Nazi persecution. Rather, after the Second World War ended, all memory of their treatment during National Socialism seemed to vanish as completely from public memory as did Germany's colonial past. Despite the fundamental differences in political systems and the GDR's official commitment to anti-racism, neither socialist East Germany nor the democratic West had any use for their black citizens. This mentality underscores the point that the perceptions of white Germans were based on concepts predating 1945 that were obviously never significantly challenged within either the socialist or the Western democrat mode of thinking.[27] Since the existence of a population that was not white but still German was as unthinkable after 1945 as it was before, history was both ignored and repeated. Old positions continued to guide discussions about non-white Germans, and this time in the West, Germans of colour were referred to as 'occupation babies'. While the vast majority of German children fathered by American GIs were white, in the public mind all 'occupation babies' were black and all black children were fathered by GIs.[28]

Simultaneously, scientific 'race studies' revived within academia. Using materials gathered during the preparation of forced sterilisations (with little reflection about their origin), studies assessed the chances of integrating 'Mulatto children' into the Federal Republic.[29] Thus, not surprisingly, during the 1950s black Germans once again were defined as unnatural, a product of extraordinary circumstances. The public again viewed black soldiers foremost as potential rapists, white women in relationships with them as whores and their children as mistakes of nature.[30] Again, removal of the children to a more appropriate surrounding – namely Africa or the USA – was seen as the preferable solution. After all, as a 1952 parliamentary debate on the issue concluded, 'the climate in this country does not suit them'.[31] Instead of accepting the existence of a black population, and one that was quickly growing, the majority of white Germany opted to deny its existence by defining black Germans as inherently 'foreign'.

White Germans remained surprisingly consistent in their attitude towards their black compatriots: from the beginning of the twentieth century to the post-World War II period, black Germans symbolised sexual and racial transgressions committed by 'real' Germans. Their outsider status prevented their social and ideological, if not legal, inclusion into the national community of citizens, depriving them of a voice even in public debates where they were the subject. Unlike African migrants who faced many of the same prejudices but repeatedly challenged their marginalisation, Afro-Germans's very Germanness paradoxically stopped them from doing the same. There was no black community Afro-Germans could fall back on – unless they created it themselves.

The Beginning of a Movement: Afro-German Women Showing Their Colours

> In the spring of 1984, I spent three months at the Free University in Berlin teaching a course on Black American women poets and a poetry workshop in English, for German students. One of my goals on this trip was to meet Black German women, for I had been told there were quite a few in Berlin. (Audre Lorde)[32]

Audre Lorde's visit to Berlin in the spring of 1984 served as a catalyst for events that would radically change Afro-German history. Lorde was relatively well known in Germany because a small Berlin-based feminist publisher, Orlanda, had issued an edited volume containing texts by Lorde and Adrienne Rich, *Macht und Sinnlichkeit* (*Power and Sensuality*) – the first German language publication on the US debate on racism within the feminist movement. A number of key texts from the US women's movement had previously been translated into German, but did not include works by black authors or works addressing racism among women. While living in the United States, Orlanda founder Dagmar Schultz had become aware of this omission but she did not yet connect it to the situation of black Germans:

> My realisation that racism was only rarely called by its name in Germany, even in the woman's [sic] movement, led me to publish the book *Power and Sensuality*, with texts by Audre Lorde and Adrienne Rich. But it was not until I worked on this book [*Showing Our Colours*] that I became aware of the racism that Afro-Germans have experienced and continue to experience.[33]

Power and Sensuality offered insights into a debate that was of particular interest to black German women and accordingly, many took the chance to meet Lorde in person when she came to Berlin. It is indicative of the German silence around race and racism Schultz described – and of the identification of the 'race problem' with the USA – that it took the presence of an African American to create a platform for black Germans to address their situation. Many were still struggling to develop a black identity vis-à-vis a society, which considered the terms 'black' and 'German' mutually exclusive and doubted black Germans' justification to claim either identity.

Lorde acknowledged these women as part of a worldwide black Diaspora. Such recognition validated their experiences in a way previously unknown to black German women and facilitated the new process of collectively exploring their similarities rather than being defined through their 'Otherness' in a white society:

> As Afro-German women almost all of us between the ages of twenty and thirty were accustomed to dealing with our background and our identity in isolation. Few of us had any significant contact with other Afro-Germans and if we attempted to discuss our thoughts and problems with friends, it was always possible that we would alienate someone or be accused of being 'too sensitive'. Meeting each other as Afro-Germans and becoming involved with each other has been a totally new experience.[34]

The new sense of community was empowering and became even more so as an admired African American poet and activist took on a mentor role, providing experience, advice and support. That the newfound energy could be transformed into a book, which is now *the* Afro-German key text, was again due to Lorde's intervention. She convinced Orlanda to take on this daring project rather than publishing texts by Lorde herself as Schultz had planned. After two years of research, *Showing Our Colours* was published in 1986 and edited by Schultz along with Afro-German activists Katharina Oguntoye and May Opitz (later Ayim). Ayim had devoted her thesis in sociology to the history of black Germans and provided background information that ranged from twelfth-century paintings of Africans in Germany to racist representations in contemporary schoolbooks. Additionally, the volume presented life stories of fourteen Afro-German women between the ages of seventeen and seventy. *Showing Our Colours* thus provided factual information on a part of German history deemed non-existent by society, politics and academia alike. Through the interview collection the anthology also contextualised experiences that had been perceived as aberrant and individual, pointing them out as collective traits in the life of a part of the population that up until that point was neither perceived nor had defined itself as a community – black Germans.[35]

The two years' research preceding the publication of *Showing Our Colours* was a major step in creating this community. The project had an effect way beyond the Berlin group of black women, influencing the first national meeting of black Germans, which took place in Wiesbaden in 1985. The meeting resulted in the founding of the Initiative Schwarze Deutsche (Initiative of Black Germans, later changed to Blacks in Germany). From the beginning, the group consisted of largely autonomous local chapters, although activists all over Germany – only a handful in the beginning – remained in close contact. Indeed, the statement of goals published by the ISD Rhein-Main in 1989 can be considered representative for the organisation's goals in general:

> We would like to contribute to a change in the general appreciation of German history – all aspects of it. This includes dealing with Afro-German (Afro-European) history, which to a great extent must be compiled and recorded for the first time. This means that we should concern ourselves with our own biographies as a basis for a special, black-identified identity. We demand that white society put an end to prejudice, discrimination, racism and sexism, perpetrated against us Black Germans/ Afro-Germans and against all other social groupings with a similar plight ... We demand that racist stereotypes and discriminatory expressions, terms, illustrations and race-slanted reports disappear from the media ... An important aspect of our work is to cooperate with groups from Black world movements, with people doing anti-racism work and other solidarity groups.[36]

In the years following the first meeting in 1985, a network of ISD chapters emerged throughout Germany.[37] Activities were wide-ranging, including an annual national community meeting (which has been attended by hundreds in recent years); Black History Month in Berlin; the publication of a magazine (*Afro Look*, preceded by the short-lived *Onkel Toms Faust*); and cooperative projects with other minorities.[38]

The translation of *Showing Our Colours* into English in 1993 by the University of Massachusetts Press and Orlanda's publishing of May Ayim's poetry and essays, resonated with US German Studies struggling to distinguish itself from the traditional 'Germanistik'. Ethnic diversity is still not part of German universities' curricula: History, Sociology and Germanistik for the most part still assume a clear division between (implicitly white) Germans and 'foreigners'. This approach leaves no space for the study of German minorities, which, of course, not only include blacks, but also Turkish Germans, Sinti and Roma, and German Jews; and programmes like 'Ethnic Studies', not to mention 'Black Studies', are non-existent. Though British and US German Studies have been instrumental in creating an awareness of Germany's inclusion in a Western discourse on race, in the current context Afro-Germans appear only as one of several German minorities, not as one of several black Diaspora communities.

Despite the links made between Audre Lorde and black German feminists in the 1980s, US and British Africana Studies still for the most part restrict Diaspora Studies to the Americas and the Caribbean. This focus was a logical and necessary first step in systematically analysing the displacement of African populations through slavery, but it is important to keep in mind that the black Diaspora experience is not identical with the black presence in the Americas. To assume this ignores the interaction of Diaspora communities across the Atlantic. Going beyond the triangle of sub-Saharan Africa, Britain and the Americas that Paul Gilroy sketched in *The Black Atlantic* as the close geographical proximity of Europe and Africa means acknowledging a continuing cultural exchange (including the exchange of humans).[39]

Whether within the African diaspora or not, political movements – progressive and reactionary – are usually dominated by men, if not in the rank and files then certainly at the level of decision-making. In many ways similar in its structure to typical male-dominated emancipation organisations, the black German movement went a different way due to its specific history. The genesis of *Showing Our Colours*, unlike many other political projects, was inextricably linked to feminism in general and US black feminists in particular. Audre Lorde's commitment to black feminism made her seek out her German sisters in the first place; for these black German women who had been told again and again that their experiences were marginal, unimportant and shameful, the support of a black woman widely recognised among German as well as US feminists was invaluable. And, following publication of *Showing Our Colours* when some of the editors and contributors did a reading/racism awareness workshop tour, feminist venues provided spaces.[40] As a result, Afro-German women, at least if they had some affinity to feminism, had access to this new movement in a way that men did not. In 1986, the black German women's association ADEFRA (Afro-Deutsche Frauen) was founded in Bremen. Similar to the ISD, with which it works closely, ADEFRA consists of affiliated but independent local groups. For several years, the organisation published its own magazine, *Afrekete*, in addition to providing a number of women-oriented activities and participating in international exchanges of women of colour. ADEFRA brought an explicitly feminist agenda and strong lesbian presence into Afro-German activism. Many in the ISD, male and female, felt uncomfortable with this development; debates on the supposed priority of racism over sexism or the 'lavender menace' that ADEFRA introduced to the movement lead to tensions not yet resolved.[41]

That women nevertheless continued to strongly affect if not dominate Afro-German activism was partly due to the fact that the feminist network which increasingly debated racism provided a platform that had no male pendent.[42] Accordingly, publications exploring the black experience in Germany often appeared in a feminist context. Sometimes this was a conscious choice as with another Orlanda publication, *Entfernte Verbindungen* (i), which was an exploration of anti-Semitism, racism and class oppression that grew out of feminist discourses, or *Aufbrüche* (*Departures*), documenting cultural productions of black, Jewish and migrant women.[43] At other times, though, the focus on women was a result of a failure of Afro-German men to contribute. This seems to be especially true for literary projects such as *Talking Home: Heimat aus unserer eigenen Feder*, an anthology by German gays of colour, or a soon-to-be published anthology of Afro-German poetry.[44]

One can only speculate as to why black German men have long been largely absent from Afro-German publications. The feminist context might have been intimidating; there could also be a relation to the content of the early works. While *Showing Our Colours* provided historical background to the black German experience, at its core were personal testimonies that often displayed a sense of isolation, insecurity, self-hate and confusion as well as pride and an insuppressible, fighting spirit. While they obviously resonated with the community as a whole, public admittance of such emotions might have been harder on male than female egos[45] – and this especially so, since the sense of isolation and traumatic experiences of most Afro-Germans growing up in the 1950s and 1960s likely remained much stronger among male activists. Feminism gave women the chance to contextualise their experiences on interrelating levels of class, race, gender and sexual orientation. How important this context and sense of community are to public artistic expression is revealed by the complete switch in 'gender visibility' that came with the advent of Hip Hop in Germany.

Brothers Keepers – Sisters Weepers? Afro-German Hip Hop and Gender

> Possibly our emerging visibility will also clear a path for those who are children today so that they can grow up feeling less isolated, marginal and exceptional than we did.[46]

Afro-German activists in the 1980s and 1990s achieved mixed results regarding the group's goal to influence media representations of black Germans. The founding of the ISD and the publication of *Showing Our Colours* generated some media interest. Newspaper articles and a number of TV documentaries reported on the fate of the grown-up 'coloured occupation babies'. Naming was a central issue from the beginning: none of the articles' authors used the terms 'black' or 'Afro-German', so clearly favoured by the subjects of their reports. Not all went as far as reviving the 'occupation baby' as did the left-liberal *Frankfurter Rundschau*, but clearly, all journalists felt that it was up to them – and not black Germans themselves – to determine how they would be called (most settled, and still do, on 'coloured').[47] By and large though, the ISD has not become the envisioned pressure group, able to expose racism in the media and in politics. This seems less due to strategic mistakes on the part of the ISD than to the continuous German myth that all non-whites must be 'foreigners' and therefore are not entitled to a voice in public discourses.

If minorities do enter the public discourse, it is usually filtered through the majority perspective.[48] Until recently, this meant a nearly unanimous focus on their 'foreignness', presenting it either as constituting a social, economic and political threat to Germany's stability or as marker of their victimisation by an intolerant society. But the distinction between implicitly white, Christian Germans and foreigners is increasingly hard to maintain. Afro-Germans, Sinti and Jewish Germans have long embodied supposedly contradictory identities. In recent decades, they have been joined by far more than a million German-born 'foreigners': the sons and daughters (and increasingly granddaughters and grandsons) of the 'guest-workers' brought to the country in the 1950s and 1960s. The first generation of young migrants organised along ethnic lines and within traditional political structures. Unions played a central role, as did (feminist) grass-roots activism in migrant neighbourhoods. The situation of the second and third generation is profoundly different: employment opportunities are slim, traditional forms of organising do not respond to their situation, and their parent's country of origin – perceived as their home-country by parents as well as by German society – is largely foreign to them. Meanwhile the Germany they have been born into continues to define them as 'foreigners' on their way out.

This disparity continues to grow within a Germany whose urban population is increasingly made up of people who might have spent their life – or a substantial part of it – in that country, but are not necessarily white, German and Christian. Within German discourses, urban centres are usually portrayed as sights of ethnic conflict and social decay; they have localised common fears around economic decline and cultural change. These are also places, though, where a new discourse on identity originated. It is a discourse that can be called authentically 'German' in that it does relate to one's predecessors' countries of origin or to other Diaspora communities. Yet focusing explicitly on the German situation, it constructs a national identity which includes hundred of thousands of Afro-Germans, more than one million 'Turks' born in Germany, and the 70,000 German Sinti, to name just a few of those usually not thought of when 'German' is defined. It is a discourse which finds its congenial expression in Hip Hop.

Created by African American, Caribbean and Latino youths, Hip Hop has long spread around the world. In Europe, minority and migrant teenagers were the first to pick up this culture, as they easily identified with Hip Hop's message. Kutlu, a Turkish German MC from Cologne remembers: 'When we saw the movies *Wild Style* and *Beat Street*, Turks and Italians and so on could immediately identify with the Puerto Ricans and Afro-Germans with the blacks. Somehow, everybody realised that right away.'[49] Meli, Skillz en Masse's female MC recalls a similar awakening:

> In Germany it starts when you enter the first institution, be it kindergarten or school – you are confronted with rejection, being different, being black. And then I heard Public Enemy, got the T-Shirts – that was a liberation for me, an outlet, to rap the lyrics, feel the energy, that just touched me. These were people 9,000 miles away from me and they said things that were relevant for my life here in Germany.[50]

Not surprisingly, then, Fresh Familee's 1990 'Ahmed Gündüz', the first rap song ever recorded in German, was the creation of 'foreigners'.[51] 'Ahmed Gündüz' reflected on the experiences of first generation migrants, thus introducing a decidedly Turkish-German point of view. During most of the 1980s, German Hip Hop crews rapped exclusively in English, and it is probably the Afro-Italian-German crew Advanced Chemistry who can be credited with first introducing German language rap in 1989. However, Fresh Familee's 'Ahmed Gündüz' was the first published and thus the most widely available rap song in German.

The nation's mainstream audience discovered Hip Hop two years later, when the (white) Die Fantastischen Vier (The Fantastic Four), who had rapped in German since 1989, published their 'Die da?!'. The song initiated enormous media hype and most accounts of Hip Hop in Germany falsely call Die Fantastischen Vier the 'inventors of German rap', completely ignoring the contribution of migrants and minorities.[52] The creativity of youth of colour, which had been central to the birth of German Hip Hop, was thus doubly marginalised: though disproportionately present within the scene since the 1980s, migrant and minority crews did not profit from the first German Hip Hop hype in the early 1990s. Instead, record deals and TV appearances went almost exclusively to white groups. And when the mainstream finally recognised their presence, rappers of colour were presented as latecomers to an established movement. Fresh Familee's Tachi, author of 'Ahmed Gündüz', recalls the beginnings of Hip Hop in Germany quite differently: 'I think, as a migrant from a poor neighbourhood, you automatically identified with Hip Hop. Just from hearing rap's rhythm and realising, someone's getting something off his chest here. You heard that immediately, for example, with "The Message", even if you couldn't understand a word'.[53] While mainstream audiences long associated German Hip Hop only with its 'whitewashed', commercially successful version, a vibrant subculture continued to exist outside the media hype, its centres often close to US army bases where the newest imports could be heard – and where traditionally a large black German population lived.[54]

Heidelberg-based Advanced Chemistry, founded in the mid-1980s as one of the first German crews, and probably the first to rap in German, were the most important proponents of a version of Hip Hop that went beyond apolitical, fun messages transported by groups such as Die Fantastischen Vier or Fettes Brot. In 1992, Advanced Chemistry's 'Fremd im eigenen Land' (Stranger in My Own Country) first proclaimed an identity which was completely ignored by mainstream society. This particular identity fit a growing part of the German population under twenty five: that of 'non-traditional' Germans with an African, Arab, Turkish, Bosnian or Asian background – 'strangers in their own country', indeed. Emerging from the everyday experiences of Germans of African and migrant descent in a post-Unification Germany that did not welcome them into the new community of citizens, the song remains one of the sharpest on the situation of Germans of colour to date. The very act of listening to 'Fremd im eigenen Land' appears recurrently in narratives by young rappers of colour as a moment of awakening and of inspiration for their own careers.[55] The tide of racist violence that swept Germany after Unification politicised many young people of colour, who could not relate to the politics of traditional migrant and anti-racist groups. For many of them 'Fremd im eigenen Land' showed that rap could be a form of political activism, and one that perfectly fit their situation.

Hip Hop, for the first time, created a broad forum of expression and exchange between marginalised communities, fostering interactions between minorities becoming aware of their similar situation. Advanced Chemistry explicitly refers to this syncretic potential. Based on African American cultural traditions of resistance, Hip Hop was created by interaction of different communities of colour, creative reaction to the inner cities' increasing pauperisation – a trend, which in Europe, too, disproportionately affects migrants and communities of colour.[56] Advanced Chemistry's Linguist applies the concept to Germany:

> In Germany you have minorities. There are minorities with a German passport. That's me for example, a black German. There are minorities in this country without a German passport. Those are Turkish Germans for example – I consciously say Turkish *Germans* – those are Yugoslavian Germans, Moroccan Germans, whoever. But we all belong together. We are all confronted with racism, not xenophobia. I am confronted with racism, but I am lucky, because I cannot be thrown out of the country. On the other hand there are no laws protecting my rights as a member of a minority.[57]

The new meta-ethnic identity created within Hip Hop culture is explored, shaped, and problematised through musical dialogue.[58] It is in this discourse – and on more than an artistic level – that the German Hip Hop scene, or rather part of it, emancipates itself from the US model through exploration of issues originating in specifically German conditions. In constructing an open, inclusive group identity based on common interests and experiences rather than shared ethnic origin, the repossession of a suppressed past is instrumental, a sense of history necessary to offensively oppose marginalisation and stereotyping by the majority.

In the cover text of their second single released in 1993, 'Welcher Pfad führt zur Geschichte' ('Which Path Leads to History'), Advanced Chemistry explicitly connects with an urban US Diaspora tradition to which they add new members:

> Each and every activist of contemporary Hip Hop, whether in Bremerhaven or Brooklyn, acts in the tradition of the Zulu Nation, no matter if he or she admits this or not … In New York, this culture was initiated primarily by African Americans, Jamaicans, Haitians, Puerto Ricans … It is no coincidence but due to its rebellious contents that in Germany many black Germans, Turks and Kurds, Yugoslavians, Roma and Sinti feel attracted to this culture and practice Hip Hop … The message should be clear: … We're going our own way![59]

While placing themselves within an international movement of artists and activists of colour and promoting inter-ethnic solidarity in Germany, Advanced Chemistry were well aware that their generation was not the first working on constructing an identity that is both black and German. Significantly, their reference to male and female Hip Hop activists in the above quote displays a sensibility towards gender representation certainly unusual for the Hip Hop community and might well be a sign of their Afro-German activism background.

The ISD and especially their annual General Meeting were important in creating a sense of community for young Afro-German Hip Hop artists and in many ways laid the foundation for the latter's 'Brothers Keepers' project. As its initiator Adé recalls:

> There [at the General Meeting] you came together for three days, watched movies together, held workshops and discussions. At these meetings, I first met people like Torch or Ebony. Many of those people I might have seen at a jam before. But in the context of the ISD-meetings, you were free of the role of 'rapper' and could really talk about yourself. You talked differently with each other in this Afro-German context.[60]

Ten years after 'Fremd im eigenen Land', 'Brothers Keepers' with their 'Adriano' raised similar issues. This time, however, the reception went beyond the Hip Hop community into mainstream society. 'Brothers Keepers' managed to break the strict division between a cultural hybrid hype around minority artists on the one side and continued political and social marginalisation of minorities on the other. 'Adriano' explicitly addresses racism in Germany, still a taboo subject in public discourse, and does so from the points of view of those under attack. This in itself is not new; numerous crews have done so since the Turkish German Fresh Familee published 'Ahmed Gündüz' in 1990. It was a new development, however, that 'Brothers Keepers' emerged explicitly as a pressure group, using the participating MCs' popularity for an Afro-German intervention into the political debate. While they have published a successful CD, members of the collective also engage in a variety of other activities, from visits to schools in East Germany and concerts for interned refugees to publicly exposing police brutality against Africans.[61] It is also new that the concept worked: media reactions went way beyond the usual interest in political Hip Hop. But while the feedback was enormous, it was not always positive, particularly in progressive circles.

Advanced Chemistry had discovered early on that the self-assured intervention of the objects of the German debate on 'foreigners' did not receive unambigiously positive reactions from white German proponents of multiculturalism. While their 'Stranger in My Own Country' had worked as a wake-up call for many young Germans of colour, the group was severely criticised for exactly this claim on being part of Germany. In the mid-1990s, Advanced Chemistry's Linguist stated:

> The crazy thing is that we are criticised, naturally, by people ideologically opposed to us, conservatives. Of course, they can't stand seeing a black guy holding up his green passport, stating offensively that he's German. On the other hand, and this is

the crazy thing, people considering themselves progressive believe that we wanted to distance ourselves from those minorities in Germany without the green passport. That accusation came very often.

Criticism of 'Brothers Keepers' was again caused by the rappers' insistence that they were *German*: failing to reflect on the privileges of uncontested national belonging that come with being white, a large part of the German left rejects any such statements as reactionary. The notoriously troubled relationship of Germans to their national identity has thus been ironically transferred unto a group whose very Germanness is continuously questioned.[62] Black Germans' attempt to make their country their home by creating a space for themselves on its imaginary map – a step which, if successful, would mean a dramatic reconfiguration of 'Germanness' – is held against them by exactly those white Germans who most decry the nation's anachronistic and exclusionary concept of identity.

'Brothers Keepers' not only face criticism for being too German, but also for being too black. That white German liberals and progressives accused the project of being exclusive, 'anti-multicultural' or even 'racist' might not come as a surprise. But criticism also came from within the Hip Hop community: Microphone Mafia's Kutla for example claimed that a Turkish 'Brothers Keepers' would have resulted in a public outcry, while the 'slavery bonus' allowed blacks to initiate such projects without provoking similar reactions, a point disproven by media reactions.[63] Skillz en Masse's Meli, participating in 'Brothers Keeper's' female version, 'Sisters Keepers', responded to the criticism:

> This project did not only raise an Afro-German voice. It raised a German, a Turkish, a Greek voice, because these were all people supporting this thing … Everybody who supported this is part of it and these are the people, too, for whom it was done … If Brothers Keepers had been multicultural from the beginning, that would have been a huge message, of course. But blacks are the most undermined, disadvantaged group in Germany. I don't know, if Brothers Keepers would have totally flopped, if there hadn't been stylish MCs involved, then people wouldn't say now that they would have liked to be part of it … I think there absolutely should be a continuation. It should be extended to MCs from different cultures who want to spread this message. But blacks in Germany don't really have a community. They meet maybe once a year in Frankfurt. The Turks for example have their people going, anyway. We are the smallest minority in Germany and the ones most threatened by racism.[64]

The criticism from all sides points to the strange, overdetermined position of black Germans: they are probably the most completely assimilated ethnic minority, growing up in largely white neighbourhoods, often in white families. At the same time, their blackness codes them as completely 'alien', they are hyper-visible, their mere presence a sore spot in Germany's perception of itself, constantly reduced to their colour and simultaneously made completely invisible, that is, 'non-German', under a constant demand to explain, justify, re-define their existence, expected to be something they are not and not allowed to be what they are, since what they are exceeds acceptable notions of Germanness.

It takes more than a successful Hip Hop project to alter notions of identity going back for more than a century. But in contemporary Germany, minorities increasingly question illusionary notions of unambiguous, pure and inalterable national identities. A number of recent developments, such as European Unification, the Social Democrat/Green government, and the new citizenship law, might work together to create an increasing receptiveness for these voices within mainstream society. Since 'Brothers Keepers' success, it seems that Hip Hop has the potential not only to mobilise those minorities not usually granted a voice, but also to motivate the majority to listen. This development cannot be overestimated: it fundamentally changed German public discourse, which can no longer unquestioningly cast minorities as mute objects, whether as scapegoats or victims. Hip Hop also fosters a dialogue among minorities, a necessary prerequisite for a concerted reaction to the Europe-wide boom of racist and xenophobic movements. The Hip Hop collective takes on the position of an Afro-German (and potentially multi-ethnic) pressure group, formerly non-existent because of the invisibility of minorities in public discourses in and about Germany.

Conclusion

The impressive success story of Afro-German Hip Hop does have its dangers too. Postmodern entertainment culture excessively borrows from subcultures, which long have become the epitome of hipness. This pseudo-openness re-establishes the mainstream as the measure of all things, while members of the fashionable subcultures are still defined as deficient: subcultural chic is an accessory only for those not belonging to it, after all; otherwise it is titillating, but less glamorous 'authenticity'. Subversive potentials can thus be domesticated into a mere sales argument. Members of minorities for the first time are massively present in Germany's mainstream cultural marketplace, with some influence on their work's content. This presence is still largely restricted to the entertainment sector though, traditionally forcing artists of colour to perform a tightrope-walk between a rare chance to express their point of view and being used to re-enforce racist stereotypes. Tyron Ricketts, actor and rapper, speaks from experience when he states: 'Fuck the slaveship – Now, I'm having a career / do the Carl Lewis runner, Eddie Murphy Imitator / play the drug dealer, basketball and football player … / The positive racism master uses clichés in his advantage, makes them his style'.[65] This strategy has its setbacks, not the least of them a state in which clichés are not used and subverted anymore but taken as the truth – and not only by the audience but by those supposedly subverting them. Afro-German MCs selling homo-phobia and sexism as authentic ghetto culture – not only in their songs but on their political agenda – is as far from subverting stereotypes about black machismo as possible.

Such an attitude, rampant in today's Hip Hop scene (though certainly not only among black rappers) is especially frustrating in the context of Afro-German activism, which had a strong feminist component since its beginning in the early 1980s. The blatant sexism of popular MCs like Samy de Luxe or Moses Pelham, who do see themselves as advocates of the black German community at large, is a betrayal of a tradition of Afro-German resistance. This tradition would have been impossible without the work of feminists and lesbians, two of the most popular objects of ridicule in German Hip Hop. The female rappers of 'Sisters Keepers', themselves an afterthought added to the successful 'Brothers Keepers' project, represent a new image of black German femininity: subdued side-kicks, usually staying in background; their song on the 'Brothers Keepers' CD, is entitled 'Liebe und Verstand' (Love and Sensibility). This is, to put it mildly, a problematic contribution. As Aziza A., one of the most pro-filed female MCs, observed: 'The guys show up like: I kick your ass, I'm the toughest. In contrast, the women appear totally clichéd. The women then offer their hand and their love. The explanation, that you always hear, that you need to listen to the songs together, doesn't make the thing any better for me.'[66] This image indeed seems too far for comfort from the unruly, self-confident and feminist attitude of their sisters fifteen years earlier. Cheap attacks on 'women's raps' like those of 'Brothers Keepers'' Samy de Luxe certainly contribute to an atmosphere in which sexism and homophobia become acceptable, thoughtless forms of 'dissing'. But it would be too easy to put the blame on the Hip Hop community alone, a community whose gender models are not far from what is presented in mainstream culture media and ads. Indicative is the story of Tic Tac Toe, a kind of Afro-German Salt 'n' Pepa and with almost three million CDs sold the most successful German rappers ever. Their rise to teenage stardom generated massive media attention in the mid-1990s. This atten-tion soon focused on one members past stint with drugs and prostitution though – and in stark contrast to the way male MCs were treated, this past did not enhance Lee's 'realness' and authenticity, but rather led to very traditional moral condemnations paired with voyeuristic curiosity. There is no doubt that Tic Tac Toe were musical lightweights, but this does not quite explain their near absence from Hip Hop histories, sexism on the part of the mostly male authors seems to play a part here, too. The group was a media product to a certain extent, with little connection to the

underground Hip Hop scene. But what makes Tic Tac Toe noteworthy is
their focus, which differed dramatically from those of their male colleagues.
Their lyrics, while not always brilliant, introduced a severely under-
represented point of view into Hip Hop: that of (black) teenage girls,
dealing with issues ranging from dating through racism to sexual abuse.[67]

Mirroring mainstream ideology of course is not what Hip Hop was
supposed to be about – nor is it what Afro-German activism aspired to.[68]
But in spite of Hip Hop's problematic structures, structures which are
even more problematic when they become part of political agendas such
as 'Brothers Keepers', Hip Hop represents the central means of articulation for 'ethnic Outsiders' in contemporary Germany. It articulates a
distinctive position that is not defined by ethnic difference but allowed
to name it, thereby successfully challenging dominant divisions between
'proper Germans' and 'foreign outsiders'. Hip Hop culture is the only area
so far where the essentialisation, ethnic stereotyping and marginalisation
of non-white Germans has been successfully challenged. Against many
odds, Afro-German Hip Hop activists have achieved a prominent position
in contemporary Germany, opening up possibilities for their communities
at large. It is to be hoped that they do not waste this well-deserved chance
by subscribing to conservative ideologies that serve only mainstream
interests in the long run. Instead, hopefully they shall honour one of Hip
Hop's central traditions by paying respect to those who paved the way and
remembering the subversive and complex tradition they come from.

Notes

1. 'Beauty', in Olumide Popoola and Beldan Sezen (eds) *Talking Home: Heimat aus unserer eigenen Feder* (Amsterdam: Blue Moon Press, 1999).
2. See, for example, '"Wir sind schwer im Kommen": Schwarze Deutsche zwischen Erfolg und Rassismus', Stern 38 (1997); [Cover] 'Fremd und deutsch. Warum die Integration von Ausländern Unsinn ist', *Spiegel Reporter* 2 (2000).
3. Turks born or residing in Germany have an equally troubled but different relationship to 'citizenship', due to separate histories of migration.
4. This is not to say that these issues went unaddressed, at least by artists of colour, who rarely appeared on German TV until 'Brothers Keepers'. See, for example, Hannes Loh and Murat Güngör (ed.), *Fear of a Kanak Planet: Hiphop zwischen Weltkultur und Nazi-Rap* (Vienna: Hannibal-Verlag, 2002), p. 128.
5. For a selection of articles on 'Brothers Keepers' see their website: <www.brotherskeepers.de>.
6. For a more detailed discussion of German post-war discourses on race see: Leslie Adelson, *Making Bodies Making History. Feminism and German Identity* (Lilncoln: University of Nebraska Press, 1993); Sara Friedrichsmeyer, Sara Lennox, Susanne Zantop (eds), *The Imperialist Imagination: German Colonialism and its Legacy* (Ann Arbor: University of Michigan Press, 1998); Uli Linke, *German Bodies: Race and Representation after Hitler* (New York: Routledge, 1999).
7. Autobiographical texts by Afro-Germans, such as those collected in *Farbe bekennen*, almost unanimously speak of an identification with African Americans as the only visible blacks in German media, children's books, films etc. See also Ika Hügel-Marshall, *Invisible Woman: Growing Up Black in Germany* (New York: Continuum, 2001).

8. For an overview of the history of 'foreign workers' in Germany see Ulrich Herbert, *A History of Foreign Labor in Germany 1880–1980: Seasonal Workers, Forced Laborers, Guest Workers* (Ann Arbor: University of Michigan Press, 1990).

9. The new Social Democrat/Green Party government in 1999 radically changed the law's exclusive *jus sanguinis* focus by granting citizenship to all persons born in Germany of parents legally living there for a certain period of time. The accompanying concept of dual citizenship had to be abandoned after mass protests, though. See Fatima El-Tayeb, 'Germans, Foreigners, and German Foreigners', in Salah Hassan and Ifikhar Dadi (eds), *Unpacking Europe: Towards a Critical Reading* (Rotterdam: NAI, 2001), pp. 72–81.

10. For an update on 'Brothers Keepers' current projects see: www.brotherskeepers.de

11. See the recent, rather symptomatic debate on a German *Leitkultur*, leading culture. For collected articles on the topic see: http://home.t-online.de/home/family.graetsch/rgmuku2b.htm

12. See, for example, Jeanine Kantara, 'Schwarz. Und deutsch', *Die Zeit* 7:9 (2000); Olumide Popoola and Beldan Sezen, *Talking Home: Heimat aus unserer eigen Feder* (Amsterdam: Blue Moon Press, 1998); Cathy Gelbin, Kader Konuk and Peggy Piesche (eds), *AufBrüche: Kulturelle Produktionen von Migrantinnen, Schwarzen und jüdischen Frauen in Deutschland* (Königstein: Ulrike Helmer, 1999); Oguntoye, Opitz, and Schultz (Hg.), *Farbe bekennen*.

13. Katharina Oguntoye, May Opitz and Dagmar Schultz (eds), *Showing Our Colours: Afro-German Women Speak Out* (Amherst: University of Massachusetts Press, 1989), p. xxii.

14. The crusades brought a number of blacks to Europe, often as servants at the numerous royal courts. Later black military drummers and pipers became increasingly fashionable among European royalty. See Peter Martin, *Schwarze Teufel, edle Mohren: Afrikaner in Bewußtsein und Geschichte der Deutschen* (Hamburg: Junius, 1993), p. 133.

15. Oguntoye et al., *Farbe bekennen*; Martin, *Schwarze Teufel, edle Mohren*.

16. A derogatory name in the early twentieth century for Namibia's Nama population, Germans still use the expression 'like the Hottentotts' to characterise inappropriate behaviour, apparently with no awareness of the word's entrance into German culture. On German rule in Namibia see Helmut Bley, *South-West Africa under German Rule 1894–1914* (Evanston: Northwestern University Press, 1971), and Horst Drechsler, *Süwestafrika unter deutscher Kolonialherrschaft* (Berlin: Akademie-Verlag, 1966).

17. See Bley, *South-West Africa*; Drechsler, *Süwestafrika*.

18. See El-Tayeb, 'Germans, Foreigners, and German Foreigners', pp. 92–118.

19. With the exception of the national socialist period, the law remained effective throughout the twentieth century, until the revised law of 2000 added *jus soli* elements, thereby for the first time granting certain persons of 'non-German blood' the *right* to citizenship. On the question of non-ethnic Germans of Jewish, Polish, African, or Turkish ancestry see e.g. Rogers Brubaker, *Citizenship and Nationhood in France and Germany* (Cambridge MA: Harvard University Press, 1992) and Zafer Senocak, *Atlas of a Tropical Germany: Essays on Politics and Culture* (Lincoln: University of Nebraska Press, 2000).

20. See BAB, R 1001, 61 Kol DKG 1077/1, 230; BAB, RKA-4457/7, 64; Katharina Oguntoye, *Eine afro-deutsche Geschichte. Zur Lebenssituation von Afrikanern und Afro-Deutschen in Deutschland von 1884 bis 1950* (Berlin: Hoho, 1997), pp. 56–60.

21. The interesting topic of African migrant organization cannot be detailed here. See Paulette Reed-Anderson, *Eine Geschichte von mehr als 100 Jahren: Die Anfänge der afrikanischen Diaspora in Berlin* (Berlin: Die Ausländerbeauftragte des Senats, 1995), pp. 38–40; Oguntoye, *Eine afro-deutsche Geschichte*, pp. 76–101.

22. See C. Fidel, *Die Widerlegung des Beschuldigungsfeldzuges gegen die farbigen französischen Truppen im besetzten rheinishcen Gebiet* (o.O., 1921). Internationally the campaign was also supported by British feminists, French socialists, the Pope, and the anti-colonial activist E. D. Morel. See Robert C. Reinders, 'Racialism on the Left: E. D. Morel and the "Black Horror on the Rhine,"' *International Review of Social History* 13 (1968), pp. 1–28 and Fidel, *Die Widerlegung des Beschuldigungfeldzuges*.

23. An inquiry conducted by the British Foreign Office in 1920, showed the vast majority of the accusations against the black soldiers were unfounded, but did not have any influence on the continuous propaganda. See Fidel, *Die Widerlegung des Beschuldigungfeldzuges*, p. 10.

24. Reiner Pommerin, '*Sterilisierung der Rheinlandbastarde*': *Das Schicksal einer fargingen deutschen Minderheit, 1918–1937* (Düsseldorf: Droste, 1979), p. 23.

25. *Artzliche Rundschau* 47 (1920) quoted in Heinrich Diestler, *Das deutsche Leid am Rhein: Ein Buch der Anklage gegen die Schanderherrschaft des französischen Militarismus* (Minden: Koehler, 1921), p. 56.

26. See Pommerin, *Sterilisierung der Rheinlandbastarde*; Robert W. Kesting, 'Forgotten Victims: Blacks in the Holocaust', *Journal of Negro History* 77 (1992), pp. 30–33; Clarence Lusane, *Hitler's Black Victims: The Historical Experiences of Afro-Germans, Afro-Europeans, African Americans, and Africans during the Nazi Era* (New York: Routledge, 2002). Often, 'Negermischlinge' ('Negro-mongrels') were included in Nazi measures against Roma and Sinti; see Romani Rose (Hg.), *Der nationalsozialistische Völkermord an den Sinti und Roma* (Heidelberg, 1995).

27. I will concentrate on the developments in West Germany. For the situation in the East see Jan C. Behrends, Thomas Lindenberger, Patrice G. Poutrus (eds), *Fremde und Fremd-Sein in der DDR. Zu historischen Ursachen der Fremdenfeindlichkeit in Ostdeutschland* (Potsdam: Zentrum für Zeithistorische Forschung, 2002); and Peggy Piesche, 'Black and German? East German Adolescents before 1989, A Retrospective View of a "Non-Existent" Issue in the GDR', in Leslie Adelson (ed.), *The Cultural Afterlife of the GDR: New Transnational Perspectives* (Washington DC: American Institute for Contemporary German Studies, 2002).

28. In 1955, of 66,730 children registered as fathered by allied soldiers, only 4,776 were black. Klaus Eyferth, Ursula Brandt, and Wolfgang Hawel, *Farbige Kinder in Deutschland und die Aufgaben ihrer Eingliederung* (München: Juventa, 1960), p. 12.

29. 'Expertise' was centred in the former Kaiser-Wilhelm-Institute for anthropology, founded 1926 in the Weimar republic and headed for sixteen years by Eugen Fischer, an anthropologist who had built his reputation on 'bastard-studies' conducted in German Southwest Africa. Despite its central role in Nazi racism, the institute was one of the few German scientific centres that was not closed down by the Allies. Seven years after the end of the war, the institute published a study on 'mixed-race children' based on research on children selected for sterilisation in the 1930s. It ended with the conclusion that '[e]specially the children's strong animalism will surely cause certain problems'. See Walter Kirchner, 'Untersuchung somatischer und psychischer Entwicklung bei Europäer-Neger-Mischlingen im Kleinkindalter unter Berücksichtigung der sozialen Verhältnisse', quoted in Benno Müller-Hill, *Murderous Science. Elimination by Scientific Selection of Jews, Gypsies and Others, Germany 1933–1945* (Oxford: Oxford University Press, 1988), p. 115.

30. Several studies conducted in the 1950's reveal negative attitudes towards 'the "niggerlovers" and their bastards': Luise Frankenstein, *Uneheliche Kinder von ausländischen Soldaten mit besonderer Berücksichtigung der Mischlinge* (Geneva, 1953), p. 29; see also Eyferth et al., *Farbige Kinder in Deutschland und die Aufgaben ihrer Eingliederung*, pp. 74–78. Magazine articles and stories of the 1950's had a less aggressive attitude towards the children, rather portraying them as 'tragic mulattos', but presented their fathers in 'Black Horror'-tradition as drunken, animal-like rapists. See Lester, in Reinhold Grimm and Jost Hermand (eds), *Blacks and German Culture* (Madison: University of Wisconsin Press, 1986), pp. 122–128.

31. Gisela Fremgen, *Und wenn du dazu noch schwarz bist: Berichte schwarzer Frauen in der Bundesrepublik* (Bremen: Edition Con, 1984), p. 98.

32. Katharina Oguntoye, et al., *Farbe bekennen*, p. vii.

33. Schultz, 'Introduction', *Showing Our Colours*, p. xxiii.

34. Oguntoye and Opitz, 'Introduction', *Showing Our Colours*, p. xxi.

35. At least not positively, as one of course could argue that colonial and national socialist policies directed specifically against persons who were both German and black did construct them as a group with common, identifiable traits.

36. 'Get to knows us. I.S.D. The Black German Initiative', 1989, original in English.

37. As of 2002 there were ten regional chapters (in Berlin, Cologne, Gießen, Frankfurt, Hamburg, Hannover, Mannheim, Munich, Nürnberg and Stuttgart).
38. In the 1990s, ISD and ADEFRA have transformed themselves into organizations aimed at representing *all* blacks living in Germany. See www.isdonline.de and www.cybernomads.net.
39. See Paul Gilroy, *The Black Atlantic: Modernity and Double Consciousness* (Cambridge MA: Harvard University Press, 1993).
40. The ensuing debate on racism within the German women's movement was often irritating and painful to black women who were reduced to 'racism experts' by white women, expected to educate them and absolve them of their guilt. Nevertheless, white feminists/lesbians probably were the *only* segment of German society sincerely attempting to confront their own racism.
41. See Leory T. Hopkins (ed.), *Who Is a German? Historical and Modern Perspectives on Africans in Germany* (Washington DC: The American Institute for Contemporary German Studies, 1999), pp. 18f.
42. The German/European left and the gay male movement only much later and with a lot more reluctance confronted the issue of racism. See Fatima El-Tayeb, 'Begrenzte Horizonte: Queer Identity in der Festung Europa', in Nina Zimnik and Mechthild Nagel (eds), *Postkolonialer Feminismus: Ein Reader* (forthcoming, 2003).
43. Ika Hügel, Chris Lange and May Ayim (eds), *Entfernte Verbindungen. Rassismus, Antisemitismus, Klassenunterdrückung* (Berlin: Orlanda, 1993); Cathy Gelbin, Kader Konouk and Peggy Piesche (eds), *Aufbrüche: Kulturelle Produktionen von Migrantinnen, Schwarzen und jüdischen Frauen in Deutschland* (Königsberg/Th: Ulrike Helmer, 1999).
44. Olumide Popoola and Beldan Sezen (eds), *Talking Home: Heimat aus unserer eigenen Feder* (Amsterdam: Blue Moon Press, 1999), Bibl. Angaben. Incidently, Gisela Fremgen's '… und wenn du dazu noch schwarz bist' ('… and if you're black, too, on top of that'), published 1984, which chronicles the experiences of African and African American migrants (and one Afro-German) also only included women's experiences.
45. As the editors reveal, this was not easy for the contributing women either: 'A major portion of our teamwork consisted of encouraging the authors to write and discussing their texts with them. For some it was easier to reveal their experiences in conversations, which we then reworked into a narrative form (at the request of one author, a pseudonym was used)'. See *Showing Our Colours*, p. xxv.
46. 'Introduction', *Showing Our Colours*, p. xxii.
47. 'Die farbigen Besatzungskinder feiern in diesem Jahr ihren 40. Geburtstag. Was macht Toxi heute?', *Frankfurter Rundschau* (2 August 1986), p. ZB 5. Apparently, many white Germans – not the least those concerned with the plight of oppressed minorities – would much rather have hundreds of thousands isolated 'tragic Mulattos' in need of white support than a vocal, self-reliant black community. For a compelling example of white Germans' patronizing attitude towards black German self-definition, see Hügel-Marshall, *Invisible Woman*, p. 122.
48. Members of ethnic minorities are severely under-represented in journalism, regional and national parliaments and public bodies supposed to reflect society's structure (e.g. the 'Rundfunkrat', advisory board for public television and radio). See for example, Christoph Butterwegge et al., *Medien und multikulturelle Gesellschaft* (Opladen: Leske + Budrich, 1999); and Ralf Koch, *'Medien mögen's weiß': Rassismus im Nachrichtengeschäft; Erfahrungen von Journalisten in Deutschland und den USA* (München: Dt. Taschenbuch-Verl., 1996).
49. Loh and Güngör, *Fear of a Kanak Planet*, p. 23.
50. Loh and Güngör, *Fear of a Kanak Planet*, p. 103.
51. The dominant perception of ethnic minorities as 'foreign' rather than German often expresses itself in discourses about language. The unwillingness or inability of (German-born) 'foreigners' to master the German language is a common argument against immigration. The dominant role of migrant and minority artists within the German-language Hip Hop scene sheds an interesting light on these claims.
52. For a more balanced and reliable history of German Hip Hop see: Hannes Loh and Sascha Verlan, *20 Jahre HipHop in Deutschland* (Wien: Hannibal, 2000).
53. Loh and Güngör, *Fear of a Kanak Planet*, p. 92.

54. For example Hamburg, Stuttgart and Frankfurt, but interestingly, not Berlin.
55. See the collection of interviews by Loh and Güngör published in *Fear of a Kanak Planet* (the title an obvious homage to Public Enemy's 'Fear of a Black Planet').
56. Since the end of state socialism in Europe, migration patterns are increasingly structured by the disparity between rich West and poor East. Eastern Europeans are by now the largest migrant group in Western Europe. Discourses on migration focus on the 'visible Other', though – Africans and Arab and Turkish Muslims. To include Eastern Europeans in the concept of 'people of color' would therefore distort differences in perception and treatment due to Eastern Europeans status as 'white' and 'European' (with the important exception of Roma). This notwithstanding, migrants from the East of Europe are subject to – sometimes racialised – patterns of discrimination in the West.
57. '"Schwarz" verstehen wir politisch. Die afrodeutsche Hip Hop-Gruppe Advanced Chemistry über ihre Erfahrungen mit alltäglichem Rassismus', *die tageszeitung* (25 März 1993), p. 16.
58. I am concerned here with the interaction of Hip Hop culture and new models of black (post-ethnic) identity in Germany, not with Hip Hop as an art form. The artists I am focusing on exemplify the new discourse, but are not necessarily 'better' artists than others not mentioned.
59. Founded in 1973 as a youth self-help organisation in New York's South Bronx, the Zulu Nation has by now become an internationally active group, trying to create an awareness among contemporary Hip Hop fans of the culture's history and political message (as they perceive it). For the German version see www.zulu-family.de
60. See Hannes Loh, '20 Jahre Afro-deutsch', www.brotherskeepers.de
61. The CD's title *Lightkultur* ('light culture'), was an ironic reference to the then-raging debate about a German *Leitkultur*, or 'leading culture', supposedly threatened by multiculturalism.
62. On the naïvité of the groups critics on their own uncontested white Germanness see Bakri Bakhit, 'Brothers Keepers, Sisters Keepers. Ich bin kein Rassist, meine Frau ist doch Jugoslawin' (30 November 2001). See also: www.inro.de/magazin/magazin&einzelartikel.htm or Hartwig Vens in *konkret* 4/01 for a symptomatic differentiation between (good) 'migrant' Hip Hop and the (assimilationist) 'so called Afro-German' 'Brothers Keepers' project.
63. Loh and Güngör, *Fear of a Kanak Planet*, p. 265.
64. Loh and Güngör, *Fear of a Kanak Planet*, p. 268.
65. Tyron Ricketts, 'Afro-deutsch', 2000.
66. Loh and Güngör, *Fear of a Kanak Planet*, p. 271.
67. See 'Allers verscheissender Gören-Rap', *biwidus* (15 April 1996); 'Tic Tac Toe – Die ganze Wahrheit', *biwidus* (11 April 1997); '… Tic Tac Toe am Scheideweg', *Rhein Zeitung* (21 November 1997); www.laut.de/wortlaut.artists/t/tic_tac_toe/biographie/index.htm
68. The idealisation of juvenile machismo also means compliance in the instrumentalisation of minorities, which in public discourses, culturally, politically and socially are inscribed with certain backwards traits or customs (misogyny, homophobia, nationalism), which then are classified as 'ethnic' rather than as part of a general conservative backlash. A projection that not only works to reaffirm the majority's cultural superiority but also allows the exclusions of 'backwards' minorities from full participation in modern, democratic societies.

5

Creole Performance in *Wonderful Adventures of Mrs. Seacole in Many Lands*

Rhonda Frederick

> While subjugated peoples cannot readily control what emanates from the dominant culture, they do determine to varying extents what they absorb into their own, and what they use it for.
>
> Mary Louise Pratt, *Imperial Eyes: Travel Writing and Transculturation*

> I have attempted, without any consideration of dates, to give my readers some idea of my life in the Crimea. I am fully aware that I have jumbled up events strangely, talking in the same page, and even sentence, of events which occurred at different times; but I have three excuses to offer for my unhistorical inexactness. In the first place, my memory is far from trustworthy, and I kept no written diary; in the second place, the reader must have had more than enough of journals and chronicles of Crimean life, and I am only the historian of Spring Hill [Seacole's store in the Crimea]; and in the third place, unless I am allowed to tell the story of my life in my own way, I cannot tell it at all.
>
> Mary Jane Grant Seacole, *Wonderful Adventures*[1]

In *Haiti, History, and the Gods*, Joan Dayan writes against accounts of Haiti that lose the country's 'complex and perplexing social history ... in exposition'.[2] Although her version of Haitian history is also susceptible to the simplifications that she wants to confront, Dayan's interpretation of Vodou allows her to maintain the 'incoherence' absent from the more familiar historical narratives. Dayan asserts the necessity of foregrounding seemingly irresolvable contradictions since 'the shock of Creole society ... resulted in strange bedfellows, spiritual connections that had as much to do with domination as resistance, with reinterpretations of laws laid down, tortures enacted, and the barbarous customs of a brute white world'.[3] In order to articulate these dynamics, Dayan creates a 'complex and perplexing' Haiti by excavating stories sustained in the myths, religious practices and the so-called unofficial stories maintained by the country's 'unlettered', majority population. Her goal is to narrate a Haiti necessarily born out of violence and expectation, hope and hopelessness; in this way, her book responds to silences in the country's official record.

Dayan supports her use of Vodou by representing Haiti's first ruler, Jean-Jacques Dessalines, as a figure who resulted from the convergence of myriad 'details': 'any attempt to reconstruct Dessalines historically involves ambiguities, obscurity, and details that do not cohere. But perhaps that is how gods are born'.[4] As this quotation suggests, spiritual and popular accounts of Dessalines – the god and the man – illustrate a comfort with complexity (contradiction, ambivalence, nonsense) that is absent from official accounts of the 1804 revolution and nationalist appropriations of this Black Jacobin. The former renditions evolved out of ambiguities surrounding Dessalines's life, but particularly his death. His deification remembers the hatred that resulted in his bullet-riddled, stabbed, stripped and dismembered body; the motivations behind his assassination; his role in the revolution; and his creation of the Haitian flag. Vodou also acknowledges the ruthless violence of his short regime, his investment in Haiti as a black republic, and the obscurity surrounding the recomposition and internment of his remains. Through this more indeterminate 'Dessalines' one can access the man's vexed historical moment; this representation also allows analysis of the politics surrounding his violent death, but also the possibilities of his vision. One could argue that his deification captures Jean-Jacques Dessalines's moment in time, his physical self and his symbolic functions, but also the fulfilled and unfulfilled potential in each.

I want to borrow from Dayan's critical use of Dessalines-the-god and of Vodou to make visible aspects of Jamaica's Creole class through an analysis of _Wonderful Adventures of Mrs. Seacole in Many Lands_, aspects that have not yet been explored.[5] Mary Seacole's 1857 autobiography is a first-person account of a New World subject in response to the capricious cultural, racial and gender-based pressures in nineteenth-century Jamaica. If, as Kamau Brathwaite poetically states, 'the unity is submarine/breathing air, our problem is how to study the fragments/whole',[6] then the method I attempt here acknowledges how various 'fragments' – those which contribute to evolving social classes in nineteenth-century Jamaica – meaningfully collide in Seacole's narrative. These collisions produce a Jamaican Creole experience that has not been central to critical treatments of the narrative. By locating my analysis of Seacole's autobiography in a Jamaican Creole context, I acknowledge its defined geographical and social spaces and, at the same time, emphasise the complexities that are symptomatic of mid-nineteenth-century Jamaica, and of the various places to which Seacole migrates.

Wonderful Adventures describes Mary Jane Grant Seacole's career as a doctress and lodging-house keeper in Jamaica, Central America and the

Crimea. Written to refill financial coffers depleted after the abrupt end of the Crimean War, Seacole begins her account by briefly discussing her Jamaican birth and parentage and then continues by describing her lifelong love of travel, offering details of her intra-Caribbean voyages and trips to England as examples. The bulk of her narrative describes her exploits in the towns of Cruces, Navy Bay, Gorgona and Escribanos in New Granada (now Panamá) during the beginning of the California Gold Rush (1849) and the construction of the Panamá Railroad (1850–55), as well as her adventures in the Crimea during the Crimean War (1854–56). Wherever her travels take her, the 'yellow doctress' builds on her medical experience (using cholera treatments learned in Jamaica[7] to excellent advantage on the isthmus[8] and in the Crimea[9]) and her entrepreneurial savvy as a self-styled doctress and lodging-house keeper. Although she attributes some aspects of her adventurous personality to her Scottish father and 'creole' mother, the narrative leaves no doubt that Seacole's autobiographical persona coalesces as the 'yellow doctress' and 'Mother Seacole' due to the author's self-authorising rhetoric.[10]

To understand *Wonderful Adventures* as subversive, some critics have highlighted the features of the memoir that resemble traditional Victorian travel and women's literatures (war memoir, travel accounts, autobiography). Other scholars have supported the latter reading by positioning Seacole's autobiography within and against slave narrative, feminist and Caribbean writerly traditions.[11] That *Wonderful Adventures* lends itself to these varied analyses testifies to its complexity. One may consider, as Bernard McKenna suggests, that Mary Seacole's account of her life embodies 'the contra-dictions of imperial expansion' because 'travel writing not only began to question English and imperial values but began to be written by figures from the periphery of society, by individuals whose claims to the masculine, protestant, and racially pure "John Bull" inheritance are questionable'.[12] McKenna also finds that Seacole's autobiography exposes fissures in the English persona by 'subtly reaffirming three important aspects of her Jamaican identity in relation to England as a colonizing force: race, spirituality, peripheral membership in the empire',[13] and by relying 'on the rhetoric of imperial expansion in order to testify to the fact that she does not carry the contagion [of otherness] with her, that she is not part of the alien'.[14] Finally, McKenna describes disruptive moments in Seacole's autobiography as points where readers can critically engage dominant discourses of Englishness (race, culture).

While she is neither male nor white, it can be said that Seacole assumes 'the tone of an English gentleman' in that she reflects 'the prejudices and mores of the class to whom the book was directed'.[15] The yellow doctress stands well beyond the bounds of Englishness but nonetheless operates in places reserved for English men (and extraordinary English women), and

thus she implicitly challenges the 'truths' promoted by Englishness, including gender norms initially prescribed for white women.[16] Yet analyses
that identify and support a subversive reading of *Wonderful Adventures* do
not thoroughly engage moments when Seacole distinguishes between
individuals whom the English might categorise as 'other'. These very
moments, however, are the sites from which my interpretation of *Wonderful
Adventures* evolves.

Seacole's autobiographical persona challenges English tenets of 'otherness' to be sure, but the author does not do so in support of everyone who
might be considered 'other' by English standards. Seacole makes no
bones about the differences between herself, on the one hand, and certain
Creoles and 'wholly black' people on the other, distinctions that resonate
differently in English colonial ideology. In constructing her brand of a
Creole identity, one that survives in a variety of chaotic geographical
spaces, Seacole articulates these differences through the rhetorical
manipulation of certain visually and behaviorally manifested identities.
Accordingly, I read her narrative as a testimony to the kind of Creole
subjectivity that developed in and travelled from Jamaica.

Although there is a difference between the author's lived reality and
the world she constructs in *Wonderful Adventures*, Seacole autobiographical
persona shares characteristics with the Euro-Creole coloured minority
described by historians of the Caribbean. Nineteenth-century Jamaican
society was stratified in ways that reflected the tumultuous contact
between indigenous, European, African and Asian peoples; Jamaica's
Creole population was no exception. Arnold Sio, for example, identifies
three 'types' of coloured people: a small minority who subscribed to a
'Euro-creole cultural complex', the majority who embraced an 'Afro-
creole' identity, and 'the middle stratum that emerged in the process of
differentiation [and who] developed a "Synthetic-creole" culture that was
a combination of elements derived from the Afro-creole and Euro-creole
patterns'.[17] Most agree that Jamaica's mixed-race population developed
out of an oppressive slave system, particularly the practice of absentee
land ownership (in that it determined the overwhelming numbers of
single white men on the island) and the racial hierarchies that enabled
white males' sexual exploitation of enslaved black women. Through
certain privileges granted them by their white fathers, the offspring of
white men and black women 'formed a separate group in Jamaican society
with their own social hierarchies',[18] though the law often did not recognise
the distinctions these people found significant. Once established, free people
of colour began to build on their inheritances from their planter fathers.
Jamaica's local assembly responded by restricting the development of
this population with laws that limited the value of their inheritances, by
preventing them from testifying in court against whites (which seriously

impeded their ability to protect their wealth) and by barring them from jobs that would have put them in direct competition with whites.[19]

Free people of colour responded to these legal restrictions by employing various means to secure their economic and social positions, one of which included shifting their political alliances between Jamaica's white planter class and its local assembly, the English colonial government, and the free black population. The relationship between upper-class whites and free people of colour seemed to influence greatly the latter's political affiliations, since Jamaica's planter class saw free browns/blacks ambivalently, sometimes as friends but often as foes.[20] Individually speaking, privileged browns were afforded limited rights in the early part of the eighteenth century, but even these were repealed when whites 'realized how much wealth was passing into colored and black hands'.[21] While exceptional browns successfully petitioned to overturn the most restrictive laws, it was not until the end of the eighteenth century (after the Haitian Revolution) that Jamaica's free coloured population worked together to change their lot, specifically those who understood themselves as the Creole élite.[22] In Barbados, for example, free coloureds responded to legislation that placed 'significant property limitations upon [them]' by stating that 'should the bill become law it would "remove the best security of our loyalty and fidelity"', and in a society structured upon the possession of property, 'death would be preferable to such a situation' of being propertyless.[23] The non-confrontational tone of these lines could not disguise the implication that free coloureds' continued loyalty to whites might depend on the outcome of this and future legislation.[24] The free coloured populations in Barbados and Jamaica challenged their respective local assemblies by openly or subtly threatening to align either with the Crown government or with local freed blacks against the white planter class to secure their status.[25] Free coloureds were also not above ingratiating themselves with the white ruling class by actively fighting against rebellious enslaved blacks, though this sacrifice often went unrewarded. Whether they enhanced their status through coalitions with free blacks or with the English colonial government, or through concessions granted by local assemblies, free coloureds worked to solidify and improve their social standing and thus began to understand themselves as a distinct group.[26]

The insecure social and political positions of free people of colour in the Anglophone Caribbean also seemed to encourage the definition and maintenance of rigid boundaries between the white, brown and black populations. Even though some whites hoped that mixed-race people would mediate between themselves and black populations, most viewed free people of colour as 'black enough' to be segregated from white society. Additionally, before emancipation the very presence of brown people as property holders in Jamaica challenged the premise on which slave society was based, because 'for the system to be successful, slaves had to associate the ownership of land and people with whites; slave-holding freedmen were dangerous because their existence suggested that browns and blacks were no different from whites'.[27] So when laws could not sufficiently de-legitimise Jamaican freedmen as a distinct social class, it became more important to deny them social access to upper class white society. Though they resented this restriction on their upward mobility, free coloureds were still dependent upon the support of whites to secure their civil rights. Not surprisingly, free coloureds' distance from the lower-class black majority became even more necessary.[28] One effect of this manoeuvring was the acquisition of behaviours that distinguished coloureds from the black majority (the inferior group that they rejected) as well as from the white élite (the superior group from which they were rejected).[29]

Thus far, this survey of Jamaica's free coloured population largely pertains to its propertied and educated males. Elite, coloured men, whose status and property afforded them access to official channels could stage their complaints publicly through formal petitions for exception to restrictive legislation or through military service. Free women of colour were denied these options and, unlike black and coloured men, the market for their skills was limited.[30] They therefore developed different ways to protect their standing.

Whether deemed legitimate businesswomen or 'prostitutes', black and coloured Jamaican women often earned their economic independence through 'proprietorship of taverns, lodging-houses and houses of pleasure … sometimes separately, often in combination'.[31] The money to set up these businesses probably came from white men, either lovers or fathers, and this, along with the fact that their patrons were mainly white military men, coloured even legitimate establishments with the taint of the illicit.[32] While there has been productive debate as to whether these business women were merely victims 'held in a sexual bind to white men who created the situation to further their own gain' or women who 'strategised rather than [give] into her circumstances',[33] like the coloured population as a whole, female hotel keepers attempted to carve out comfortable social and economic positions for themselves. Indeed, their status was further complicated because they had no 'natural' allies; their colour, personal relationships and economically-enhanced social position made for tense – though nonetheless interdependent – relations between these women and white men and women, as well as black women and men.[34] It is not clear whether these women's realities directly influenced the political standing of coloured people in Jamaica, but the influence wielded by female boarding-house keepers has had a lasting social effect.

In the light of these histories, when Mary Seacole promotes herself as other than 'other', she confirms her position as Jamaican, and as African descended, but significantly as a *Creole woman*. Through her strident proclamations, as well as her celebration of certain African-descended people, Seacole affirms 'creole' as a distinct social category, seeks the benefits that accrue to Creole status (particularly 'doctress-ing' and hotel-keeping), and shuns limiting meanings that attach to black skin. The author's investment in communicating marked differences between wholly black and Creole peoples can be seen in the distinctions she makes between identities that only manifest visually (physical characteristics) and those that are revealed as behaviour (rhetorically described 'actions'), the latter being that which significantly determines Seacole's self-selected social position. In other words, Mary Seacole asserts her creoleness by highlighting those behaviours that affirm this desired social position, in spite of her ambiguously raced and stereotypically gendered physical appearance and the meanings attached to them. Yet her strident attestations may also reflect the difficulties she confronts in occupying a Creole subject position as she travels outside of Jamaica; however, as Seacole promotes it in her memoir, her self-styled identity stands firm.

The re-situation of Seacole's narrative within Caribbean social and literary milieux challenges 'the literary establishment's desire to categorize "national" literatures into easily recognizable genres'.[35] To counter the effects of this kind of categorisation, Belinda Edmondson argues that 'it is only by returning Caribbean women's texts to their cultural points of origin that the textual pieces that have fallen in between the cracks of European and American literary theory start to emerge as definitive to their structure as a whole'.[36] *Wonderful Adventures* has been subject to the treatment Edmondson describes, confirming that Seacole's book usefully informs Western literary and critical concerns.[37] However by attending to the uniquely local aspects of this autobiography, I can complicate rather than devalue previous interpretations. Rather than viewing *Wonderful Adventures* as either representative of 'diasporal solidarity between African peoples' or only the product of a self-interested, locally oriented subject,[38] one might consider the autobiography more productively as both. This point can best be understood by positioning Seacole's Creole performance as central to the story she tells rather than attending to the ways that her narrative techniques expose the fallacies of Englishness. From this literary critical perspective, the yellow woman's self-authorising process does not merely reveal the false limits placed on a non-white, female, colonised subject, or lay bare the 'constructedness' of the English persona. It also establishes the complexity of her Jamaican subject position. While nineteenth-century colonial ideology informs Seacole's persona, its evolution into a Jamaican social category importantly signifies the unique culture that evolved there. It is by identifying and negotiating the ambiguities of her historical moment that Mary Seacole can narrate the story of her life in her own way. Her autobiographical manoeuvres distinguish her from wholly black people, 'manly' women and the white English adventurer, and allow her to claim the privileges of a particular kind of creoleness. This involves exception from the 'wholly black' category and claim on spaces occupied by Creole women and the white men they often served.

Seacole manipulates categories set by race, gender, geography and adventure – not to mention several literary genres – to articulate a Jamaican, Creole, female subjectivity; however, it is important to emphasise that her self-representation neither reduces contradictions nor coheres into a 'Totality'.[39] Instead, her manner of self-presentation draws attention to the fact that both these narratives and her autobiographical persona are disorderly.[40] It follows, then, that the sophistication of Seacole's Creole performance is made visible through the very stereotypes she uses in the narrative to varying effect.

In their introduction to *Wonderful Adventures*, Ziggi Alexander and Audrey Dewjee collect and comment on the many references to Seacole that appear in memoirs written by her English, male contemporaries. One such man, the 'illustrator William Simpson', offers the following characterisation:

> Mrs. Seacole, an elderly mulatto woman from Jamaica, was a well-known character in the Crimea, all the soldiers and sailors knew her. She had a taste for nursing and doctoring, but she added to this a business as a sutler. *She told me that she had Scotch blood in her veins. I must say that she did not look like it, but the old lady spoke proudly of this point in her genealogy.*[41]

In my focus on the author's rhetorical performance, I see her assertions of her 'yellow' or otherwise 'Creole' self as defining points in her autobiography. The import of my emphasis can be seen in comparison to the myriad ways scholars describe Seacole and her mother. Sandra Paquet and Faith Smith describe Mrs. Seacole's mother as 'a free black Jamaican'[42] and Evelyn Hawthorne asserts that *Wonderful Adventures* is 'a paradigmatic black woman's text' but later identifies the doctress as 'a woman of color' and cites a source that identifies her as a 'Black Briton'.[43] Sandra Gunning describes Seacole as a 'mulatta' and as a 'black entrepreneur'.[44] Finally, Aleric Josephs comments on – and adds to – this range of descriptors by identifying Seacole as quadroon and her mother as mulatto.[45] By returning to the autobiography and the author's description of her persona, I am particularly interested in how she displays, dislocates, and relocates the meanings of her visually and geographically-defined self. The fact that she might not have 'looked like' the child of a Scot and a Jamaican 'creole' contributes to the idea that, visually speaking, her claim to creoleness is uncertain. This point is all the more interesting since Seacole, as a child of a 'creole' woman and a Scottish man, would have been a quadroon and not a mulatto. This distinction is significant because it offers insight into why Seacole might be so strident about her creoleness (if she did not 'look like' a mulatto, she certainly did not 'look like' a quadroon), but it also speaks to the problems of defining the emergent mixed-race segment of Jamaican society solely in terms of visual markers. Nevertheless, although she might be – to some degree – visually indeterminate, the narrator is vociferously – and, therefore, clearly – Creole. If one considers that writing in a definitive manner can be construed as 'performance', then Seacole is a Creole because she rhetorically affirms this identity. She is also Creole because she behaves as Jamaican Creole women have long behaved: as lodging-house keepers and doctresses.

Taking the above historical and critical assessments as examples, Mary Seacole might be mistaken for wholly black, thereby making her aggressive assertion of her creoleness and attention to her Creole behaviour understandable. Consequently what she negotiates may not be the 'other' category per se, but visual manifestations of 'otherness' that militate against her inclusion within the Creole caste. If, as Edmondson claims, Victorian manhood can be defined and made 'real' through the performance of 'gentlemanliness', when male Caribbean writers duplicated gentlemanly behaviours, they were, in fact, Victorian men.[46] Similarly, Mary Seacole makes herself Creole because she performs this identity. Of course, there are tensions between the performed persona and her visually raced and geographically situated one, yet these are what make *Wonderful Adventures* meaningful in Jamaican literary and critical contexts.

The contradictory ways Seacole depicts other characters in the autobiography complement the manner in which she 'makes' herself into an entrepreneur, adventurer, sutler and Creole. Indeed, her representations of 'others' manifest the process through which she writes herself into Jamaica's Creole caste. The author's 'unhistorical inexactness', her triumphant and stereotypical representations of wholly black people, and her depictions of gendered and raced norms derive authority from, but do not simply duplicate, English mores. She re-deploys them, but not to privilege Englishness or otherwise affirm colonial and racial ideologies as such prejudices had done. Seacole's focus on visual and behavioural markers directs attention toward her successful performance rather than on her bodily appearance and its significance, features over which she has no control.

That which distinguishes Seacole-the-character, as she is wont to inform readers, is her incomparable creoleness. But, within the context of her memoir, her literal claim to creoleness is ambiguous at best. This, in addition to the convoluted way that she identifies with enslaved African peoples, requires close scrutiny. Seacole says that she is 'only a little brown – a few shades duskier than the brunettes whom [the English] all admire so much' and that she has 'a few shades of deeper brown upon my skin which shows me related – and I am proud of the relationship – to those poor mortals whom you once held enslaved, and whose bodies America still owns'.[47] Seacole undoubtedly wants her readers to know that her skin is *light brown* and that she is *related to*, but *not* one of, Jamaica's black and formerly enslaved population.

The author's emphasis on her Scottish father and traits inherited from him stands in contrast to her awkwardly depicted, dusky self. Of her father and his legacy, the doctress has a lot to say:

> I am Creole, and have good Scotch blood coursing in my veins. My father was a soldier, of an old Scotch family; and to him I often trace my affection for a camp-life, and my sympathy with what I have heard my friends call 'the pomp, pride, and circumstance of glorious war'. Many people have also traced to my Scotch blood that energy and activity which are not always found in the Creole race, and which have carried me to so many varied scenes: and perhaps they are right.[48]

This revelation is followed by Seacole's description of her inheritance from her mother. She says: 'my mother kept a boardinghouse in Kingston, and was, like very many of the Creole women, an admirable doctress'.[49] Seacole thus asserts her mother's creoleness by linking it to her status as doctress and (by association) boarding-house keeper. Readers can only consider, therefore, that the mother is Creole because she inhabits these occupations, despite the fact that both black and coloured women worked in these professions. Seacole's mother's status as 'mother' is also questionable since another woman mothers the narrator. Seacole reports that 'when I was a very young child I was taken by an old lady, who brought me up in her household among her own grandchildren'.[50] Readers never learn why this arrangement is necessary.

In light of Seacole's definitive description of her father, this characterisation of her mother's creoleness is strangely imprecise, a fact that makes one question the 'fact' of the mother's, but also the author's, stated social position. Since it is through Mary Seacole's statements about her mother's occupations that readers can name her creoleness, the certainty about the doctress's Jamaican Creole self must also derive from her rhetorical reiterations. At the same time, the deliberateness of *Wonderful Adventures*' autobiographical persona disguises its unsettling features. Consider for instance, that if the author is a quadroon because of her Scotch father and her 'creole' mother, then she must be culturally black because of her surrogate mothering.[51] Seacole chooses to proclaim biology and behaviour over upbringing and culture, and she also chooses to impose an ordered Creole identity on her ambivalent one, all of which suggests how much is at stake in Mary Seacole's self-representation.

   The conviction of the author's rhetorical performance is also observable when we look at how other characters define her. 'Tired to death of life in Panama',[52] the author seeks passage to Kingston, Jamaica on an available American steamer rather than wait on an English vessel. Availing herself of the private on-board saloon, Seacole is accosted by two North American ladies:

> 'Where air you going?'
> 'To Kingston'.
> 'And how air you going?'
> 'By sea'.
> 'Don't be impertinent, *yaller* woman. By what conveyance air you going?'
> 'By this steamer, of course. I've paid for my passage'.
>   They went away with this information; and in a short time eight or nine others came and surrounded me, asking the same questions. My answers – and I was very particular – raised quite a storm of uncomplimentary remarks.
>   'Guess a *nigger* woman don't go along with us in this saloon', said one. 'I never travelled [sic] with a *nigger* yet, and I expect I shan't begin now', said another ...[53]

In this exchange, Mary Seacole's accusers use 'yaller' and 'nigger' interchangeably, indicating that they do not make the colour/caste distinctions that the doctress finds crucial. By contrast, an earlier moment in the autobiography augments this point. At Seacole's going-away party (she moves from Cruces to Gorgona, New Granada), one of her North American customers attempts to verbalise his appreciation of her. This nameless white man announces to the room: "'I calculate, gentlemen, you're all as vexed as I am that she's not wholly white, but I du reckon on your rejoicing with me that she's so many shades removed from being entirely black; and I guess, if we could bleach her by any means we would, and thus make her as acceptable in any company as she deserves to be'".[54] Through her recounting of this speech and the ship-board conflict, Seacole locates racial prejudice firmly within a North American context and also, in her use of phonetically correct spelling, marks North Americans as crude.[55] It is important to note, however, that in her 'unhistorical inexactness', she remembers the speech in a way that mirrors her own portrayal of her Creole self. However, the same reasoning does not neatly explain the interchangeable use of 'yaller' and 'nigger' by the occupants of the American ship. I argue, then, that location might be the significant feature here. On board the ship, a space unequivocally defined as 'American', it appears that North Americans hold fast to racial categories that are rigidly upheld in the United States. On the other hand, the isthmus and, later, the Crimean war zone can support Seacole's Creole persona better than the USA because the former are 'rendered almost uninhabitable by war, social upheaval, and pestilence'.[56] To put it another way, the narrator can interpolate her uniquely New World subjectivity within spaces that resemble the one from which she originates.

Occupying isthmian ground, the nameless North American speech-maker affirms the identity that the author goes to great lengths to project; still, Mrs Seacole uses her response to establish her subject position more firmly. After attributing her isthmian success to 'Providence', the author avers, 'I must say, that I don't altogether appreciate your friend's kind wishes with respect to my complexion. *If* it had been as dark as any nigger's, I should have been just as happy and as useful'.[57] The importance of location is affirmed since Seacole professes her creoleness when inhabiting a North American space, but also when circulating in an English one. These locations are without a doubt the *least chaotic* spaces represented in the memoir. As with the North Americans onboard the American steamer, the English in England need reminding that while 'wholly black' and 'creole' are related, they are by no means the same.

After being rejected for Crimean service by the War Office, the yellow woman intimates that the problem might lie with English people's lack of familiarity with her 'kind':

> Now, I am not for a single instant going to blame the authorities who would not listen to the offer of a motherly yellow woman to go to the Crimea and nurse her 'sons' there, suffering from cholera, diarrhœa, and a host of lesser ills. *In my country, where people know our use, it would have been different; but here it was natural enough – although I had references, and other voices spoke for me – that they should laugh, good-naturedly enough, at my offer.*[58]

Though the narrator testifies to the 'naturalness' of this mistake, her tone (not to mention her references and the 'voices' that speak for her) signifies the opposite. What this scene marks as unnatural is the failure to recognise Seacole's 'kind' as well as the maintenance of an 'emblematic, unitary English subject'[59] of the female variety. The persona that Mary Seacole embodies at the War Office has distinctly Jamaican, female and Creole behaviours (as can be deduced from the word 'use'), the knowledge of which, the narrator implies, should recommend her. Despite the fact that the yellow woman is out of (her geographical) place, her expectation that her Creole-self be recognised suggests that this identity should be transportable. It is important to note that it is only un-chaotic locations (the American ship, England) that cannot accommodate the narrator's selected persona. It is reduced to 'wholly black' in the former and 'wholly black female' in the latter.

By repeatedly asserting her exceptional colour and professional skill, Seacole reconstructs her self, but in and on her own terms. On the isthmus, she is Creole, a hotel keeper and a doctress. In Sebastopol, she is all of these things, but importantly with a textual emphasis on the first two characteristics, since the English cannot accept her as nurse (although she still occupies this role). Yet she achieves her rhetorical negotiations in part by identifying the 'not her' that nonetheless defines her.[60] In the memoir, she references her 'nigger'[61] cooks and additional kitchen helpers who are identifiable because of their big, white teeth.[62] In describing her battle with 'Russian rats' at her British Hotel in the Crimea, Seacole states that:

> when hard pressed they more than once attacked the live sheep; and at last they went so far as to nibble one of our black cooks, Francis, who slept among the flour barrels. On the following morning he came to me, his eyes rolling angrily, and his white teeth gleaming, to show me a mangled finger ... a few mornings later he came in a violent passion this time, and gave me instant notice to quit my service ... This time the rats had ... been bolder, and attached his head, in a spot where its natural armour, the wool, was thinnest.[63]

When she introduces black men who are not servants (one is a priest, another a local mayor), she predictably portrays them as lazy.[64] Finally, one can gauge the deliberateness of Seacole's distancing strategy by the following example. In Escribanos, a mining town on the isthmus, the doctress expresses her disgust with native food by saying 'with what pleasure, for instance, could one foreign to [native] tastes and habits dine off a roasted monkey, whose grilled head bore a strong resemblance to a negro baby's?'[65] However stereotypical her representations of pheno-typically black peoples may be, the yellow doctress's treatment of them highlights the difference between blacks as merely visually represented subjects and her own rhetorically-defined image. The self-described doctress counters depictions of her self as 'other' by advertising the extreme otherness of the individuals described above.

The sutler/doctress is aware of her English reading audience and positions her text by playing on the celebrity she garners in New Granada and the Crimea. Seacole acknowledges the image of herself as a 'female Ulysses',[66] but the usefulness of this characterisation does not hinge on her audience's knowledge of Ulysses's textually defined adventures, but rather their familiarity with Greek stereotypes. When people so describe Seacole, she believes they intend 'it as a compliment; but from my experience of the Greeks, I do not consider it a very flattering one'.[67] Nonetheless she accepts other kinds of labels. The narrator describes herself as a 'hot-blooded Creole' when she quickly recovers from her husband's death and as 'one of an impulsive people' who finds 'it hard to put that restraint upon my feelings which to you [English] is so easy and natural' when she cries after her attempts to serve in the Crimea are twice thwarted.[68]

While these Creole characteristics render her 'knowable' in a limited way to English readers, they nonetheless facilitate the performance of her broader subjectivity. 'I have often heard', Seacole states, 'the term "lazy Creole" applied to my country people; but I am sure I do not know what it is to be indolent'.[69] Not only is she – unlike other Creoles – naturally industrious, she demonstrates her industry by putting it in service of 'English people':

> I think all who are familiar with the West Indies will acknowledge that Nature has been favorable to strangers in a few respects, and that one of these has been in instilling into the hearts of the Creoles an affection for English people and an anxiety for their welfare, which shows itself warmest when they are sick and suffering.[70]

While this quotation is not unique in its use of flattery, Seacole deploys the Creole stereotype for both her narrative and financial ends. The passage can also be interpreted as an example of the author's Anglophila, but this does not account for her skill as a writer nor for the more nuanced readings the latter perspective makes available. The passage, for example, demonstrates Seacole's manipulation of her readers, but it also allows for a more layered analysis of 'the English' themselves.

The people with whom Mrs Seacole associates are her 'kind', not only because they are English but also because they mirror some part of her entrepreneurial, adventurous or migratory spirit. Their Englishness can therefore be read in a more complex way. Early in the narrative, Seacole acknowledges the 'friends' she encounters in her travels: 'I met with some when my adventures had carried me to the battle-fields of the Crimea; and to those whose eyes may rest upon these pages I again offer my acknowledgements for their past kindness, which helped me to be useful *to my kind* in many lands'.[71] She ends her tale of Crimean life by destroying the most valuable stock at her British Hotel for 'there was no more of *my own people* to give it to, and I would rather not present it to our old foes'.[72] Obviously, these 'friends' are (mainly) English, but they are significantly *soldiers*, individuals who share behavioural traits with the narrator.

One can also assert that Seacole's 'kind' includes 'wholly black' people but, again, only with qualification. Describing prejudices that citizens of New Granada hold against all Americans, Seacole compliments African-descended people who, after escaping slavery in the US, settle and thrive in Central America. She claims that:

> many of the negroes, fugitives from the Southern States, had sought refuge in this and the other States of Central America, where every profession was open to them; and they were generally superior men – evinced perhaps by their hatred of their old condition and their successful flight – they soon rose to positions of eminence in New Granada. In the priesthood, in the army, in all municipal offices, the self-liberated negroes were invariably found in the foremost rank; and the people [of New Granada], for some reason – perhaps because they recognised in them superior talents for administration – always respected them more than, and preferred them to, their native rulers.[73]

This quotation clearly notes the behaviour of these formerly enslaved people, and remarks on the fact that 'the people' of New Granada recognise and encourage it through their patronage. While living on the isthmus, the author comes across as a black *alcalde* (mayor) who freed himself from slavery in the United States. (The *alcalde* reaps the rewards of this freedom by obtaining a white wife and producing a 'pretty' daughter with her.)[74] Seacole further illustrates her interest in those who were formerly enslaved:

> Against the Negroes, of whom there were many in the Isthmus, and who almost invariably filled the municipal offices, and took the lead in every way, the Yankees had a strong prejudice; but it was wonderful to see how freedom and equality elevate men, and the same Negro who perhaps in Tennessee would have cowered like a beaten child or dog beneath an American's uplifted hand, would face him boldly here, and by equal courage and superior physical strength cow his old oppressor.[75]

This quotation complicates previous analyses that simply map Seacole's self-authorising tactics onto all who the English might consider 'other'.[76] The author represents 'wholly black' men as individuals who elevate themselves by escaping from and prospering beyond US slavery. By calling attention to the yellow woman's interest in particular behaviours exhibited by wholly black people, I similarly call attention to her rhetorically described behaviour and narrative feats: she 'talks' herself into Jamaica's Creole class, into the Crimea and into the categories of 'doctress' and 'mother' to her soldier 'sons'. As a result, Seacole's autobiography demonstrates that narrative performances can authorise subjectivities; importantly, her narrative persona manifests how inefficiently visual markers define the self.

The import of this interpretation becomes clear in Seacole's narration of the following event. Before travelling to the Crimea the author and her companions stop at the coastal town of Balaclava. Finding wounded soldiers in need of her ministering, Seacole begins to comfort an artillery-man without waiting to be invited. Seacole describes how she cared for the wounded lying on the dock: 'I do not think that the surgeons noticed me at first, although, as this was my introduction to Balaclava, I had not neglected my personal appearance, and wore my favorite yellow dress, and blue bonnet, with the red ribbons; but I noticed one coming to me, who, I think, would have laughed very merrily had it not been for the poor fellow at my feet'.[77] Dress is obviously a yardstick against which she measures women in her environment despite the gore and dirt. Describing the isthmus as practically a 'classless' society (almost everyone is coarse, venal, and dirty), Seacole opines:

> the women alone kept aloof from each other, and well they might; for, while a very few seemed not ashamed of their sex, it was somewhat difficult to distinguish the majority from their male companions, save by their bolder and more reckless voice and manner. I must say, however, that many of them adopted male attire for

the journey across the Isthmus only, as it spared them many compliments which their husbands were often disposed to resent, however flattering they might be to their choice.[78]

And she continues:

> although many of the women on their way to California showed clearly enough that the life of license they sought would not be altogether unfamiliar to them, they still retained some appearance of decency in their attire and manner; but in many cases … the female companions of the successful gold-diggers appeared in no hurry to resume the dress or obligations of their sex.[79]

The women Seacole notices appear and behave as roughly as men. However, their coarseness might be mitigated by the retention of 'some appearance of decency' but also by their assumption of the obligations of their sex – whatever Seacole believes these might be.

Within the context of nineteenth-century women's travel and auto-biographical narratives this emphasis on dress and deportment is familiar. Women writers invested in establishing their legitimate authority took pains to distinguish themselves from so-called whores and manly women; as a woman of African descent from an English colony, Seacole's adherence to such codes is understandable. Still, if dress can establish a woman's authority then Seacole's use of the word 'obligation' implies that behaviour might be used to do the same. Thus far, the author's behaviour defines her as a Jamaican Creole in that she keeps a well-stocked boarding house and doctors those in need. Significantly, these are services predominantly performed by Creole women in Jamaica; thus Mary Seacole ably achieves the 'obligations' of her sex. In this way, her performance is not merely that of a Jamaican, female or a Creole, but simultaneously all of these identities.

While her observance of established literary gender codes serves the writer's purposes, this view can be complicated by attending to Seacole's performance of her gendered obligations, especially if one interprets dress as costume. If Seacole can undermine the meanings that confine blackness through written/behavioural performances of creoleness, then her fashion choices might constitute another scene in the same act. One might similarly interpret *Wonderful Adventures*' two scenes of passing. The narrator notes that Christmas celebrations in the Crimea included peculiar kinds of holiday entertainment, including theatrical productions staged for the entertainment of soldiers and other attendees. Seacole offers her kitchen as a 'green room' for one such show and assists with the costumes. She 'lent [performers] plenty of dresses' and 'the ladies of the company of the 1st Royals were taught to manage their petticoats with becoming grace, and neither to show their awkward booted ankles, nor trip themselves up over their trains'.[80] Her ministrations were not altogether successful, however, because 'although [Seacole] laced them in until they grew blue in the face, their waists [and hips] were a disgrace to the sex'.[81] Later, soldiers transported part of the culture of home to the warfront in the form of horse races and blackface minstrelsy. Mrs Seacole observes that 'in order that the course should still more closely resemble Ascot or Epsom, some soldiers blackened their faces and came out as Ethiopian serenaders admirably, although it would puzzle the most ingenious to guess where they got their wigs and banjoes from'.[82]

Seacole's representation of these scenes might divert attention away from her intentional performance, but can arguably be understood as a critique of the tenuous link between how one looks and how one defines oneself. Inattention to such details restrains interpretive possibilities such as the one that qualifies her recognition of blacks in her narrative. Yet Mary Seacole is always aware of how she differs from the people she serves and from whom she earns her living. While she positions herself as substitute mother/wife to English soldiers, she recognises her deviation from the real: the 'mother' in 'Mother Seacole' is most often depicted in scare quotes. Seacole 'is well aware that these men are not her "sons" and that she is not their "Mother", and yet she uses this language in the context of her attempt to authorize her behaviour in the Crimea'.[83] This particular technique has the effect of making the private, domestic space (then the province of women) portable as she migrates into various public places. Though this strategy certainly affects Mary Seacole's ability to operate in spaces set aside for white and English men, it effectively authorises her brand of Creole identity within the spaces she inhabits.

Amy Robinson argues that 'models of inversion suggest the possibility of new social organization, but, on the other hand, they often end in a conservative trajectory because flipping cultural categories does nothing to alter the systemic binary structure which produces them or, in [the case of Seacole's autobiographical self], produces the exception to the rule'.[84] However, the analysis I attempt above puts Mary Seacole's autobiographical self outside of the typical black/white binary. It is crucial to recognise the author's ambiguous position as an author, as a woman of colour and as a person in dire financial straits. On the other hand, the autobiography shows her as a woman unused to imposed limitations and as one who feels obliged to challenge barriers that confine her. Attempting to identify some purpose to the narrator's often contradictory representations of creoleness, blackness, Englishness and femaleness forces one to be attentive not only to her reconstructed self but also to the processes of categorisation and the limited nature of these categories. Seacole, an 'other' in the English frame of reference, claims the travel narrative and the 'authentic' Englishness that it articulates. She is, simultaneously, a healer, mixed race and female. I concur with Robinson when she states that 'in [Seacole's] acknowledged "difference" from the "real" British subject, it is possible to locate a new value, one which repudiates the "real" and therefore initiates a dislocation of the fiction of power with which Great Britain authorized its colonial policies'.[85] But rather than position Mary Seacole's narrative persona within a binary, it might more productively be understood as a seminal articulation of a particularly Jamaican subjectivity produced at a particular moment in history. Seacole's narrative self is an example of a Creole identity that highlights the inherent complications in master narratives and that exemplifies an emergent Caribbean subjectivity.

Notes

1. Mary Louise Pratt, *Imperial Eyes: Travel Writing and Transculturation* (London: Routledge, 1992), p. 6; Mary Seacole, *Wonderful Adventures of Mrs. Seacole in Many Lands* (New York: Oxford University Press, 1988), pp. 146–7.
2. Joan Dayan, *Haiti, History, and the Gods* (Berkeley: University of California Press, 1995), p. xvii.
3. Dayan, *Haiti*, p. xvii.
4. Dayan, *Haiti*, p. 24.
5. For examinations of definitions of 'creole', see Gad J. Heuman, *Between Black and White: Race, Politics, and the Free Coloreds in Jamaica, 1792–1865* (Westport: Greenwood Press, 1981), pp. xix–xx; Hilary Beckles, 'On the Backs of Blacks: The Barbados Free-Coloureds' Pursuit of Civil Rights and the 1816 Slave Rebellion', *Immigrants and Minorities* 3 (1984), p. 185, endnote 1; Sandra Gunning, 'Traveling with Her Mother's Tastes: The Negotiation of Gender, Race, and Location in *Wonderful Adventures of Mrs. Seacole in Many Lands*', *Signs: Journal of Women in Culture and Society* 26 (2001), p. 949, footnote 1.
6. Edward Kamau Brathwaite, 'Caribbean Man in Space and Time', *Savacou* 11/12 (1975), p. 1.
7. Seacole, *Wonderful Adventures*, pp. 8–9.
8. Seacole, *Wonderful Adventures*, pp. 24–5.
9. Seacole, *Wonderful Adventures*, p. 125.
10. For additional biographical scholarship on Seacole see Ziggi Alexander's and Audrey Dewjee's introduction to *Wonderful Adventures of Mrs. Seacole in Many Lands* (Bristol: Falling Wall Press, 1984), pp. 9–41; Aleric Josephs' 'Mary Seacole: Jamaican Nurse and "Doctress", 1805/10-1881', *Jamaican Historical Review* 17 (1991), pp. 48–65.
11. See Evelyn Hawthorne, 'Self-Writing, Literary Traditions, and Post-Emancipation Identity: The Case of Mary Seacole', *Biography* 23 (2000), pp. 309–31; Amy Robinson, 'Authority and the Public Display of Identity: *Wonderful Adventures of Mrs. Seacole in Many Lands*', *Feminist Studies* 20 (1994), pp. 537–57; Sandra Pouchet Paquet, 'The Enigma of Arrival: The *Wonderful Adventures of Mrs. Seacole in Many Lands*', *African American Review* 26 (Winter 1992), pp. 651–62; Cheryl Fish, 'Voices of Restless (Dis)continuity: The Significance of Travel for Free Black Women in the Antebellum Americas', *Women's Studies* 26 (Summer 1997), pp. 475–95; Catherine Judd, *Bedside Seductions: Nursing and the Victorian Imagination, 1830–1880* (New York: St. Martin's Press, 1998); Paul Edwards and David Dabydeen, *Early Black Writers, 1760–1890* (Edinburgh: Edinburgh University Press, 1991).
12. Bernard McKenna, '"Fancies of Exclusive Possession": Validation and Dissociation in Mary Seacole's England and Caribbean', *Philological Quarterly* 76 (Spring 1997), p. 222.
13. McKenna, 'Fancies', p. 220.
14. McKenna, 'Fancies', p. 221.
15. Alexander and Dewjee, Introduction, *Wonderful Adventures*, p. 39.

16. For detailed discussions of black, coloured, and white women and their roles in Anglophone Caribbean societies, see Paulette A. Kerr's 'Victims or Strategists?: Female Lodging-House Keepers in Jamaica', *Engendering History: Caribbean Women in Historical Perspective*, ed. Verene Shepherd, Bridget Brereton, and Barbara Bailey (New York: St. Martin's Press, 1995), pp. 197–212; Barbara Bush's 'White "Ladies", Coloured "Favorites" and Black "Wenches": Some Considerations on Sex, Race and Class Factors in Social Relations in White Creole Society in the British Caribbean', *Slavery and Abolition* 2 (1981), pp. 245–62; Heuman's *Between Black and White*; and Gunning's 'Traveling with Her Mother's Tastes'.

17. Arnold Sio, 'Marginality and Free Coloured Identity in Caribbean Slave Society', *Caribbean Slave Society and Economy: A Student Reader*, ed. Hilary Beckles and Verene Shepherd (New York: Ian Randle Publishers, 1991), pp. 153, 152. For an early investigation of Jamaican social classes, see Edward Kamau Brathwaite, *Contradictory Omens: Cultural Diversity and Integration in the Caribbean* (Mona, Jamaica: Savacou Publications, 1974) and *The Development of Creole Society in Jamaica* (London: Oxford University Press, 1974).

18. Heuman, *Between Black and White*, p. 4; see also Gunning, 'Traveling', p. 955; Bush 'White "Ladies"', pp. 248–89, 251, 258; and Beckles, 'On the Backs', p. 168.

19. Heuman, *Between Black and White*, p. 5.

20. Heuman, *Between Black and White*, pp. 6, 10–11; Beckles, 'On the Backs', pp. 177–8.

21. Heuman, *Between Black and White*, p. 6.

22. Heuman, *Between Black and White*, p. 23; Sio, 'Marginality', p. 154.

23. Beckles, 'On the Backs', p. 170.

24. Beckles, 'On the Backs', p, 171.

25. Heuman, *Between Black and White*, pp. 23, 40–1; Beckles, 'On the Backs', pp. 172, 175.

26. Heuman, *Between Black and White*, pp. 11–12, 24; Beckles, 'On the Backs', pp. 169, 180, 177; Sio, 'Marginality', p. 153.

27. Heuman, *Between Black and White*, p. 6.

28. Sio, 'Marginality', p. 156.

29. Sio, 'Marginality', pp. 153–4; Heuman, *Between Black and White*, p. 11.

30. Kerr, 'Victims', p. 202.

31. Josephs, 'Mary Seacole', p. 50.

32. Gunning, 'Traveling', p. 957; Kerr, 'Victims', pp. 204, 206; Josephs, 'Mary Seacole,' pp. 51, 57–60; Heuman, *Between Black and White*, pp. 12–13.

33. Kerr, 'Victims', p. 198.

34. Bush, 'White "Ladies"', pp. 245–6.

35. Belinda Edmondson, *Making Men: Gender, Literary Authority, and Women's Writing in Caribbean Narrative* (Durham: Duke University Press, 1999), p. 2.

36. Edmonson, *Making Men*, p. 5.

37. See Gunning, 'Traveling', p. 950; Faith L. Smith, 'Coming Home to the Real Thing: Gender and Intellectual Life in the Anglophone Caribbean', *South Atlantic Quarterly* 93 (1994), p. 916.

38. Gunning, 'Traveling', pp. 967–8.

39. For an important discussion of the need to recognise contradiction and disorder as creative forces in Caribbean literature, see Maryse Condé , 'Order, Disorder, Freedom, and the West Indian Writer', *Yale French Studies* 83 (1993), pp. 121–35. Her celebration of disorder directly challenges Jean Bernabé, Patrick Chamoiseau and Raphaël Confiant in their essay 'In Praise of Creoleness', *Callaloo* 13 (1990), pp. 886–909, who argue that 'Creoleness is *'the world diffracted but recomposed'*, a maelstrom of signifieds in a single signifier: a Totality' (p. 892).

40. Edwards and Dabydeen accurately identify the 'divided loyalties' that can result from being 'of mixed blood and heritage' in a colonial context, but they attribute them to Seacole's 'split personality' instead of a predictable consequence of the history of Jamaica's Creole population. See their 'Introduction', p. 169.

41. Introduction, *Wonderful Adventures*, pp. 26–7, emphasis added.

42. Paquet, 'Enigma', p. 652; Smith, 'Coming Home', p. 901.
43. Hawthorne, 'Self-Writing,' p. 309.
44. Gunning, 'Traveling', pp. 955, 949.
45. Josephs, 'Mary Seacole', p. 48.
46. Edmonson, *Making Men*, p. 6.
47. Seacole, *Wonderful Adventures*, pp. 4, 14.
48. Seacole, *Wonderful Adventures*, pp. 1–2.
49. Seacole, *Wonderful Adventures*, p. 2.
50. Seacole, *Wonderful Adventures*, p. 3.
51. As mentioned above and throughout the text, Seacole obsessively identifies characters' race and/or colour as she determinedly constructs her own creoleness. That she does not mention either the race or colour of the 'old lady' who raises her suggests that she did not find this woman's features commendable. I interpret this particular omission as resulting from the adoptive mother's less-than-remarkable blackness.
52. Seacole, *Wonderful Adventures*, p. 56.
53. Seacole, *Wonderful Adventures*, p. 57, emphasis added.
54. Seacole, *Wonderful Adventures*, p. 47.
55. Paquet, 'Enigma', p. 654.
56. Gunning, 'Traveling', p. 953.
57. Seacole, *Wonderful Adventures*, p. 48, emphasis added.
58. Seacole, *Wonderful Adventuers*, p. 78, emphasis added.
59. Gunning, 'Traveling', p. 952.
60. Smith, 'Coming Home', p. 914.
61. Seacole, *Wonderful Adventures*, p. 20.
62. Seacole, *Wonderful Adventures*, p. 141.
63. Seacole, *Wonderful Adventures*, pp. 115–16.
64. Seacole, *Wonderful Adventures*, pp. 35, 44–5.
65. Seacole, *Wonderful Adventures*, p. 69.
66. Seacole, *Wonderful Adventures*, p. 2.
67. Seacole, *Wonderful Adventures*, p. 2.
68. Seacole, *Wonderful Adventures*, pp. 6, 80.
69. Seacole, *Wonderful Adventures*, p. 2.
70. Seacole, *Wonderful Adventures*, p. 60.
71. Seacole, *Wonderful Adventures*, p. 8, emphasis added.
72. Seacole, *Wonderful Adventures*, p. 196, emphasis added.
73. Seacole, *Wonderful Adventures*, pp. 50–1.
74. Seacole, *Wonderful Adventures*, p. 66.
75. Seacole, *Wonderful Adventures*, pp. 42–3.
76. See McKenna, '"Fancies"', p. 221.
77. Seacole, *Wonderful Adventures*, pp. 97–8.
78. Seacole, *Wonderful Adventures*, p. 18.
79. Seacole, *Wonderful Adventures*, p. 20.
80. Seacole, *Wonderful Adventures*, p. 180.
81. Seacole, *Wonderful Adventures*, p. 181.
82. Seacole, *Wonderful Adventures*, p. 183.
83. Robinson, 'Authority', p. 547.
84. Robinson, 'Authority', pp. 545–6.
85. Robinson, 'Authority', p. 555.

6

Colonial Matriarchs: Garveyism, Maternalism, and Belize's Black Cross Nurses, 1920–1952

Anne Macpherson

In her novel *Beka Lamb*, part of the canon of West Indian women's fiction, Zee Edgell claims that '[i]n Belize, to be able to work like a woman was an honourable thing'.[1] For most poor Creole and Garifuna women in the first half of the twentieth century, the honour of labour lay in providing for themselves, their children and households; they often legitimised their political activism in terms of this same combative womanhood and motherhood.[2] Elfreda Reyes, a veteran activist, paid domestic and childcare worker, recalled her nationalist militancy of the early 1950s as an effort 'to get from under the claws of this British Empire ... All we wanted – justice. It was for the children more than any other thing'.[3] Working-class black women in Belize, mothers or not, based their self-respect on minimising economic dependency and political exclusion. The combative woman and/or mother, then, was a strongly resistant subject, one common to the British Caribbean. Mimi Sheller has found that Jamaican freed women in the apprenticeship transition made labour and broader political demands 'as mothers who were struggling to support their families'. She hypothesises a 'long-term continuity in the forms and style' of African Diaspora women's 'political participation and leadership'. Indeed, Olive Senior has summarised the widely-shared view of present-day working-class Caribbean women of children's emotional and material importance and the value these women place on economic and political independence over respectability.[4] Combative motherhood emerged as a characteristic political strategy out of evolving post-emancipation realities of female household leadership, British definitions of proper womanhood and poverty.

Practitioners of combative motherhood in Belize were maligned by British colonial authorities as well as by the Belize Town local of the

Universal Negro Improvement Association (UNIA) and its Black Cross Nurses organisation, both formed in 1920 by progressive middle-class Creoles. The UNIA, founded by Marcus Garvey and Amy Ashwood in Jamaica in 1914 and re-launched in Harlem in 1917–1918, was a mass movement for black liberation, mobilising thousands across the African Diaspora for separate black economic progress, and the establishment of a black-run state in Africa.[5] The conservative politics of the Belize UNIA makes sense within the growing scholarly critique of the movement's radicalism.[6] Belize's Creole middle class – a small but pivotal group of shopkeepers, artisans and civil servants – was largely descended from free coloured and black families in economic decline since the nineteenth century. Its leaders emphasised social respectability, and sought an end to Crown Colony rule (1871–1936) that had extinguished the colonial legislature.[7] Garveyites, like the middle class as a whole, opposed autonomous working-class mobilisation for labour rights, universal suffrage and national independence, and they repeatedly eschewed alliances with popular organisations. In parallel, the Nurses' Garveyism emphasised a maternalist politics of racial uplift through modern scientific motherhood, and nurtured 'persistent fantasies of sovereignty over the "colonized" female body … modern household', and infant body, countering combative motherhood with a comparatively passive, obedient subjectivity.[8] The Belize UNIA's 'respectability[,] unmatched in any other colonized country',[9] thus stemmed from its acceptance of British executive authority and other colonial hierarchies, but also from the espousal of a maternalism aimed at increasing middle-class women's rights and their control over working-class women.

Garvey scholarship has documented women's work in the UNIA's membership and leadership and has analysed with deepening insight the gender culture and politics of the movement. Early claims that women 'enjoyed equal status' with men – based on separate male and female structures of authority – or that they broke with middle-class black women's ideal of respectability, have given way to a more nuanced view.[10] Barbara Bair, the leading feminist scholar of Garveyism, has noted that the UNIA did challenge 'dominant definitions of Black womanhood'[11] – especially those that cast black women as sexually degenerate, ugly and dangerous to civilisation – but did not break with the bourgeois and imperial paradigm of progress.[12] That paradigm centrally defined civilisation in terms of the male-headed nuclear family, nurtured by an educated but domestic mother and housewife. It was this 'companionate, supportive' ideal of black womanhood that Garvey promoted, while condemning birth control, single motherhood, illegitimacy, female-headed households and interracial sex.[13] Self-sufficiency through education and capitalist enterprise would form the basis for black female domesticity and proper public service. The UNIA's Black Cross Nurses movement, modelled on the Red Cross nurses of World War I, was launched in early 1920 as an arena for respectable female community service.[14] The maternalist politics of Belize's Black Cross Nurses exemplified such service, even as their own practices went well beyond the companionate domestic ideal.

Feminist Garvey scholarship has concentrated on the women at the centre of Garvey's life and of the UNIA, principally his second wife, Amy Jacques Garvey, a pattern mirroring the general literature's focus on the New York 'Parent Body'.[15] Bair and Jamaican activist-scholar Honor Ford-Smith have suggested that Garveyite women resisted or simply moved beyond Garvey's ideal of the black woman.[16] Jacques Garvey certainly struggled with it very publicly, developing a praxis that Ula Y. Taylor has dubbed 'community feminism' – essentially a race-uplift activism asserting women's political equality while demanding fulfilment of traditional male roles.[17] Without an adequate knowledge of local UNIA histories, however, it is difficult to know how or to what extent the majority of Garveyite women 'broadened the internal debate over what women should do and be', or developed ideologies and practices 'that to some extent [belie] the dominant construction of womanhood presented by Garvey and by many of the women themselves'.[18] Judith Stein's study of several US UNIA branches finds that each was a marriage 'between the traditions of local racial communities and the ... culture of New York Garveyism'.[19] The farther from headquarters, the more those marriages drew on local dynamics; branches were never simply the childlike creations of the Parent Body.[20] The slim scholarship on the gendered worlds of Garveyism beyond New York finds a strong emphasis on middle-class respectability and other imperial norms.[21] This study, the first to examine in depth the practice and ideology of one local's Black Cross Nurse branch, confirms that maternalist politics were not uncommon in the movement, though they were never simply imposed by Garvey.

Research on maternalism and female reform during the late-nineteenth and early-twentieth centuries has developed with a comparative bent, yet focuses on the industrialising nations of the North Atlantic. Enlarging the comparative field are rapidly maturing literatures on Latin America and Europe's colonial empires.[22] The latter in particular shows the importance of viewing European women's movements and maternalist politics as being formed within imperial contexts. Confirming the claim that 'Europe was made by its imperial projects', Antoinette Burton finds that '[m]iddle class Victorian feminists not only identified their cause with the British imperial mission, they helped to shape a modern Western feminism which was profoundly influenced by the imperial assumptions of its day'.[23] Studies of similar processes in post-1898 US imperial expansion are proliferating.[24]

The British Caribbean, however, receives relatively little attention in feminist scholarship on the British Empire or comparative imperialism.[25] Countering this lacuna, Clare Midgley argues that post-1865 'imperial feminism' (or 'maternalist imperialism') had strong roots in the anti-slavery activism of British women from 1780 to the mid-nineteenth century.[26] That activism focused on enslaved women in the Caribbean, constructed by abolitionists as victimised sisters in need of moral uplift within Christian male-headed families.[27] Crucially, the rising biological racism that Midgley tracks across the nineteenth century was in part a British reaction to freedmen's and women's refusal to abide by emerging bourgeois morality, as labourers or family members.[28] The British Caribbean was thus a key site in the ongoing production of wider imperial racism.

In examining Belize's Black Cross Nurses, this article brings the British Caribbean more squarely into comparative scholarship on gender, empire and maternalism. It also contributes to a sorely-needed analysis of non-European and/or non-white women's maternalist politics, particularly in colonised areas. While some work has been done on middle-class Indian maternalists, they tended toward nationalism, unlike their race-uplift counterparts in the British Caribbean who espoused the region's middle-class tradition of colonial accommodation.[29] '[B]rown, middle-class' Jamaican girls were disciplined, in a Foucaultian sense, by colonial schools, becoming 'social managers of the black working class' by internalising imperial racism and splitting themselves off from a resistant, or indeed any, black identity.[30] This colonised subjectivity has been very marked in the Caribbean, where racialised slavery bred a free-coloured attachment to whiteness.[31] The deep historical roots of middle-class West Indians' culture of respectability contrast sharply with colonial efforts to jump-start such a culture in Africa, in part through maternalist training.[32] The Black Cross Nurses – mature, self-motivated, imbued with Protestant bourgeois morality, and hostile to popular black politics – were far more reliable agents of imperial reform than native African midwives or British nurses in colonial Africa.[33] The British Caribbean, then, is indispensable to comparative scholarship on imperial reform and maternalism, both as a site where imperial ideologies were produced through ongoing social and political struggle, and as a region shaped by non-white, middle-class female reformers, whose agency was never entirely produced or bounded by colonial norms.

Scholars generally acknowledge that maternalists' promotion of motherhood as grounds for public action challenged male political authority and brought some benefits to poor mothers through welfare-state expansion. But most also scrutinise the limits of their politics as white class-privileged women who sought legitimacy with the state, and assumed superiority over working-class, colonised, immigrant and/or non-white women. Often constructing themselves as puritanical saviours or rehabilitators, they could act autocratically and accept state authoritarianism.[34] The terms 'maternalism' and 'social motherhood' thus seem to answer Nancy Cott's call for ways to describe non-feminist women's activism.[35] Yet maternalism and feminism were 'different but not mutually exclusive rhetorical strategies and perspectives', and the same women could dispute male domination while placing class-race hierarchy above equal women's rights.[36] Belize's Black Cross Nurses were maternalists who occasionally addressed larger issues of women's equality and rights in a feminist praxis compromised by its moralistic class exclusivity. Significantly, they developed no discourse of black sisterhood, consumed, like the African-American club women Eileen Boris analyses, by a fear 'that their sameness (race and gender) would obscure their differences (class and education)' from the working-class women whom they sought to uplift.[37] Their politics, then, differed from Taylor's relatively classless 'community feminism' through which Jacques Garvey encouraged other black women to speak.[38]

I further the mapping of the gendered worlds of Garveyism and the colonial worlds of maternalism, first by overturning the view that the Belize UNIA was ever radically anti-colonial, and sketching Creole middle-class politics from the 1890s to 1920. For Garveyism became a vehicle for those existing politics of colonial reform. I then illuminate the dynamics of the Black Cross Nurses' maternalist politics in four arenas: collaboration with the colonial state; their didactic stance toward poor mothers; the Nurses' harmonious but autonomous relations with male Garveyites; and their tempered feminist support for divorce and women's suffrage. In the mid-1930s and early 1950s the Nurses opposed popular labour and nationalist mobilisations against the colonial state, in which women like Elfreda Reyes were central. When nationalism eclipsed that state in the 1950s, the Nurses lost the class-bound political clout that they had accrued over three decades as possibly one of the strongest, most autonomous and most politically involved female divisions of any Garveyite local.

Interest in British Honduras among Garvey scholars has focused on links between the July 1919 anti-white, anti-colonial riot in Belize Town and the founding of its UNIA local in April 1920. These events are assumed to have been carried out by the same people, particularly World War I veterans, and are linked to the banning of *Negro World*, Garvey's newspaper, by the colonial authorities in January 1919. Thus, the historiography suggests a radical continuity among the paper's local readership, the veterans, their joint protest of July 1919 and the founding of the local.[39] This impression is strengthened by a focus on Samuel Haynes, who was a leading veteran, founder of the local, and UNIA chief in the US from 1921. In fact, Haynes played a crucial role in clearing the streets and

ending the protest – and its potential to yield labour or nationalist organisation. A decade later he recalled having 'silenced the radicals' and saved
the whites from 'savage massacre' in 1919.[40] Peter Ashdown has documented Haynes's role, but nonetheless sees the UNIA local as continuing
the radical spirit of the riot and as politically 'emasculated' primarily by
Haynes's departure to the US. He is thus puzzled by Garveyites' *volte face*
in opposing popular nationalism in the 1950s.[41] But Ashdown's interpretation misplaces the discontinuity in Belizean Garveyite history.

Claims that Garveyism, through the *Negro World*, fuelled popular race-
conscious anti-colonialism among Belize Town's labourers in 1918–1919
are, in all likelihood, correct.[42] The paper provided a language to articulate
frustrations over chronic poverty and political exclusion as well as extreme
wartime price inflation, which gave looting during the riot a political edge.
Days after the riot was put down by Haynes's band of veterans and British
sailors from the HMS *Constance*, domestic servant Annie Flowers hoped
for its resumption in provocative, if not black nationalist, terms: '[T]his
country belongs to the blacks. The next night there is a row my strong
arms will shove hat pins in the eyes of the bloody white men, for they have
to get out of this town now … When the ship goes we will know what to
do with the white bastards'.[43] Strikingly, Flowers anticipated Jacques
Garvey's conclusion that black women could not wait for their men to
lead the fight for liberation. Her bitter condemnation of black men as
having 'no pluck' can certainly be read as a critique of Haynes and his
post-riot negotiations with the Governor. If this was British Honduran
Garveyism in 1919, it was working-class, violently anti-colonial, and the
intellectual property of women as well as men.

The moment of disjuncture in British Honduran Garveyite history must
be located *between* the riot and the founding of the UNIA local in early
1920. In the riot's aftermath, during the period of martial law when both
the local and Black Cross Nurses were organised, progressive middle-
class Creoles appropriated the ephemeral but radical popular Garveyism
and harnessed it to their long-term campaign to end Crown Colony rule.
By so doing, Creoles sought to restore middle-class legislative representation without popular suffrage or labour agitation. But even as Garveyism
became implicated in these older struggles, it afforded new legitimacy to
'respectable' Creole women in public race-uplift work, thus strengthening
women's position in middle-class political culture. Indeed, the Black
Cross Nurses became the most successful element of the middle-class
takeover of Garveyism in British Honduras. For the UNIA local itself
declined within a decade, not only because of Haynes's departure and
financial disputes, but also because it neither represented nor sought
to organise British Honduran labour. Most importantly, Garveyite
leaders opposed universal suffrage – one labelled the masses as

'riff-raff'[44] – and promoted a cultural conservatism more anglophile than Pan-African.

This middle-class version of Garveyism was gendered and had roots in the empire loyalty practiced by the middle class since at least the 1890s. Unwilling to ally with workers and mistrustful of the white merchant élite, middle-class leaders lobbied British officials to restore their 'native' rights as legislators speaking for the masses. They did so by creating an origin myth that posited harmonious but hierarchical racial fraternity as the colony's central political tradition, thus making it safe for Britain to empower middle-class Creole men. In the first decade of the twentieth century, the middle class gained neither popular nor state allies, though it did win a restricted municipal franchise in Belize Town in 1911 (for men) and 1912 (for women).[45] During the later 1910s through wartime loyalty and in the 1920s through post-riot collaboration, a stronger alliance was forged with the colonial state, which had begun to see the middle class as vital in combating both popular protest and the élite's repressive responses to it.

The Black Cross Nurses were central to both the Garveyite and general middle-class alliances with British officials. The Nurses organised somewhat independently and existed at least a month before the Belize Town local was inaugurated in April 1920.[46] This early mobilisation of the Nurses may have stemmed from a prior impetus for community health work when the global influenza epidemic reached Belize in late 1918. The Influenza Committee chose Miss Eva Cain (a Methodist schoolteacher) and Mrs Wallace, both Creole 'ladies', to hire and supervise a 'brigade [of] women' to locate and care for 'flu victims at one dollar per day'.[47] None of the first Nurses worked with Cain and Wallace, nor were they among the sixteen women hired in 1919. Thus when Cain, the founding Secretary of the UNIA's Ladies Division and a relative of H. H. Cain, publisher of the Garveyite *Belize Independent*, pointed Garveyite women toward health activism a year later, she apparently did so as a means to quiet post-riot resentments among poor Creole women.[48]

The Nurses began with at least nine members, and twenty took nursing classes in 1921. Most were Methodist and Baptist women in their thirties and forties, lower middle-class (only 21 per cent qualified as voters in the 1918–1948 period) and included wives, widows and single women.[49] Although some of these women must have worked, all had sufficient leisure to invest in training and extensive volunteer hours. Their leader, Mrs Vivian Seay (1881–1971), who was also Treasurer of the Ladies' Division, was an elementary schoolteacher; her switch to nursing and social work covered the full professional range then open to middle-class Creole women.[50] Hailed as the 'matriarch of maternal mothers' at her death, Seay possessed ambition, determination, a 'strict code of ethics' and sympathy for the poor that did not condone disrespect, disorder or irresponsibility.[51] She forged her Nurses into a cohesive unit that developed its maternalist politics, with approval from the colonial authorities and middle-class men but had little success in building popular support for itself or the larger middle-class project.

The Black Cross Nurses sought to influence the colonial state through negotiation and alliance – as did maternalists elsewhere – rather than through frontal assault. Not only was confrontation inimical to middle-class politics, but it was also unnecessary given the state's post-riot search for reform collaborators. These dynamics explain why the Nurses, unlike early African-American clubwomen, enjoyed a positive relationship with the state – though they never came under its full control.[52] Health care was an obvious arena for cooperation, for the pro-reform medical staff viewed Belize Town as unhygienic, breeding a host of endemic diseases. Efforts to vaccinate newborns against smallpox were one means of lowering an infant mortality rate that averaged 125 per 1000 live births in the 1918–52 period – a rate comparable to that in other British Caribbean colonies – with alarming periodic spikes.[53] But British doctors did not attribute infant mortality solely to tropical disease. Dr Thomas Gann, the Principal Medical Officer from the mid-1910s to 1923, blamed a pattern of men leaving families destitute during seasonal bush work, mothers' preference not to breastfeed and illegitimacy, which ostensibly lead to neglect.[54] Similarly, the Black Cross Nurses' 1920 housing survey in Belize Town's poor neighbourhoods found intense overcrowding and 'maternal neglect' leading to infant mortality.[55]

By 1952 the Nurses had worked with seven colonial governors, maintaining excellent relations with six.[56] Collaboration began in 1921 with the failed efforts of Matron Lois Roberts, recently arrived from England, to recruit young nurse probationers 'of superior status and education' to pay $10 per month for training at the Belize Public Hospital.[57] Dr K. Simon, who also wished for trained midwives and ante-natal clinics, was by May 1921 giving 'lectures on midwifery to young women of the Universal Negro Improvement Association'; they paid 20 cents per week each and Simon ordered them textbooks and uniforms. Gann supported Simon's plan for practical training under Matron Roberts in 'general hospital work, with special reference to cleanliness and asepsis, with a view to their ultimate employment as midwives or public nurses'. Simon and UNIA leader William Campbell insisted that the women 'would prove simply invaluable in child welfare work, and in teaching the people the rudiments of domestic sanitation'. By July, Governor Sir Eyre Hutson backed the project, and when seventeen of twenty Nurses passed their examinations in November, Gann envisioned them working with poor mothers as 'midwives and monthly nurses in Belize and even in the districts'.[58] When infant mortality soared to 215 per 1,000 in 1922, Hutson reportedly asked the Nurses to focus on maternity care.[59] In 1923, Seay assigned each Nurse – there were now 24 – to a neighbourhood of Belize Town where she was to visit poor households weekly.[60] Seay and four other Nurses completed midwifery training on the Hospital's new maternity ward five years later.[61] Indeed, succeeding colonial administrations continued to train small numbers of Garveyite women as nurses into the 1950s.

The Nurses sought and received consistent support from officials for their most visible project, the annual Baby Exhibition. Begun in 1923, the Exhibition was a didactic competition, designed to reward the healthiest infants in various age groups and thus to display modern infant bodies and to model proper parenting to the masses. While the Nurses themselves selected those entries fit to compete, colonial medical officers served as inspector-judges, and the wife of the Governor, or other top official, presented the prizes.[62] In 1934, the Exhibition expanded to Stann Creek Town; the governor and his wife travelled there to preside several times.[63] The ritual of the Exhibition renewed the state–Nurses alliance each year, providing the authorities with a unique access to part of the public, and the Nurses with a fresh stamp of approval in their efforts to improve mothering.

Cooperative relations took several other forms. In September 1931, a hurricane wrecked Belize Town, causing a tremendous health and housing crisis. The Nurses volunteered to help and worked as laundresses at the Public Hospital, nurses at a temporary hospital and 'as Cooks, Bakers and Nurses' at a relief camp. The latter group received $15 per month, the first instance of state employment of the Garveyite nurses.[64] Governor Sir Harold Kittermaster expressed his approval of the Nurses in 1933 by appointing Seay as the first woman to serve on the Belize Town Board; one columnist then described the Nurses as 'a body that has for years commanded the attention of succeeding Governors'.[65] Crucially, in the midst of popular anti-colonial mobilisation during 1934, led by the Labourers' and Unemployed Association (LUA), Seay became a close collaborator of Governor Sir Alan Burns.[66] In return for her loyalty, Burns proudly presented her Member of the British Empire award, and at the celebratory meeting he contrasted Seay's record of community service with the 'talkative critics' who contributed nothing. He thus distinguished her from the working women and men who led and supported the LUA.[67]

When the West India Royal Commission visited the colony during its investigation of regional labour disturbances in 1938, the Nurses were one of the local organisations invited to speak. Their presentation, based on substantial research carried out by 20 Nurses and introduced by Seay in a printed report, documented the abysmal housing, income and diets of 35 'poor respectable families' in Belize Town.[68] Given the minimisation of female-headed households in the sample, and the Nurses' defence of men as unable to provide due to general economic collapse, the report constituted a defence of the male breadwinner ideal.[69] Like the Baby Exhibition, the report skirted direct moral criticism of the masses' gender 'disorder', but instead of exhibiting model families, it displayed virtuous victims in need of imperial aid.

The Nurses were not threatened by the colonial state's expansion in the 1940s, an expansion based on imperial 'development and welfare' funds stemming from the Royal Commission's recommendations.[70] Seay became a colonial civil servant in 1941 when Governor Sir John Hunter appointed her Inspector of Midwives; several of the Nurses followed suit three years later, as recruits in the new Rural Health Nurse programme. One Nurse even started a Baby Exhibition at her village posting in 1946.[71] State expansion could also strengthen the Nurses' numbers: in 1948 a woman just back from British-funded training in Jamaica to work in the Social Welfare Department, also joined the Nurses. In 1952 she spoke on the government-controlled radio station, reiterating that the Nurses were motivated by mothers' 'ignorance' leading to high infant mortality.[72]

In the early 1950s, the Nurses defended the colonial order against mass nationalism, a stance consistent with the UNIA's politics of colonial collaboration and with the Nurses' 30-year partnership with the state. The Nurses expanded ameliorative aid to the restless working class as through the Red Cross, organised by Governor Sir Roland Garvey's wife, and were known as anti-nationalists.[73] Seay again broadened her participation in formal politics by joining with prominent middle-class men in 1951 to found the anti-nationalist party. She attempted to woo working-class women away from the nationalists and was given access to the government's radio station in making her pitch. The party's efforts to stem the tide of popular hostility to colonial rule proved fruitless, however.

The second set of relationships defining the Black Cross Nurses' maternalism were those with working-class mothers. The Nurses' commitment to 'uplift' led them to act as instructors and disciplinarians, but not without a sympathetic spirit of Creole commonality. They never openly denounced prevailing high rates of illegitimacy, unwed motherhood and female employment, in part because to provoke popular opposition would weaken middle-class claims to represent the docile masses. But, in practice, the Nurses created a contrast between such gender 'disorder' and the male breadwinner ideal.[74] Perhaps like the female volunteers in WWI Britain who monitored soldiers' wives receiving state allowances, they assumed that they were 'fit to offer guidance' and that their interventions would be welcomed. Yet the Nurses' cooperation with a colonial state increasingly opposed by working women muted possibilities for class levelling through maternalist practices. While African-American clubwomen, for example, 'accepted the working mother as a worthy mother' and worked on day-care services, the Nurses endorsed the male breadwinner model and opposed womanhood suffrage. While they likely considered themselves to be enlightening poor mothers, their efforts to build middle-class hegemony foundered on the necessity of treating poor mothers as not only voiceless dependants, but as morally suspect ones.[75]

Although prior accounts have portrayed the Nurses as admired role models for young Creole girls, there is also evidence of popular aversion to them, particularly during the class-polarised mid-1930s. In 1935, Nurse Cecilia Douglas acknowledged that they had not always been encouraged by those they aimed to help: 'We are glad to say however that we are slowly but surely getting the Community to understand that our principal business is to be of Service'. More explicitly, when addressing young girls at a health lecture later that year, Seay 'told them that there are many in this community who criticize and ignore the Black Cross Nurses, but those criticisms must go behind us'. Those criticisms apparently had class content, for Seay maintained that 'creed, colour' and poverty were merely 'inconvenient,' but that 'lack of principle and decency, is a thorough disgrace'.[76] In short, a moral woman would rise above poverty and racism. But the Women's League of the LUA – at the height of its strength in 1935 – chose to confront rather than rise above, calling for womanhood suffrage in the bill to restore the colonial legislature. The League challenged Seay's and the Nurses' presumption in claiming a higher standard of womanhood and greater political rights, for supporting income restrictions on the vote.[77] Finally, while some families were willing to expose their poverty to the Nurses for their 1938 research, the lack of female-headed households in the study might indicate single mothers' resistance to further intervention.

That involvement began with the Nurses' 1920 housing survey in poor urban neighbourhoods, which blamed 'maternal neglect' as well as overcrowding for poor health conditions. It continued with their home visiting. A sense of their instructions to poor mothers can be gleaned from a 1921 government leaflet titled 'Don'ts for Mothers'.[78] It advocated breastfeeding to nine months, vaccination and daily bathing of infants, and the purchase of mosquito nets for babies as well as 'nourishing food' for mothers. Most working women earned meagre wages and could not continue to breastfeed or afford nutritious diets or netting, nor were their water supplies plentiful, given urban landlords' delinquency in providing vats. All were dependent on buckets and the canals for waste disposal. It is doubtful that they either complied with the Nurses' advice, or felt gratitude, for the visitors supplied no state benefits, nor any concrete aid until they qualified as midwives, a service that required payment. During the drought of 1922, a band of angry women created their own benefits by marching onto Government House grounds to take water from the governor's vats.[79] The one thing that poor mothers could give freely, affection, was itself prohibited, with a ban on kissing to avoid infecting infants with tuberculosis. The Nurses' emphasis was clearly on combating maternal 'ignorance' and setting higher standards of cleanliness and infant care.

The Baby Exhibition, while a less direct means of contact with poor mothers, was expressly didactic nevertheless. In rewarding the babies of middle-class and expatriate families, the Exhibition stigmatised infants who were sick, underweight or illegitimate. While most working-class parents probably did not submit their infants to scrutiny, at least from 1932 the Nurses routinely weeded out 'unfit' entries prior to judges' inspections. Twenty-five per cent of entries were rejected as too ill in 1932 and 1943, while in 1937 almost one third were excluded due to colds, fevers and skin diseases.[80] In 1930, the *Independent* applauded those families whose babies won year after year, a pattern that confirms the exclusive nature of the ritual through which the Nurses 'controlled the way maternal values were celebrated in public'.[81] In 1933, with unemployment sky-high, competition standards were raised in order to 'improv[e] the general standard of the health of the babies, which means that closer attention will have to be given by parents to their care in every detail'.[82]

The Nurses also offered traditional charity to poor mothers by giving away toys, sewing clothing for needy 'deserving' schoolchildren, and holding parties for 'indigent children' and their mothers.[83] One effort in this category – notable for its acknowledgement of women as household heads – was the Palace Unemployed Women's Fund, a joint effort of the Nurses and the Palace Theatre. The Fund provided 200 unemployed mothers with $1 of groceries each between January and April 1934.[84] This charity evidently failed to thwart popular revolt, for the LUA launched its anti-colonial campaign in March. Working-class women who had received little solidarity from the Nurses or middle class flocked to the LUA, making it a vehicle for confronting the Nurses' moralistic class exclusivity.

In a third arena, the Black Cross Nurses' maternalism developed with significant autonomy from Garveyite men, but in relative harmony with them. In the wider UNIA, Black Cross Nurse locals were established as the womanly counterpart to the Universal African Legions, which was modelled on black soldiers in WWI and embodied 'the [masculine] ideas of power and dominance and the military might necessary to achieve and maintain Negro nationhood'.[85] Belize's Garveyite men organised no Legion, thus distancing themselves from the riotous veterans of 1919 and projecting through the local's male executive a non-militant masculinity that did not aim for 'Negro nationhood'. They found the Nurses' respectable activism, especially their influence with colonial leaders, perfectly accept-able in gendered cultural and political terms. In short, the Nurses' auton-omy from the theoretical structure of male authority in the UNIA led to little overt friction, even as they grew more explicitly political. Maternalists in Latin America, Britain and the United States experienced more contentious relations with male peers, because they dealt with men who controlled the state and because many had to compromise their more strongly feminist agendas in negotiating with the state.[86]

The most telling example of the Nurses' cooperative independence from Garveyite men is the growth of their political voice. The Nurses avoided the constitutional debates of 1921–25, which dealt with ending Crown Colony rule and restoring a partially elected legislature, leaving UNIA participation to the small artisan-led Progressive Party (PP). The PP advocated a broader franchise than other middle-class organisations and included women in its proposals, but opposed enfranchising mahogany labourers, and kept women's voting age at thirty.[87] While the debates ended in stalemate, it is notable that the Nurses accepted both their male colleagues' role as spokesmen and their exclusion of workers.

A decade later Seay and her most experienced Nurses entered the fray. Demonstrating her political autonomy, Seay campaigned in 1933 for an independent male candidate for the Belize Town Board, rather than the PP slate. Not only did her man win, but the governor then appointed Seay to the Board, a move welcomed by the *Independent*'s editor and columnists. She soon proposed a municipal employment bureau for women. Although such a bureau never operated, it was not intended to broaden economic opportunities, but to save laundresses and domestics the 'shame' of beg-ging for work door-to-door. Not even this breach of the male breadwinner ideal raised any male ire, for like the Palace Unemployed Women's Fund, the bureau pragmatically aimed at containing rising popular unrest in early 1934.

Finally, by the early 1950s, Seay's political confidence and influence led her to join with five leading middle-class men, one of them the head of the UNIA local, in founding the anti-nationalist party.[88] The party opposed rapid decolonisation and universal suffrage, wanting first to 'build up a sense of real responsibility in the people'.[89] Its male leaders probably hoped that Seay and the Nurses would be able to build female responsi-bility by dissuading women from joining the nationalists. This Seay tried to do in a speech delivered over the government radio station, in which she exhorted Belizean women to behave like late eighteenth-century heroines who had encouraged their men to defend the settlement against Spanish attack. Yet she linked those women's courage, in risking sexual virtue as well as life, to the modern-day 'inner graces, the softer sentiments' and beauty of young women, mostly middle-class, who were competing in a pageant to mark the historic victory over Spain.[90] Even as Seay and the Nurses expanded their activism into party politics, they remained committed to class interests shared with Garveyite and other middle-class men, and eschewed dialogue with increasingly anti-colonial working-class women.

That basic stance shaped the Nurses' forays into feminist politics, the fourth arena that illuminates their maternalism. In the mid-1930s, Seay – possibly emboldened by her new authority as a Town Board member, but also concerned to contain working-class women's mobilisation within the LUA – led the Nurses into debates on divorce and women's suffrage. An emergent Garveyite feminism was tempered by the Nurses' moralism in both cases. In early 1934, Seay and the Nurses, like Garveyite men, backed the colonial administration's bill to confirm the legality of divorce in the colony. They did not contest their Roman Catholic opponents' focus on morality, but rather than revile divorce as immoral in itself, they argued that it was necessary to prevent the evils of adultery and illegitimacy. Seay, who spoke at the UNIA's and Nurses' public meetings, a Town Board meeting, and an outdoor rally, argued repeatedly that divorce would improve community morality. When a Town Board member opposed divorce, she retorted: 'I rise being much disappointed in the remarks of the last speaker ... He spoke as if women were the only ones to commit fornication. We are the ones who need divorce ... Divorce would mean a better moral community'.[91] Here Seay verged on an argument for women's right to divorce for happiness and self-respect, even on a critique of male behaviour, but she nevertheless ended by legitimising divorce in the name of marital stability and morality, not women's rights to economic or legal independence. At the Nurses' pro-divorce public meeting one invited speaker was Mrs E. Trapp – then the name of Elfreda Reyes, quoted at the beginning of this essay. Trapp represented a potential for feminist alliance between the Nurses and working-class women, a potential lost with the emergence of the LUA and the Nurses' hostility to its labour militancy.[92]

By early 1935 Trapp and Seay stood opposed across a polarised political terrain, for Trapp was a leader of the LUA Women's League and an organiser of the League's public meeting in support of womanhood suffrage. Seay and other middle-class women, including Nurses Cecilia Douglas and Effie Ferrel Briton, made a case for women's suffrage that was qualified by income restrictions on the franchise. Their argument was, moreover, couched less in terms of innate political rights than of women's competence in education, household management and child-rearing – a classic maternalist position. Educated, domesticated middle-class women, who met both the conventional and Garveyite ideals of womanhood should, according to such a maternalist posture, have a political voice and be empowered to represent the supposedly silent, ignorant and irresponsible majority of women. The restored legislative franchise ultimately included only propertied women over age thirty and, ironically, almost none of the Nurses qualified by income or property with the majority entering the legislative franchise only in 1953, once the nationalists forced the passage of universal suffrage. Given their existing access to state power, the Nurses did not feel the need to risk the social levelling implied in arguing for wider voting rights.

The Belize Black Cross Nurses did not broaden an internal Garveyite debate over what women should be, though they likely read and discussed with interest Amy Jacques Garvey's *Negro World* women's pages of the mid-1920s. There, Jacques Garvey attempted to define a more egalitarian Garveyism, yearning both for equal political rights and reliable black male family and race leadership.[93] The Nurses did develop, however, a set of practices that simultaneously reinforced and violated the Garveyite ideal of the educated, domesticated black woman in service to the community. On the one hand, their activism always focused on mothers, children and community morality – accepted female issues. On the other, as their training deepened and their service expanded into the arena of formal politics, their personal domesticity virtually disappeared. They never legitimised such a violation of the womanly ideal for their poor clients, whose 'uplift' was not to include wage labour or political voice. The conclusion that throughout the movement Black Cross Nurses were 'highly respected members of their communities' – a claim which relies in part on a problematic study of the Belize Nurses – must be re-examined, or the boundaries of their communities redefined.[94]

If such maternalist politics were widespread through the locals of the UNIA, they certainly limited the movement's capacity to be a vehicle for either black feminism or black liberation as a whole. Whatever their critiques of Creole men – and for the most part these remained private – the Nurses sustained the movement's prescribed gender complementarity, even as they became more overtly politicised within their 'sphere'. Most importantly, they did not bring poor Creole women into the positive paradigm of motherhood unconditionally; they simply argued that black women could be uplifted into proper motherhood.[95] While this stance was distinct from the more harshly eugenic views of some white maternalists, the weakness of any discourse of cross-class sisterhood or racial solidarity in the Nurses' history is notable.

That frailty underscores how the maternalist politics of colonised and non-white women as well as European and North American women developed in imperial contexts. Most broadly, the UNIA leadership's gender ideals represented a desire to overcome black men's and women's exclusion from 'the … Victorian ideology of true women and real men' that was embedded in transatlantic imperial culture.[96] Given that Belize's Creole middle class aimed to overcome a similarly racist political exclusion, it is little wonder that properly bourgeois gender norms became important to proving their worth to the British. Women's community uplift work through maternal education and infant healthcare would thus prove Garveyite and broad Creole middle-class fitness for expanded political power within the colonial framework. The marriage of existing middle-class politics and Garveyism in the aftermath of the 1919 riot was easily effected; both the Nurses and their male colleagues found it uncomplicated to avoid the movement's strongest and most resistant expressions of black identity and connection to Africa. To some degree they seem to have shared the British association of blackness with working-class poverty, ill health, single motherhood and illegitimacy, but they may also simply have found it difficult to create a positive public definition of blackness other than by emulating Victorian norms. The UNIA's endorsement of those norms, particularly the male breadwinner ideal, clearly had origins in the movement's 'periphery' as well as in the New York headquarters.

Nurse Cecilia Douglas, Seay's second-in-command for many years, died in 1950. She was hailed as a 'great hearted social worker … and midwife … a humble servant of God, a good mother, a faithful wife, a good neighbour, and a loyal citizen of her country'.[97] Thus idealised, her role – and that of the Nurses – in reproducing class and race hierarchies and perpetuating colonial rule was obscured. It was in popular movements against colonial rule and middle-class ambition, which after 1919 developed outside and indeed in *opposition* to Garveyism, that working-class women like Annie Flowers and Elfreda Reyes could articulate a proud black female identity linked far more to combative than to properly 'modern' motherhood.

Notes

1. Zee Edgell, *Beka Lamb* (London: Heinemann, 1982), p. 27. Belize – officially British Honduras until 1973 – gained independence in 1981. Belize Town, the largest urban centre and capital until 1970, became Belize City in 1943.
2. In Belize, Creoles are descendants of Europeans and/or enslaved Africans who arrived in the 1600s and 1700s. The Garifuna, previously labelled Black Caribs, are descendants of indigenous Windward Islanders and enslaved Africans, exiled to Central America at the turn of the nineteenth century. In the period under study, Belize Town was predominantly Creole, while Stann Creek Town (now Dangriga) and District on the southern coast were predominantly Garifuna.
3. Author's interviews with Elfreda Reyes, 10 and 11 July 1991.
4. Mimi Sheller, 'Quasheba, Mother, Queen: Black Women's Public Leadership and Political Protest in Post-emancipation Jamaica, 1834–65', *Slavery and Abolition* 19 (1998), pp. 90–117. Olive Senior, *Working Miracles: Women's Lives in the English-speaking Caribbean* (Cave Hill: ISER/UWI, 1991), chapters 4 and 8.

5. On the scale of the movement, see Tony Martin, *Race First: The Ideological and Organizational Struggles of Marcus Garvey and the Universal Negro Improvement Association* (Westport: Greenwood, 1976), pp. 15–16.

6. Prominent in developing this critique have been: Wilson Jeremiah Moses, *Black Messiahs and Uncle Toms: Social and Literary Manipulations of a Religious Myth* (University Park: Pennsylvania State University Press, 1982), chapter 8 and *Afrotopia: The Roots of African American Popular History* (New York: Cambridge University Press, 1998), pp. 193–8; Judith Stein, *The World of Marcus Garvey: Race and Class in Modern Society* (Baton Rouge: Louisiana State University Press, 1986).

7. On the development of this class see Anne S. Macpherson, 'Imagining the Colonial Nation: Race, Gender and Middle-Class Politics in Belize, 1888–1898', in *Race and Nation in Modern Latin America*, ed. Nancy Appelbaum, Anne S. Macpherson and Karin Alejandra Rosemblatt (Chapel Hill: University of North Carolina Press, 2003) pp. 108–31.

8. Antoinette Burton, 'Introduction', in *Gender, Sexuality, and Colonial Modernities*, ed. Burton (New York: Routledge, 1999), p. 10.

9. Theodore Vincent, *Black Power and the Garvey Movement* (Berkeley: The Ramparts Press, 1972), p. 175.

10. The early optimists included Vincent, p. 130, and Mark Matthews, '"Our Women and What They Think", Amy Jacques Garvey and *The Negro World*', *Black Scholar* 10 (1979), pp. 7–8. A recent reiteration is Tony Martin, 'Women in the Garvey Movement', in *Garvey: His Work and Impact*, ed. Rupert Lewis and Patrick Bryan (Trenton NJ: Africa World Press, 1991), pp. 67–72.

11. Barbara Bair, 'Universal Negro Improvement Association', in *Black Women in America: A Historical Encyclopedia*, ed. Darlene Clark Hine (Brooklyn: Carlson Publishing, 1993), p. 1188.

12. Barbara Bair, 'Pan-Africanism as Process: Adelaide Casely Hayford, Garveyism, and the Cultural Roots of Nationalism', in *Imagining Home: Class, Culture and Nationalism in the African Diaspora*, ed. Sidney Lemelle and Robin Kelley (New York: Verso, 1994), p. 122; Honor Ford-Smith, 'Women and the Garvey Movement in Jamaica', in *Garvey: His Work and Impact*, p. 73; Robert A. Hill, 'General Introduction', in *The Marcus Garvey and Universal Negro Improvement Association Papers*, vol. 1, ed. Robert A. Hill (Berkeley: University of California Press, 1983), pp. i–ii (hereafter referred to as *The Garvey Papers*); Stein, *The World of Marcus Garvey*, p. 246.

13. Bair, 'Universal', p. 1188; Barbara Bair, 'True Women, Real Men: Gender, Ideology, and Social Roles in the Garvey Movement', in *Gendered Domains: Rethinking Public and Private in Women's History*, ed. Susan Reverby and Dorothy O. Helly (Ithaca: Cornell University Press, 1992), pp. 154–66; Ford-Smith, 'Women and the Garvey Movement', p. 76; Honor Ford-Smith, 'Making White Ladies: Race, Gender and the Production of Identities in Late Colonial Jamaica', *Resources for Feminist Research/Documentation sur la Recherche Feministe* 23 (1994/95), p. 65.

14. Ula Taylor, 'Universal African Black Cross Nurses', *Black Women in America*, p. 1187 and Bair, 'True Women', p. 157.

15. On Jacques Garvey see Karen S. Adler, '"Always Leading our Men in Service and Sacrifice": Amy Jacques Garvey, Feminist Black Nationalist', *Gender and Society* 6 (1992): pp. 346–75; Bair, 'True Women', pp. 162–3; Winston James, *Holding Aloft the Banner of Ethiopia: Caribbean Radicalism in Early Twentieth-Century America* (New York: Verso, 1998), pp. 141–55; Matthews, 'Our Women'; Ula Y. Taylor, '"Negro Women are Great Thinkers as well as Doers": Amy Jacques-Garvey and Community Feminism in the United States, 1924–1927', *Journal of Women's History* 12 (2000), pp. 104–26. In addition see William Seraile, 'Henrietta Vinton Davis and the Garvey Movement', *Afro-Americans in New York Life and History* 7 (1983), pp. 7–24; 'Ashwood, Amy', in *Marcus Garvey: Life and Lessons*, ed. Robert A. Hill and Barbara Bair (Berkeley: University of California Press, 1987), pp. 358–9; Lionel M. Yard, *Biography of Amy Ashwood Garvey, 1897–1969* (Associated Publishers, Inc., nd).

16. Bair, 'True Women', pp. 155, 160–66; Ford-Smith, 'Women and the Garvey Movement', p. 77.
17. Taylor, 'Negro Women', p. 105.
18. Bair, 'Universal', p. 1188; ibid., 'True Women', p. 166.
19. Stein, *The World of Marcus Garvey*, p. 246.
20. On locals' struggles for autonomy see Rupert Lewis, *Marcus Garvey: Anti-Colonial Champion* (Trenton NJ: Africa World Press, 1988), p. 67, and Stein, *The World of Marcus Garvey*, p. 223.
21. Bair, 'Pan-Africanism as Process'; Ford-Smith, 'Women and the Garvey Movement in Jamaica'; Rhoda Reddock, *Women, Labour and Politics in Trinidad and Tobago: A History* (London: Zed Books, 1994).
22. On Latin America see Karen Mead, 'Beneficent Maternalism: Argentine Motherhood in Comparative Perspective, 1880–1920', *Journal of Women's History* 12 (2000), pp. 120–45 and Karin Rosemblatt, '"What we can Reclaim of the Old Values of the Past": Sexual Morality and Politics in Twentieth Century Chile', *Comparative Studies in Society and History* 43 (2001), pp. 149–80.
23. Ann Laura Stoler and Frederick Cooper, eds, *Tensions of Empire: Colonial Cultures in a Bourgeois World* (Berkeley: University of California Press, 1997), p. 1; Antoinette Burton, 'The White Woman's Burden: British Feminists and "The Indian Woman", 1865–1915', in *Western Women and Imperialism: Complicity and Resistance*, ed. Nupur Chaudhuri and Margaret Strobel (Bloomington: Indiana University Press, 1992), pp. 137–8.
24. Eileen Suárez Findlay, *Imposing Decency: The Politics of Sexuality and Race in Puerto Rico, 1870–1920* (Durham: Duke University Press, 1998); Francesca Miller, *Latin American Women and the Search for Social Justice* (Hanover: University Press of New England, 1991), chapter 4; Rosalyn Terborg-Penn, 'Enfranchising Women of Color: Woman Suffragists as Agents of Imperialism', in *Nation, Empire, Colony: Historicizing Gender and Race*, ed. Ruth Roach Pierson and Nupur Chaudhuri (Bloomington: Indiana University Press, 1998), pp. 41–56.
25. Anne McClintock, *Imperial Leather: Race, Gender, and Sexuality in the Colonial Context* (New York: Routledge, 1995), does not mention the Caribbean beyond Columbus's arrival in the New World. Important anthologies with no Caribbean coverage include: Chaudhuri and Strobel, eds, *Western Women and Imperialism*; Stoler and Cooper (eds) *Tensions of Empire*; Burton (ed.) *Gender, Sexuality, and Colonial Modernities*.
26. Clare Midgley, 'Anti-slavery and the roots of "imperial feminism"', in *Gender and Imperialism*, ed. Midgley (Manchester: Manchester University Press, 1998), pp. 161–79. 'Imperial feminism' is Burton's term, while Barbara Ramusack expresses the same concept as 'maternalist imperialism' ('Cultural Missionaries, Maternalist Imperialists, Feminist Allies: British Women Activists in India, 1865–1945', in *Western Women and Imperialism*, pp. 119–36).
27. Catherine Hall, 'Gender Politics and Imperial Politics: Rethinking the Histories of Empire', in *Engendering History: Caribbean Women in Historical Perspective*, ed. Verene Shepherd, Bridget Brereton, and Barbara Bailey, (New York: St. Martin's, 1995), pp. 48–59.
28. Thomas Holt, *The Problem of Freedom: Race, Labor, and Politics in Jamaica and Britain, 1832–1938* (Baltimore: Johns Hopkins University Press, 1991). See also Catherine Hall, 'Competing Masculinities: Thomas Carlyle, John Stuart Mill, and the case of Governor Eyre', in *White, Male and Middle Class: Explorations in Feminism and History* (New York: Routledge, 1992), pp. 255–95.
29. See Mary Hancock, 'Gendering the Modern: Women and Home Science in British India', in *Gender, Sexuality, and Colonial Modernities*, p. 153. On West Indian colonial accommodation, see C. L. R. James, 'The West Indian Middle Classes', in *Spheres of Existence: Selected Writings* (Westport: Lawrence Hill & Co., 1980), pp. 131–40.
30. Ford-Smith, 'Making White Ladies', pp. 65, 55, 61.
31. On a similar pattern in Sierra Leone see Bair, 'Pan-Africanism as Process', pp. 122–24; on self-alienation see Frantz Fanon, *Black Skin, White Masks*, trans. Charles Lam Markmann (New York: Grove Press, 1967).

32. Nancy Rose Hunt, 'Domesticity and Colonialism in Belgian Africa: Usumbura's *Foyer Social*, 1946–1960', *Signs* 15 (1990), pp. 447–74, and Carol Summers, 'Intimate Colonialism: The Imperial Production of Reproduction in Uganda, 1907–1925', *Signs* 16 (1991), pp. 787–807.

33. Summers, 'Intimate Colonialism', pp. 803–06; Dea Birkett, 'The "White Woman's Burden" in "The White Man's Grave": The Introduction of British Nurses in Colonial West Africa', in *Western Women and Imperialism*, pp. 177–88.

34. My analysis draws on: Eileen Boris, 'The Power of Motherhood: Black and White Activist Women Redefine the "Political"', in *Mothers of a New World: Maternalist Politics and the Origins of Welfare States*, ed. Seth Koven and Sonya Michel (New York: Routledge, 1993), pp. 213–45; Findlay, *Imposing Decency*, chapter 2; Margaret Jolly, 'Introduction: Colonial and postcolonial plots in the histories of maternities and modernities', in *Maternities and modernities: Colonial and postcolonial experiences in Asia and the Pacific*, ed. Jolly and Kalpana Ram (New York: Cambridge University Press, 1998), pp. 1–10; Seth Koven and Sonya Michel, 'Womanly Duties: Maternalist Politics and the Origins of Welfare States in France, Germany, Great Britain, and the United States, 1880–1920', *American Historical Review* 95 (1990), pp. 1076–1108; Asunción Lavrin, *Women, Feminism, & Social Change in Argentina, Chile & Uruguay, 1890–1940* (Lincoln: University of Nebraska Press, 1995), pp. 82–3; Jane Lewis, 'Motherhood Issues', in *Delivering Motherhood: Maternal Ideologies and Practices in the 19th and 20th Centuries*, ed. Katherine Arnup, Andrée Lévesque, and Ruth Roach Pierson (New York: Routledge, 1990), pp. 1–19; Susan Pedersen, 'Gender Welfare and Citizenship in Britain during the Great War', *American Historical Review* 95 (1990), pp. 983–1006; Susan Pedersen, 'National Bodies, Unspeakable Acts: The Sexual Politics of Colonial Policy-making', *Journal of Modern History* 63 (1991), pp. 647–80; Wayne Roberts, '"Rocking the Cradle for the World": The New Woman and Maternal Feminism, Toronto 1877–1914', in *A Not Unreasonable Claim: Women and Reform in Canada, 1880s–1920s*, ed. Linda Kealey (Toronto: The Women's Press, 1979), pp. 15–45; Terborg-Penn, 'Enfranchising Women of Color'; Mariana Valverde, review essay in *Signs* 20 (1994), pp. 209–15; Patrick Wilkinson, 'The Selfless and the Helpless: Maternalist Origins of the U.S. Welfare State', *Feminist Studies* 25 (1999): pp. 571–97.

35. Nancy Cott, 'Comment on Karen Offen's "Defining Feminism: A Comparative Historical Approach"', *Signs* 15 (1989), pp. 203–05. On social motherhood see Miller, *Latin American Women*, chapter 4.

36. Seth Koven, 'The Ambivalence of Agency: Women, Families, and Social Policy in France, Britain, and the United States', *Journal of Women's History* 9 (1997), p. 168.

37. Boris, 'The Power of Motherhood', p. 226.

38. Taylor, 'Negro Women', p. 111, finds that Jacques Garvey moved beyond black club women's genteel methods, and thus, presumably, their class views.

39. Vincent, *Black Power*, pp. 36, 128, 175; Martin, *Race First*, pp. 12, 58, 95; James, *Holding Aloft*, pp. 51–66. The notes following 'Report of UNIA Meeting' (Philadelphia, 28 April 1920), in *The Garvey Papers*, vol. 2 (1983), p. 303, imply the same continuity.

40. *Belize Independent*, 18 June 1930. This was the local Garveyite paper, founded in 1914. There are no extant copies for the period 1914–30.

41. Peter Ashdown, 'Race Riot, Class Warfare and Coup d'etat: The Ex-Servicemen's Riot of July 1919', *Belcast Journal of Belizean Affairs* 3 (1986), pp. 13–14; and 'Marcus Garvey, the UNIA and the Black Cause in British Honduras 1914–1949', *Journal of Caribbean History* 15 (1981), pp. 46–7, 54.

42. Peter Ashdown, 'The Growth of Black Consciousness in Belize 1914–1919: The Background to the Ex-Servicemen's Riot of 1919', *Belcast Journal of Belizean Affairs* 2 (1985), pp. 1–5.

43. CO 123/296/65699, 'Riot at Belize. Report of the Riot Commission, Appendix P: List of Persons alleged to have committed offenses. Annie Flowers: inciting to crime, testimony of William Hoar ... September 22, 1919'.

44. *Belize Billboard*, 27 June 1948.

45. On strained relations between colonial administrators and middle-class critics, see Mark Moberg, 'Crown Colony as Banana Republic: The United Fruit Company in British Honduras,

1900–1920', *Journal of Latin American Studies* 28 (1996), pp. 357–81. Qualifications for the municipal franchise included having reached age twenty-one (males) or thirty (females) and either owning property worth $60/year, paying $96/year in rent, or earning $300/year. *Consolidated Laws of British Honduras*, revised edition (1924), cap. 118, p. 704, originally an ordinance passed 25 July 1911.

46. The Nurses celebrated their anniversary in March each year, while the local was inaugurated on 22 April 1920. *Clarion*, 29 April 1920.

47. Belize Archives, Minute Paper 534–1919.

48. Richard E. Hadel, SJ, 'Builders of Belize (3): Nurse Seay', *National Studies* 2 (1974), pp. 8–11; Eleanor Krohn Herrmann, 'Black Cross Nursing in Belize: A Labour of Love', *Belizean Studies* 8 (1980), pp. 1–7; Eleanor Krohn Herrmann, *Origins of Tomorrow: A History of Belizean Nursing Education* (Belize: Ministry of Health, 1985), chapter 3. For information on Cain, see *Clarion*, 29 April 1920.

49. Of 35 Nurses identified, only eight qualified as municipal or legislative voters in this period, according to lists published in the *British Honduras Gazette*.

50. For more on Seay, see Herrmann, 'Black Cross Nursing', and *Origins of Tomorrow*.

51. *Belize Times*, 18 July 1971; *The Reporter*, 23 July 1971.

52. Boris, 'The Power of Motherhood', p. 229. Deborah Gray White, *Too Heavy a Load: Black Women in Defense of Themselves, 1894–1994* (New York: W.W. Norton, 1999), chapter 5, shows that organised middle-class African-American women developed a better relationship with the state in the 1930s.

53. John Everitt, 'The Growth and Development of Belize City', *Journal of Latin American Studies* 18 (1986), pp. 75–112; on vaccination and infant mortality see British Honduras Colonial, Medical, and Vital Statistics Reports. O. Nigel Bolland, *The Politics of Labour in the British Caribbean* (Markus Weiner, 2001), pp. 126–27, lists Jamaica's infant mortality rate as 174.2 per 1,000 (1916–20) and 85.5 (1946–50), and Guyana's as 121.83 per 1,000 in 1935.

54. Belize Archives, Minute Paper 1406–1921, Medical Report for 1920.

55. Herrmann, *Origins of Tomorrow,* p. 40, citing *Belize Independent*, 19 March 1941.

56. Relations with Governor Sir John A. Burdon (1925–31) were positive but somewhat strained by his suspicions of the UNIA, and his and Lady Burdon's support for the Infant Welfare League, an élite female-volunteer group founded in 1928. See Belize Archives, Minute Papers 1-, 52-, and 522–1928 and 824–1929; 'John Burdon, Governor, British Honduras, to L.C.M.S. Amery, Secretary of State for the Colonies', 3 March 1928, in *The Garvey Papers* vol. 7 (1990), pp. 134–35; *The Clarion*, 26 April 1928 and 12 and 19 February 1930.

57. This paragraph draws on Belize Archives, Minute Papers 715–1920, 1348–1921, 1406–1921, 3531–1921; *British Honduras Annual Medical Report for the Year 1920* (Belize Prison, 1922); *Clarion*, 29 November 1923.

58. Hutson indicated his support to Marcus Garvey, then visiting the colony. 'Report of Interview', in *The Garvey Papers*, vol. 3 (1984), pp. 508–9.

59. Herrmann, *Origins of Tomorrow*, p. 42, citing *The Reporter*, 1 November 1968.

60. *Belize Independent*, 26 June 1935.

61. *British Honduras Annual Medical Report for the Year 1927*, p. 11; *Clarion*, 1 November 1928.

62. *Belize Independent*, 24 December 1930, 21 December 1932, 29 November 1933, 7 August 1935.

63. *Belize Independent*, 11 and 18 April 1934, 6 May 1936.

64. *Belize Independent*, 26 June 1935; Hadel, 'Builders', p. 10.

65. *Belize Independent*, 29 November 1933.

66. *Belize Independent*, 21 November 1934 and Belize Archives, Minute Paper 1628–1934.

67. *Belize Independent*, 26 June 1935.

68. Black Cross Nurses, *Compendium of the Living Conditions and Dietary Statistics of the Labouring Classes in the Town of Belize, British Honduras* (Belize, 1938). (Belize Archives, Miscellaneous Collection no. 164).

69. See note 74 for percentages of single mothers in British Honduras. Only four of the families were female-headed.

70. Reddock, *Women, Labour and Politics*, pp. 218–21, describes the similar Côterie of Social Workers in Trinidad, which felt threatened by the Social Welfare Department's direct connections with poor rural women, and succeeded in closing it down.

71. *Clarion*, 17 August 1952, reported the sixth annual Gales Point exhibition, led by Nurse Cleopatra White.

72. *Clarion*, 16 and 24 January, 6 February 1948; 3 April 1952.

73. Author's interview with Miss Adelia Dixon and Mrs Hortense Garbutt, June 1992.

74. Illegitimacy ran at 41–46.5 per cent colony-wide in this period, and at 45–50 per cent in the heavily Creole and Garifuna Belize and Stann Creek Districts. Colony-wide, 40 per cent of mothers were unwed in 1946, split evenly between single women and common-law wives. Official female employment in the Belize and Stann Creek Districts ran at 22–24 per cent; in 1946, colony-wide, 47.8 per cent of single women aged 25–44 were employed. See British Honduras Medical Reports and Jamaica Central Bureau of Statistics, *West India Census 1946, Part E: Census of Population of British Honduras* (Department of Statistics, Kingston 1948), pp. xxiii, xxxi.

75. Pedersen, 'Gender, Welfare, and Citizenship', pp. 992–3; Boris, 'The Power of Motherhood', pp. 214–5.

76. *Belize Independent*, 26 June and 13 November 1935.

77. *Belize Independent*, 6 and 13 February 1935.

78. Belize Archives, Minute Paper 1348–1921.

79. *Clarion*, 11 May 1922.

80. *Belize Independent*, 21 December 1932, 1 September 1937, 14 August 1943.

81. Mead, 'Beneficent Maternalism', p. 121.

82. *Belize Independent*, 29 November 1922.

83. *Belize Independent*, 18 October 1933, 9 January and 26 June 1935, 29 July 1936.

84. *Belize Independent*, 21 February and 11 April 1934.

85. Bair, 'True Women', pp. 157–8.

86. See, for example, Mead, 'Beneficent Maternalists'; Pedersen, 'National Bodies'; and Wilkinson, 'The Selfless'.

87. *Clarion*, 12 and 26 March 1925.

88. Cedric Grant, *The Making of Modern Belize: Politics, Society and British Colonialism in Central America* (Cambridge: Cambridge University Press, 1976), p. 148.

89. *Clarion*, 12 January 1952.

90. *Clarion*, 3 September 1952.

91. *Belize Independent*, 31 January, 7 and 14 February 1934.

92. Research in British Honduran legal records on legalised divorce and working-class women is still to be done.

93. Taylor, 'Negro Women', p. 107, dubs this uneasy mix 'community feminism'.

94. Bair, 'True Women', pp. 157–58. In footnote 3 Bair cites Herrmann's laudatory 'Black Cross Nursing in Belize'.

95. Boris, 'The Power of Motherhood', pp. 220–2.

96. Bair, 'True Women', p. 156.

97. *Belize Billboard*, 22 January 1950.

7

'Wearing three or four handkerchiefs around his collar, and elsewhere about him': Slaves' Constructions of Masculinity and Ethnicity in French Colonial New Orleans

Sophie White

In New Orleans, in 1766, a case was brought against a thirty-year-old runaway slave known as 'Francisque' for the theft of articles of dress stolen from a modest white household and from a black slave household.[1] In the course of the investigation and trial that lasted from April to August of 1766, five witnesses, including the accused, were called to testify about Francisque's movements; three of the witnesses were black. In their testimonies we find Francisque's appearance dissected, his performance of masculinity and ethnicity exposed, and the cross-cultural reception of these facets laid bare. Dress and appearance were crucial tools in this dissection. They made manifest gendered performances that were built on contested notions of African diasporan homogeneity anchored by the particular experience of African slavery in Louisiana.

Francisque was accused of the theft of bundles of laundry and other clothing taken from a certain laundry woman, Madame St Germain. He was also accused of the theft of a hat and earrings from a black female slave of his acquaintance. Francisque admitted the theft of the laundry goods, which consisted of both male and female dress and included some children's items. Among the missing laundry items were some strictly functional long breeches (ankle-length, wide-legged trousers commonly found in slave or working wardrobes) as well as some more fanciful clothing, such as ruffled shirts, handkerchiefs and ribbons.[2] Although Francisque's testimony fluctuated in the details, this appears to have been a theft of opportunity, since St Germain's open window gave Francisque easy access to the pile of clothes. Francisque denied the theft from the female slave. There is no record of her testifying in the case, but other (black) witnesses reiterated the accusation. No more was said about this slave or any restitution of her property in the court record.

Francisque was formally introduced to the court as a Catholic, and in the ownership of Jean Pierre Robert Gérard, Chevalier de Vilemont, a member of the colonial and military élite.[3] In the course of his interrogation, Francisque identified *himself*, in a pointed assertion of self-naming, as an 'Englishman from Philadelphia' who had come to the Colony via Havana.[4] It is not known how long he had been in the Colony or in the ownership of Vilemont. He claimed to have been in Louisiana before this particular stay, suggesting a cosmopolitan background, possibly as a mariner.[5] These personal statements about his origins denoted his conception of himself within the colonial order while hinting at the complexity – and the fluidity – of slave identities. A runaway for about one-and-a-half months before his capture, Francisque had been leased by Vilemont to St Maxent, a prominent merchant and fur trader, and one of the founders of St Louis. He was reported to have deserted the convoy between New Orleans and the Illinois Country, after setting fire to St Maxent's boat.[6]

No whites were called to testify against Francisque, but the white owners of the stolen goods, Madame St Germain and one of her laundry customers, Jean Rousset, were brought in to make depositions about what was stolen and to identify the goods found in Francisque's possession. Another runaway, a thirty-five year old Creole slave named Jacques, was also interrogated as an accomplice ('Creole' being a term used to describe anyone of foreign extraction born in the Colony, whether of African or European descent). He was a recent acquaintance, his and Francisque's statements contradicted each other's, and charges against Jacques were ultimately dropped, not necessarily for lack of evidence. Crucial testimony against Francisque was offered by one of the members of a group of New Orleans slaves, Demoirité, who described Francisque's appearances at a series of private slave gatherings. Demoirité's statement freely expressed the male members' of the group's resentment at Francisque's intrusions. This Ibo slave provided a lengthy statement that provided far more than the cursory information required by the court and thus merits close scrutiny. Demoirité singled out for criticism the runaway's ostentatious attire, lavish spending on music and flirtation with the women present. Francisque had initially succeeded in having these gestures negotiate his admittance into the group, but his subsequent actions had betrayed the community's social conventions. In his testimony Demoirité drew attention to Francisque's status at once as insider and outsider even within diasporan communities, by putting the spotlight on the newcomer's sartorial performance of ethnicity and sexuality.

Through the records of this case, the very premise of black diasporan boundaries and inclusions in one 'Atlantic' colony is examined, elucidated through the analysis of Francisque's deployment of dress. This article takes as its broad subject the significance of sartorial culture to the lives of New Orleans's slaves. It is anchored by one criminal investigation, centred upon the slave known as Francisque, although reference will be made to other cases. In the absence of any runaway slave advertisements (and newspapers) in the Colony, criminal investigations into slave infractions offer the single most comprehensive, if problematic, source of evidence on the material lives of Africans in French Colonial Louisiana.[7] Louisiana did not have a separate slave court to deal with slave infractions; rather, investigations and prosecutions of slaves were tried in the Superior Council of Louisiana and integrated within the mainstream judicial system.[8] Criminal cases against slaves presented eyewitness testimony by blacks, among these the accused, fellow accomplices, witnesses and bystanders; varied voices that provide an alternative window into the meanings of goods for Africans in New Orleans. The use of such slave testimony as a primary source is not without difficulty. Complicated by the larger framework of slavery and colonisation, it highlights the reflexes of prosecutors and court clerks. These cases therefore necessarily tell us much about whites' perspectives on slaves and their anxieties about slaves' use and display of goods. Yet, this exceptional body of material can also be read as foregrounding the voices of slaves and freed blacks, not merely that of their masters. Indeed, we can locate an alternative standpoint in the testimony of select slaves who attempted to articulate a more nuanced relationship to material goods, premised less on a static vision of West African culture than on variable notions of ethnicity and gender. It is to this refusal of the homogeneity of the diasporan experience, illustrated in the interplay of masculinity and ethnicity raised in one criminal case, that this article is addressed.[9]

The case against Francisque followed standard procedures for the decade: investigation, interrogation of accused, interrogation of witnesses, confrontation of accused with witnesses, judgement and sentence. As in the majority of the trials conducted by the Superior Council, no torture was carried out.[10] The evidence from the records of his trial, in which he and other slaves testified directly, like other criminal investigations where slaves of African origin gave first-person accounts, establish a few preliminary points. First, that European-manufactured cloth and clothing were the commodities of choice selected for theft or purchased illegally by slaves in New Orleans. Second, while some of this apparel was slated for resale to whites, the bulk of it was reserved for personal consumption, or intended for gift-giving or trading to fellow members of the black community.

Thirty-nine investigations and/or prosecutions of blacks accused of theft in French Colonial New Orleans have survived; these date from 1723 to 1767, each of the cases involving one or more black transgressors, and occasionally their white and Indian accomplices. (While seemingly low, the ratio of criminal cases to the combined colonist and slave population level – which remained below 5,000 in Lower Louisiana, with blacks outnumbering whites by almost two to one by the 1760s – was not altogether inconsistent.)[11] Of these extant cases 82 per cent involved clothing (stolen, or acquired with stolen money), while at best only 36 per cent involved food, guns or alcohol. Studies of slave dress in the mainland English Colonies have likewise stressed the deployment of apparel and appearance in slave self-fashioning. I propose that slaves' interest in dress, as revealed in these figures, was in fact directly linked to their status as property-less chattel. Indeed, if slaves were prohibited by Article 22 of the 1724 Black Code (which regulated slavery in Louisiana) from property ownership, the next article moderated this by granting slaves the ambiguous right to acquire and dispose of property, if not to own it.[12] In practice, slaves' private possession of certain household goods – namely clothing – was tacitly acknowledged, and underscored a process through which once in their possession, slaves' goods (even those handed them by their masters) were perceived as their personal and private property.[13] Thus, it is my contention that dress was the primary tool for slaves precisely because it was one of the few arenas in which they could exert ultimate control over material goods. Hence dress must take centre stage in any analysis of the meanings of goods for slaves.[14] This is not to discount the place of individual masters and other instruments of the colonial order in handing out dress and dictating its broad parameters; nor is it to ignore the potential for control deriving from other cultural outlets. Yet I wish to emphasise that dress – even supplied dress – was open to manipulation and interpretation, and that this process was played out with greater immediacy and on a wider stage than other forms of material culture. As detected in the actions of other marginalised groups as well as in the vested consumer interests of wider swathes of the population, the deployment of clothing thus constituted a rich, perhaps unique medium for complex cultural elaboration.[15]

For authorities, the supplementation of clothing rations was perceived as the main motivation for the thefts of garments and the theft of other goods to purchase apparel. A contemporary commentator, Le Page du Pratz, believed that there was 'nothing surprising in seeing Negro thiefs when they are short of everything, as I have seen them badly nourished, badly dressed and made to sleep on the ground'.[16] Indeed, this view of slaves as intrinsically criminal was so widespread that the Superior Council invoked it in defence of meting out a minor sentence to two slaves convicted of stealing sacks of rice, arguing that 'if we were to hang all the negro thieves not one would have his life saved, for they are all, more or less, thieves'.[17] Yet, to ascribe all thefts of clothing to pure necessity was to underestimate the meanings attached to it. Dress could denote, construct or contest status; serve as an instrument of economic agency; facilitate or disrupt interracial and intra-racial power relations. Indeed, beyond personal gain, clothing stolen or secured by means of other licit and illicit activity fulfilled a specific function in the initiation and maintenance of sexual and non-sexual kin relations. Thus, in the case against Jupiter belonging to Sr Pradel, and Alexandre belonging to Sr Dumanoir, they each admitted to giving items of apparel to their mistresses, claiming to be motivated by the desire for sexual favours.[18] Non-sexual kin relations were similarly cemented by gifts of clothing, such as when Faÿ was pressured by the slave who was harbouring him, Margueritte, to steal apparel and money, some of which she used to buy herself a skirt. As in this case, often the circle of recipients of stolen goods were punished, in addition to the criminals and their accomplices.[19] Clothing was presented as a core commodity in these records of illicit transactions and gift practices amongst slaves. Yet, there is no reason to believe that these were anomalous treatments of dress limited to testimony from criminal investigations. Indeed, the boundaries between licit and illicit activities were not clearly delineated and the informal local economy ensured that slaves could function *as legitimately* as whites, both as consumers and suppliers.

Clearly, dress was a valuable channel for social and economic agency. It achieved this status by virtue of being a staple commodity in both the black market and the more legitimate market place, and indeed, often served as intermediary between the two. In French Colonial Louisiana, the cloth and clothing available to slaves was European in style, form and manufacture, in effect a shared commodity with cross-over potential between slave and free, white, black and Indian. For, in spite of official condemnation from France and local ordinances formulated in the Colony, whites (including the military), Indians and blacks interacted together in an informal market economy. Such interactions had been a defining feature of the 'frontier exchange economy' that characterised the early and middle parts of the French régime, and had resulted in blacks establishing a constant if marginalised presence in the market place.[20] Against a background of formal probate auctions which redistributed white colonists' goods (occasionally to blacks), used- (or stolen) clothes dealers and those individuals who actively participated in the black market made the recycling as well the exchange of goods an essential feature of Louisiana's economy. These conditions of supply were played out against a harsh economic climate in which constant supply problems resulted in the colonial population's dependence on alternative sources of provision.[21] These were the conditions of consumption that underpinned blacks' consumerism in New Orleans and provided the backdrop for Francisque's sartorial transformation through the theft of a bundle of clothes.

On one level, participation in the local exchange economy meant open access to a market for the goods and services which slaves produced in their free time, giving them in turn the means to barter for goods and services. Conversely, their participation in this informal economy, as producers, suppliers and consumers, gave slaves a quasi-legitimate foothold in the marketplace, simultaneously providing cover for illicit transactions. Thus, in a rare case that targeted a female slave, a twelve-year-old Creole 'negritte' named Babette was brought before the court in October 1765 where she faced charges of stealing a sum of money. Babette confessed to the theft during the interrogation and described what she had done with the money:

> She bought a cotton skirt and a jacket from Sir Nicolet and another skirt from Mistress St Martin; a gold cane handle from La Rochelle, the army drummer; a silk handkerchief and a blue handkerchief from the merchant next to the jail, known as Cassale; some confectionery and pecans from Mistress de Lorier; and a pair of shoes for one piaster from Mistress Olivier Pecherit.[22]

In other words, we have the case of a slave child openly going to different shops and approaching various traders (established and otherwise), to make cash purchases of apparel goods and treats. It is against such a backdrop of pervasive involvement in the formal and informal consumer economies that we should understand Francisque's explanation for the clothing he was wearing at his court hearing, for he described himself as dressed in a hat and sleeveless waistcoat that had *cost* him 50 *sols*.[23] While his statement was later contradicted by other slaves, his openly claiming a consumer act (notably a cash purchase like Babette) reiterated the fact of slaves' presence as customers in the market place, with sartorial display as a valid means of advertising their ownership of material goods.[24] Furthermore, it illustrated slaves' necessary immersion within European styles and forms of dress, here signalled by the professed purchase of two distinctive components of European dress, a waistcoat and a hat.

While there is some sparse evidence of African sartorial retentions, I suggest that the pronounced identification with European models documented here is significant.[25] One likely cause for this lies in the specific character of African slavery in the Colony, namely, the demographic patterns of slave importation and creolisation that meant that no great new population influxes into Louisiana, slave or free, took place after 1731, though new immigrants continued to trickle into the Colony. With shipments of new slaves all but stopping after 1731, the increase in the Colony's black population was the product of childbearing within Louisiana itself. The ensuing creolisation of the black population was to become a defining feature of slaves' demographic make-up.[26] This creolisation and corresponding separation from native African cultures was a factor in slaves' heightened engagement with non-African sartorial culture, made manifest in the case against Francisque.

By 1766, when Francisque was brought before the Superior Council of Louisiana, New Orleans was undergoing a shift from 'frontier exchange economy' to hegemonic white plantation society, and the Colony was in thrall to a sweeping attempt to clamp down on the movement of slaves and limit their trading interactions with the white populace. Officials in the Colony, conscious of the loss of social control heralded by slaves' economic interactions and autonomous sartorial expression, articulated their resistance in a variety of ways. Fortified by the shifting concerns of the growing slave-holding planter class, local officials enacted new legislation (notably the police code of 1751) that sought to control the movements of slaves, including their access to the market place and the ownership of material possessions.[27] They also prosecuted whites who engaged in commercial transactions with slaves, a hitherto commonplace occurrence condoned by masters.

The white populace – also concerned about the loss of control, but primarily preoccupied with their immediate livelihood – remained ambivalent in their responses. For instance, none of the traders accused of selling to the girl Babette, all of whom knew her to be a slave, had queried her possession of money, or the suitability of her wearing new finery. It was in fact on this basis, that they had knowingly made sales to a slave, that the sellers in twelve-year-old Babette's case were prosecuted and either fined heavily or banished from town.[28] Indeed, the chronology of the investigation makes clear that the prosecution was set off with a complaint about the theft of the money (for which Babette was the obvious suspect) rather than her flouting of her new acquisitions, which seems not to have elicited any reaction. And the court record in fact stated that the main motivation for bringing a case against the girl was neither her transgression of rules of (white) property, nor her flagrant display of the goods, as argued elsewhere.[29] Rather, the Court asserted that it was in the public interest to know how and why merchants had flouted the laws concerning the sale of goods to slaves, thus clearly ascribing responsibility to these (white) traders. That whites repeatedly put themselves in a position to be thus prosecuted underlined the Colony's reliance on economic interactions between the different members of that diverse society, with apparel as a key commodity for all of these groups, and stolen clothing and textiles as a common feature of their exchanges.

Convicted slaves could face severe, and even lethal, sentences for their infractions. Yet, they were usually spared the death penalty (but not corporal punishment) since owners of slaves sentenced to die were entitled to financial compensation for the loss of their chattel.[30] Babette's sentence – commuted to 40 lashes as a result of her youthfulness – was considered light.[31] Yet, that slaves, by their transgressions, put themselves in a position where they could be harshly punished raises additional questions about their motives for doing so, especially when the end product was the possession of European clothing. Indeed, I would argue that it is through their willing assimilation of European dress that slaves at once conformed to yet subverted their subservient position. They conformed by making their commodity of choice European standards of dress. This gave them a staple product that was common to whites and some Indians.[32] They resisted by subverting authority in assuming ownership of goods that they were not legally entitled to and putting a distinctive stamp on these. In the process, this clothing could be deployed for quite distinct purposes and the testimony from criminal investigations sometimes hinted at the role of dress in managing social relations among slaves.

The dress of slaves served as a site of contestation between whites and blacks, yet this sartorial discourse should be seen as primarily predicated on internal slave dynamics rather than reduced simply to slave–master power relations. For example, in spite of the willingness on the part of some whites to continue to profit from illegal trading activities with blacks, as Babette's case exemplifies, there is evidence of social tensions brought about by that most visual form of class antagonism – the perception of an 'inappropriate' use of dress. Thus, a free black involved in an altercation with a local white resident, had asserted that he was 'a person of quality, from Paris'. Although he had allegedly been arrested for carrying a sword, this free black he had been harassed because of his appearance, and in particular his hat, which was trimmed with braid and a gold button.[33] That there were growing moves by whites to regulate slaves' independent deployment of material goods is intrinsic to these personal confrontations, new laws and increasing prosecutions. Yet, I suggest that there is evidence, in their testimonies before the court, that slaves enacted their *own* standards of conduct with reference to the deployment of material culture by fellow blacks, testimony to the ability of slaves to negotiate power relations among themselves. Establishing rules of social conduct was not the prerogative of the white hegemony alone. And for blacks, it was dress, more than any other element of material culture, I argue, that was at the core of the internal debates about belonging and exclusion. Thus, if articles of apparel and adornment could be used to signal distinctions between slave and master, between French, African and American, these could also be deployed to distinguish *among* individual slaves or groups of slaves. The analysis of the eyewitness testimony of individual slaves is crucial to unravelling this process, and in the case against Francisque, these accounts bring to the fore questions of ethnic and gender performance, and the multifaceted reception of these.

For clothing was used to signal distinctions among slaves and the testimony of one slave, Demoirité, against Francisque revealed a marked ambiguity about the norms of appearance acceptable to slaves. In his testimony, the forty-year-old Demoirité, acting as spokesman for his immediate community, described four encounters with Francisque. Francisque first surfaced, an unknown, at the Saturday evening festivity held by Demoirité and his group, impressing them all with his munificence. After dancing, lavishing his money on the drummers and his attention on the women, Francisque left, only to return a few days later with a basket to purchase some eggs, ostensibly for the account of his master. Brandishing only a large note in payment, Francisque left without paying, promising to return as soon as he had made change. He next appeared as another dance was underway, but this time, Demoirité asserted, Francisque was both generally impertinent and insulting towards the women. At this point, another male slave, Hector, had stepped in saying 'there is a b. [sic] who comes here to fool around that we don't know. Leave, go away, we don't need you to pay the drum, keep your money and leave'.[34] At their next encounter, according to Jacques' testimony, Demoirité and an unnamed associate attacked Francisque and tried to pry the bundle of stolen laundry that he was carrying, whereupon Demoirité received a knife-wound in the arm.[35]

Demoirité provided a vivid description of Francisque as he was dressed for the dances; he was perceived by the onlookers as 'a pretty rich negro'. He carried a large silver-accented snuff-box and Demoirité stated: 'when he went dancing he was like a Gentleman, ruffled shirt, blue waistcoat, white hat, and wearing three or four handkerchiefs around his neck, and elsewhere about him'.[36] In some respects, Francisque's behaviour and dress at this dance paralleled that of other slaves in French Colonial Louisiana and beyond. The Chevalier de Pradel's description of his slave St Louis La Nuit's infractions offer a mirror image of the concerns expressed in the new, repressive police code enacted in 1751. This former military officer was a plantation- and slave-owning minor French noble who had settled in the Colony and made his fortune there. He described the temporary fall from grace of his favoured slave in a letter from 10 April 1755. In this letter, Pradel attributed his slave's wrongdoing to the latter's airs and pretensions – need and functionality scarcely featured in this reading of slave dress: 'He acted the little master when he got here and to keep up this condition he stole from me: sheep, poultry of every kind, and maybe even some other things that I did not find out about, although the appearance of this is there to see'.[37] St Louis had been charged with going each morning to the New Orleans slaughterhouse on behalf of his master. Instead, he allegedly went in the evening, first spending the night dancing with free blacks in New Orleans, and paying for the music and refreshments. Like Francisque, St Louis assumed a specific role in these gatherings – sponsor of the music and dance partner – that proclaimed his identity through a precise execution of prescribed masculine rituals. The close parallel with Francisque's role performance shown in St Louis's example was multiplied in the weekly slave gatherings that took place in this and other American colonies.[38] The commonality and universality of some features of the African diasporan experience were thus underscored and reinforced by the ubiquity of these social events and the gendered performances that they called for.[39]

In one of the testimonies against the slave Louis from Illinois (by way of Martinique), he too was described as being well-dressed, wearing a white shirt and like Francisque, a hat.[40] In contrast to his dress-up garb of ruffled shirt, blue waistcoat, white hat and multiple handkerchiefs, Francisque's everyday dress was described by one witness as consisting of cheap, worn-out clothing, 'one gingham shirt with a vest no hat and a torn pair of linen long breeches'.[41] This testimony was taken by the court as corroborating evidence that Francisque had stolen the clothing which Demoirité described him as wearing at the festivities. The difference between the description of Francisque in poor, used workday clothing, and his flashy appearance at the festivity, brings into sharp focus the differences between slaves' dress in their free time and on working days.[42] This finer apparel would have been paraded for Saturday and Sunday festivities rather than for workdays, thus minimising the likelihood of whites being confronted with blacks' conspicuous display, and reserving this special act of dressing for a non-white (or non-master) audience.[43] The free black sailor from Paris had flouted this tacit convention by parading, uncontained, around whites in clothing deemed above his station, causing resentment and unease in his aggressor. In this example, class and race issues were blurred.[44] In Francisque's case, his ostentation at the dances appeared to have evoked feelings of resentment amongst the male slaves present, who felt they were being shown up to their female audience by someone outside of their usual acquaintance who had assumed a position of social and economic superiority. Francisque further alienated members of the local black community by his theft from a fellow slave, the female acquaintance from whom he had purportedly stolen some earrings and a hat.[45] His ploy to avoid paying for the eggs purchased from the group in spite of having the means to do so (where other local runaways might have relied on community support in times of need) had further compounded his offence.[46] Such tensions among slaves were not rare, and in Louisiana may have occurred because of differences in ethnic or cultural backgrounds. Evidence of ethnic strife emerged from a number of investigations. For example, the slave Pierrot, described as a 'Bambara' (likely shorthand for non-Muslim) refuted the testimony of a Creole slave who had named him as his accomplice, stating that 'he was no friend of the creoles'.[47] Demoirité was Ibo, while Francisque had lived a peripatetic life that had blurred knowledge of his ethnic origin, leaving him open to marginalisation within the diasporan community. Indeed, concomitant with its precocious and sweeping creolisation, the African slave experience in French Colonial Louisiana was underpinned by a second distinguishing demographic factor, namely the apparent divisions of West African ethnic and religious origins. Together, these unusual patterns of ethnic removal and creolisation gave shape to a distinctive diasporan character in the Colony, one that we find reflected in slaves' deployment of material culture in that environment.

Two-thirds of the slaves sent to Louisiana between 1719 and 1731 came from the area of Senegambia, in West Africa, the bulk of the Colony's remaining slaves originating in Juda. Africans arriving, like Francisque, from the French West Indies, or from the English or Spanish colonies of America (sometimes as runaways) were sporadic occurrences.[48] One influential historian of African slavery in Louisiana, Gwendolyn Midlo Hall, has argued that in spite of its ethnic diversity, Senegambia can be characterised as a culturally homogenous region. Hall argues that this factor served to facilitate the cohesiveness of Louisiana's black population, and the retention there of inherited and shared cultural values made the more acute by the rapid creolisation rate.[49] An opposite interpretation, that the inhabitants of these West African regions were entrenched in their ethnic and religious differences, and that they carried these over to Louisiana, is made by Thomas N. Ingersoll in his study of colonial New Orleans.[50] Hall has relied on the analysis of detailed French records which suggest that members of the Bambara, Ibo, Mandinga and Wolof nations made up the largest proportion of the cargoes sent to Louisiana from Senegambia, with the Bambara as numerically superior. Yet, official French records on slave ethnicities are themselves unreliable in some respects. According to Peter Caron, French naming and identifying practices are deceptive, based as they sometimes were on misleading African ethno-labels. The term Bambara, for instance, likely was a generic ethno-label for slave or non-Muslim rather than referring to members of the inland Bambara state. In other words, according to this account, the designation 'Bambara', rather than indicating one ethnic nation, encompassed instead the members of a wide range of ethnic groups; the supposed Bambara majority of Louisiana's slaves (and hence their homogeneity) was a fiction.[51] The diasporan experience in Louisiana can thus, at best, be characterised by the homogeneity of the creolised black slave population, complicated by the heterogeneity of ethnic African origins with potential for fomenting dissent along ethnic lines. The evidence from the criminal case brought in 1766 against Francisque suggests a yet more subtle articulation of diasporan identities predicated on gendered sartorial expression.

Francisque's various transgressions and transformations distinguish him as the 'artful fellow' or 'con man' type familiar from the runaway advertisements of the English Colonies.[52] Indeed, officials and fellow slaves could not even fix on his name: he was intermittently known as Francisque, Francisco or François; similarly, when asked if he had offered to show a female slave how to cook, he admitted that his specialties included both 'des Ragouts anglois et espagnols', English and Spanish stews. In one sense, it was precisely the transgressive character of his sartorial ostentation that cost Francisque his freedom and very nearly his life – he was condemned to be hung, but his sentence was commuted to a beating, branding with the letter 'V' for 'voleur' (thief) and banishment from the Colony.[53] Francisque had reserved his flashy dress for his appearance at the slaves' weekly gathering, a private affair sheltered from the gaze of whites. It was not whites, therefore, who had witnessed Francisque's behaviour and dress, raised questions about his ownership of fine clothing and accessories, and ultimately, who caused him to be sentenced by the authorities. This role was left to fellow black slaves, envious of Francisque's apparent affluence and offended by the runaway's impact on the established social and gender hierarchy of the group. Free of any kin or ethnic loyalty, they had worked to defuse his power through the intermediary of whites, a previous attempt by Demoirité and his ally to appropriate the means to Francisque's sexual and material affluence (by attempting to snatch his stolen bundle of laundry) having failed. Here was an example of slaves engineering social control within black spaces by manipulating the apparatus of the white hegemony, the Superior Council of Louisiana.

Reserved for an audience of his fellow slaves and his fellow Africans, Francisque's gestures cannot thus be reduced to the familiar trope of dress as means of subaltern resistance and transgression. The case against the twelve-year-old Babette similarly raises pointed questions about the girl's consumerism and the intended audience for the display of her new purchases. These can be read as articulating her taste and desires beyond the merely functional purposes they served, as Babette had according to one merchant made a specific request for some red cloth with which to make herself a skirt. Although none was available, this request – punctuated by her successful acquisition of treats and refined (or 'populuxe') clothing such as a silk handkerchief and a gilded ornament – heralded Babette's consumer interests in material goods.[54] This girl's purchases accentuate that the practicality of dress cannot be dissociated from its potent role as material manifestation of the socialised body.

The fact that Babette openly purchased her goods from both established traders and 'fly-by-night' operators suggests that she was indifferent to her sartorial transformation being witnessed by respectable law-abiding white settlers, and that her (white) audience was similarly impervious to this. On one level, the differing receptions of Francisque and Babette's transgressions can be attributed to gendered notions of sexual relations that acknowledged, and privileged, slave women's access to material goods procured via relations with white males. The identity of one of her shopping companions, Marie Louise, the daughter of the two girls' master with one of his slaves, would seem to underscore this. Indeed, were it not for Babette's direct testimonial in court about the theft and her admission to the shopping spree, the case against her could have been construed as a cover-up for the activities of the slightly older and more privileged Marie Louise, whose father and master, a military lieutenant, was the son of the late Attorney General of Louisiana and a future member of the court under Spanish colonial rule.[55] However, Babette was not always accompanied by Marie Louise, but on one occasion by a much younger child, and on another, by a girl of twelve named Françoise belonging to a different master. Neither these girls nor Marie Louise's mother, who was also implicated, were called to testify. But their awareness of Babette's ownership of a sum of money hints at the extended community network that supported slaves who transgressed against whites and that benefited from these. Our focus thereby shifts from the 'individual' to the 'collective', from the personal benefit derived by slaves' from their infractions, to the wider community's gain.[56] For Francisque, his marginal status and self-serving practices foiled his attempt at immersion into the New Orleans slave community he had infiltrated. Yet his flouting of that community's standards was contradicted by his attempts to conform and be absorbed, as witnessed in his deployment of a prevalent West African convention of masculinity suggested by his manipulation of handkerchiefs.

The evidence of slaves' familiarity in Louisiana with European sartorial practices tends to underscore their assimilation into the dominant white culture, to the detriment of any consideration of their actual treatment of European clothing. In part this is due to our reliance on the evidence constructed by whites. Less tangible to these white onlookers – and hence less documented in the extant sources – was the retention by blacks of any features of their native or ancestral modes of dress. Africans in Louisiana maintained links to their originating culture in the way of naming practices, religion, technology, food practices and social relations.[57] Yet there are no explicit references in Louisiana's records to the retention by blacks of africanisms in their dress and appearance. However, echoes of shared West African aesthetics can be detected, and in Louisiana may have included an emphasis on the head, adornment with certain kinds of metallic and non-metallic jewellery and ornaments, or the prevalence of certain colours, such as red, popular across a spectrum of Senegambian nations.[58] Such sartorial characteristics of West African dress feature in the depictions of maroon slaves by a French military engineer, Alexandre de Batz, dating from the 1730s.[59] In one of these images (see Figure 1), the black figure wears a variant on a turban-like head wrap, paired with a breech-clout, the latter in itself evidence of the carry-over of sartorial preferences for unrestricted and unstructured styles of clothing. Indeed, while the breech-clout is usually associated with indigenous Indian dress, there are African antecedents of such a style, these two sartorial traditions merging in the dress of slaves of African origin in French Colonial Louisiana.[60] Ironically, all of the constituents of the figure's apparel – in other words the cloth for the turban and the blanket for the breech-clout – would have been of European manufacture (the tell-tale white *point* or stripe of his breech-clout is clearly visible). I suggest that it is in this context, where the assimilation of European *forms* of apparel is inseparable from the retention of African *modes* of dress, that we should read the twelve-year-old Babette's unfulfilled request for red cloth with which to make herself a skirt, and perhaps also her interest in a gold cane handle – an unusual item certainly suitable for adaptation into an ornament. As in other instances of cultural confrontation and 'bricolage' – for example those experienced by whites and Indians in French Colonial Louisiana – some elements were absorbed, others discarded and others still reinvented.[61] For blacks, this synthesis was facilitated by their widespread participation in Louisiana's frontier exchange economy, as producers, providers of goods and services and as consumers. This offered them a twofold way of asserting autonomy in the face of severe constraints mandated by their state of bondage. Consumerism became a channel for contesting the immediate authority of the hegemonic master-figure and the institutional structures that validated slavery. By providing a vehicle for expression within the framework of a diasporan communal identity, slave consumerism in the Colony formulated itself as a syncretic amalgam of European and non-European values.

The dress of Francisque exemplified this process. Francisque created a jarring element in his use of European dress, revealing an unusual use and interpretation of European clothing mores that can be ascribed a diasporan character. When he went out dancing, he wore not one handkerchief around his neck, as was usual in European dress, but 'three or four handkerchiefs around his neck, and elsewhere about him'.[62] We find

Figure 1: Alexandre de Batz, 'Dessein de Sauvages de Plusieurs Nations', New Orleans, 1735 (Peabody Museum of Archaeology and Ethnology, Harvard).

a possible clarification for his appearance in an anonymous image from South Carolina of a slave gathering, 'The Old Plantation', dating to c. 1800 (Figure 2). Here, to the tune of African musical instruments, the slaves perform a traditional dance, the men brandishing sticks as the women wield handkerchiefs of the kind that Francisque had borne.[63] There are further parallels in the works of Agostino Brunias, a prolific artist who was a regular visitor to the West Indies and produced ubiquitous images of slave and free blacks in Dominica.[64] In one such painting, a scene similar to that from South Carolina is reproduced, with a woman holding up a handkerchief while dancing with her male partner who is garbed in a checked head-wrap with a handkerchief wound around his waist (Figure 3). In an engraving made from another Brunias painting again showing a group of slaves or free blacks gathered together for a dance, the male dancer in the foreground sports a handkerchief on his head, with another asymetrically draped across one shoulder.[65] The sexual overtones of such courtship performances are encapsulated in the surfeit of handkerchiefs seen in these images – the very feature of Francisque's appearance which was singled out and denounced by his rivals when they described him as wearing 'three or four handkerchiefs' draped around his body. Simultaneously means of adornment and gift token, presentation and self-presentation, these handkerchiefs were the objects of Demoirité's envy and desire, which he had unsuccessfully sought to appropriate, literally and metaphorically, from Francisque, by fighting him for possession of the bundle of laundry at the cost of a wounded arm. Francisque's appearance was aimed at appealing to a shared notion of masculinity common across diasporan communities, the handkerchiefs symbolising his attempt at diasporan membership through the performance of maleness and masculine eroticism. Yet this gender performance, for all its conventionality and ubiquity across widely divergent diasporan communities built from ethnically fractured origins, failed to ensure Francisque's acceptance in one cohesive slave community in New Orleans.

The simultaneous success and failure of Francisque's sartorial enterprise highlighted the fragmentation and mutability of African values yet underscored the authority of diasporan models. Influenced by the conditions of slavery in a colony that foregrounded European models of dress, yet cognizant of a shared diasporan language of modes and manners, Francisque's deployment of dress remained exactly that: a performance that played on the notion of a shared affinity and communal empathy while simultaneously putting into question the very possibility of a consistent gendered and diasporan identity across ethnic, religious and kinship lines.

Figure 2: Anonymous, 'The Old Plantation' c. 1800 (Collection of the Abby Aldrich Rockefeller Folk Art Center, Williamsburg).

Figure 3: Agostino Brunias, 'Scene with Dancing in the West Indies' ca. 1770–80 (Present whereabouts unknown, after Hugh Honour, *The Image of the Black in Western Art, IV From the American Revolution to World War I* (Harvard University Press, 1976), plate 3 p. 33.)

Notes

I would like to thank David Waldstreicher, the anonymous readers for this article, and the audience members of the 'Speaking in Signs' conference at the McNeil Center for Early American Studies (Philadelphia, September 1999) and the Early Americanists in Britain and Ireland Colloquium (Brunel University, July 1999), where I presented earlier versions of this paper.

1. The records of this investigation are found in the Records of the Superior Council of Louisiana, Louisiana Historical Collection, Louisiana State Museum, New Orleans (hereafter RSCL): see RSCL 1766040202, 1766070401, 1766070402, 1766070403, 1766072302, 1766072502, 1766072904, 1766072905, 1766073106, and 1766080204.
2. On long breeches, see RSCL 1765091602.
3. On Vilemont, see Fontaine Marin, *A History of the Bouligny Family and Allied Families* (Lafayette: University of Southwestern Louisiana, 1990), pp. 81–96.
4. Unless otherwise specified, all translations from the original French are my own. In an important article on African ethnicity in Colonial Louisiana, Peter Caron correctly cautions against blindly using the ethnic labels used in official records including criminal investigations, arguing that these were sometimes generic labels imposed by whites. However, he over-generalises in suggesting that 'in the majority of cases the slave's identity was probably already known and it was therefore likely that the preliminary questions as to name and "nation" of origin were not asked'. In the case against Francisque, the court recorder did provide an opening statement about the slave's age, ownership and religion. However, Francisque was then asked directly about his origins and he provided that information himself. See 'Of a nation which the others do not Understand': Bambara Slaves and African Ethnicity in Colonial Louisiana, 1718–60' in *Slavery & Abolition* 18 (1997), pp. 98–121, especially pp. 108–9.
5. On (free and enslaved) black sailors in the Atlantic world, see W. Jeffrey Bolster, 'An Inner Diaspora: Black Sailors Making Selves' in Ronald Hoffman, Michel Sobel and Fredrika J. Teute (eds) *Through a Glass Darkly: Reflections on Personal Identity in Early America* (Chapel Hill: University of North Carolina Press, 1997) and Peter Linebaugh and Marcus Rediker, *The Many-Headed Hydra: Sailors, Slaves, Commoners, and the Hidden History of the Revolutionary Atlantic* (Boston: Beacon Press, 2000), pp. 143–73.
6. Convoys were regularly manned by slaves: see Carl J. Ekberg, 'Black Slavery in Illinois, 1720–1765', *Western Illinois Regional Studies* 12 (1989), pp. 5–19; also RSCL 1738040901.
7. Runaway advertisements have proved to be exceptionally rich bodies of evidence for the study of the slave experience in Anglo-America. See notably Jonathan Prude, 'To Look upon the "Lower Sort": Runaway Ads and the Appearance of Unfree Laborers in America, 1750–1800', *The Journal of American History* 78 (1991), pp. 124–59; Shane White and Graham White, 'Slave Clothing and African-American Culture in the Eighteenth and Nineteenth Centuries', *Past & Present* 148 (1995), pp. 149–86, and 'Slave Hair and African American Culture in the Eighteenth and Nineteenth Centuries', *Journal of Southern History* 61 (1995), pp. 45–76; and David Waldstreicher, 'Reading the Runaways: Self-Fashioning, Print Culture, and Confidence in Slavery in the Eighteenth-Century Mid-Atlantic', *William and Mary Quarterly*, 3rd Series, 56 (1999) pp. 241–72. Runaway reports were occasionally filed with the Superior Council but these contained no references to dress or appearance (save for age in some rare cases, for example RSCL 1744013101 and RSCL 1748052101), suggesting that they existed to fulfill a legal requirement for accounting of property rather than as a tool to aid in the recapture of runaways.
8. Thomas N. Ingersoll, 'Slave Codes and Judicial Practice in New Orleans, 1718–1807', in *Law and History Review*, 13 (1995), pp. 23–62.
9. Few studies of French Colonial New Orleans have fore-grounded gender as a category of analysis; most have focused on the question of women: see Emily Clark, '"By All the Conduct of Their Lives": A Laywomen's Confraternity in New Orleans, 1730–1744', *William and Mary Quarterly*, 3rd Series, 54 (1997), pp. 769–94; Emily Clark and Virginia Meacham Gould, 'The Feminine Face of Afro-Catholicism in New Orleans, 1727–1852', *William and Mary Quarterly*, 3rd Series, 59 (2002), pp. 409–48; Jennifer M. Spear, '"Whiteness and the

Purity of Blood": Race, Sexuality, and Social Order in Colonial Louisiana' (Ph.D. dissertation, University of Minnesota, 1999) and 'Colonial Intimacies: Legislating Sex in French Louisiana', *William and Mary Quarterly*, 3rd Series, 60 (2003), pp. 75–98; Sophie White, "'This Gown ... Was Much Admired and Made Many Ladies Jealous:" Fashion and the Forging of Elite Identities in French Colonial New Orleans' in *George Washington's South*, ed. Greg O'Brien and Tamara Harvey (Gainesville: University Press of Florida, 2003).

10.   But see a near contemporary trial, RSCL 1764072403, when torture was applied as part of the investigation.

11.   Charles R. Maduell, comp. and trans., *The Census Tables for the French Colony of Louisiana from 1699 through 1732* (Baltimore: Genealogical Publishing Company, 1972), pp. 113–41 and 150, and Jacqueline K. Voorhies, comp., *Some Late Eighteenth-Century Louisianans* (Lafayette: University of Southwestern Louisiana, 1973), pp. 5–103.

12.   Louisiana Historical Collection, Louisiana State Museum, New Orleans, III 2852.23 March 1724. See Ingersoll, 'Slave Codes', p. 37.

13.   See for example RSCL 1723071301, 1724072701, 1736090903, 1744032103, 1765080204, discussed in Sophie White, 'Trading Identities: Cultures of Consumption in French Colonial Louisiana, 1699–1769' (Ph.D dissertation, University of London, 2000), pp. 181–4.

14.   Here I am drawing on Amanda Vickery's reading of the consumerism of another disenfranchised group, gentlewomen, in eighteenth-century Britain. See, *The Gentleman's Daughter: Women's Lives in Georgian England* (New Haven: Yale University Press, 1998).

15.   See for example, Beverly Lemire, 'The Theft of Clothes and Popular Consumerism', *Journal of Social History* 24 (1990), pp. 255–76.

16.   Le Page du Pratz, *Histoire de la Louisiane, contenant la découverte de ce vaste pays*, vol. 1 (Paris: Debure *l'aîné*, 1758), p. 348 (author's translation). See RSCL 1764041201 for a rare confirmation of this view.

17.   Archives Nationales Colonies, France (hereafter ANC), Ser. C13A vol. 17, fol. 152: 18 July 1733.

18.   RSCL 1744032103.

19.   RSCL 1765090902.

20.   Daniel H. Usner, Jr., *Indians, Settlers, and Slaves in a Frontier Exchange Economy: The Lower Mississippi Valley Before 1783* (Chapel Hill: University of North Carolina Press, 1992). See also James T. McGowan, 'Creation of a Slave Society: Louisiana Plantations in the Eighteenth Century' (Ph.D. dissertation, University of Rochester, 1976).

21.   See White, 'Trading Identities'.

22.   RSCL 1765101001.

23.   The currency used in French colonial Louisiana was the *livre* (one *livre* = 20 *sous* and 1 *sol* = 12 *deniers*) although the value of treasury bills and specie fluctuated wildly; see N. M. Surrey, *The Commerce of Louisiana During the French Regime, 1699–1763* (New York: Columbia University Press, 1916), pp. 102–53.

24.   Dylan Penningroth offers a subtle articulation of the dynamics of slaves' ownership of property as mediated through an 'informal system of display and acknowledgement'. See 'Slavery, Freedom, and Social Claims to Property among African Americans in Liberty County, Georgia, 1850–1880', *The Journal of American History* 84 (1997), pp. 405–35.

25.   The wearing of European cloth in Africa was already well-established by the start of the eighteenth century, with consumer preferences in different parts of Africa playing an important role in the changing tastes for European goods, just as they did elsewhere, in Europe and in America. See John Thornton, *Africa and Africans in the Making of the Atlantic World, 1400–1680* (1992; repr. Cambridge: Cambridge University Press, 1998), pp. 48–53 and 230–34; Valérie Bérinstain, 'Les toiles de l'Inde et la Compagnie des Indes XVIIe – XVIIIe siècles', *Cahiers de la Compagnie des Indes*, No. 2 (1997), pp. 25–32; and John Picton, *The Art of African Textiles: Technology, Tradition and Lurex* (London: Barbican Art Gallery, 1995).

26.   Hall, Africans, Appendix A, pp. 381–97; also Ingersoll, *First Slave Society*, 94–5.

27.   ANC Ser. C13A vol. 35 fol. 39: New Orleans, 28 Feb–1st March 1751. See Ingersoll, 'Slave Codes'; also White, 'Trading Identities', 189–91.

28.   See RSCL 1766112204 for another banishment resulting from the 1751 Police Code.

29. RSCL 1765100901. See Ingersoll, *First Slave Society*, p. 85.
30. For a discussion of the differences between the punishment meted out to whites and to blacks in Louisiana, see Mathé Allain, 'Slave Policies in French Louisiana', *Louisiana History* 21 (1980), pp. 136–7; also Ingersoll, 'Slave Codes', pp. 34–5 and 40–1.
31. RSCL 1765101207 and RSCL 1765101210.
32. Pointed evidence of the function of apparel as commodity can be seen in the pawning of a ring by the slave Jupiter (RSCL 1744032103).
33. RSCL 1765101501 and 1765101802.
34. RSCL 1766072904.
35. RSCL 1766070401. In his own testimony, Demoirité denied that Francisque had been carrying any goods (RSCL 1766072904).
36. RSCL 1766072904. On the sartorial transgressions of slaves in English Colonies, and particularly on the effect of their adoption of élite items of clothing, see White and White, 'Slave Clothing', pp. 156–8 and 162.
37. A. Baillardel and A. Prioult, *Le Chevalier de Pradel: Vie d'un colon français en Louisiane au XVIIIe siècle d'après sa correspondance et celle de sa famille* (Paris: Maisonneuve Frères, 1928), p. 260.
38. In Louisiana, see the references to slave assemblies found in the Black Code of 1724 and Police Code of 1751, as always, useful indicators of existing behaviour. See also RSCL 174609, C0309 and 1764081001. On music and dancing in African American culture, see Philip D. Morgan, *Slave Counterpoint: Black Culture in the Eighteenth-Century Chesapeake & Lowcountry* (Chapel Hill: University of North Carolina Press, 1998), pp. 580–94; Shane White, '"It Was a Proud Day": African Americans, Festivals, and Parades in the North, 1741–1834', *Journal of American History* 81 (1994) pp. 13–51; Prude, 'To Look upon the "Lower" Sort' and Waldstreicher, 'Reading the Runaways'.
39. For a sophisticated reading of the ubiquity of gestures across diasporan communities, see W. T. Lhamon, Jr., *Raising Cain: Blackface Performance from Jim Crow to Hip Hop* (Cambridge: Harvard University Press, 1998).
40. RSCL 1764073101.
41. RSCL 1766072502.
42. No sumptuary legislation existed for French colonial Louisiana but in the French West Indies, a 1720 statute restricted the wearing of white cloth to freedmen alone. See Gabriel Debien, *Les Esclaves aux Antilles françaises, XVIIe–XVIIIe siècles* (Société d'histoire de la Guadeloupe, 1974) p. 240, and Chaela Pastore, 'Consumer Choices and Colonial Identity in Saint-Domingue', *French Colonial History* 2 (2002), pp. 77–92.
43. For an alternative reading of slaves' Sunday dress, see Penningroth, 'Slavery, Freedom, and Property', pp. 420–21.
44. On the social unease caused by servants dressing above their station in Paris in this period, see for example Daniel Roche, *La Culture des apparences: Une histoire du vêtement XVIIe–XVIIIe siècle* (Paris: Flammarion, repr. Paris: Le Seuil, 1989), pp. 101–4.
45. For further references to thefts committed by blacks from other blacks see RSCL 1744122604, 1746112701, 1748040601, 1758071001, 1760090301, 1765030201, 1765080204 and 1766063001.
46. Community support was clearly perceived as a form of community service; see for instance RSCL 1764041201, 1741011001 and 1741011101.
47. RSCL 1748011101. On these generic ethno-labels, see Caron, 'Bambara Slaves'. Also relevant is the investigation into the murder of Marboux, which Caron has persuasively interpreted as stemming from conflict between non-Muslim and Muslim Africans (ibid., p. 114). Other allusions to ethnic strife are related in Hall, *Africans*, 163.
48. For example, a former runaway slave, John Mingo, who arrived from Carolina in August 1726, settled in New Orleans where he was hired as a free man and married a slave whose freedom he bought (RSCL 1729102102 and 1730112501).
49. Hall, *Africans*, pp. 29–34. See also Philip D. Curtin, *The Atlantic Slave Trade: A Census* (Madison: University of Wisconsin Press, 1969), pp. 163–202.

50. Ingersoll, *First Slave Society*, pp. 67–71. Morgan offers a nuanced reading of this issue in the Chesapeake, which also had relatively few influxes of new African slaves after about 1740, resulting in the necessity for extensive contact with black Creoles. See, *Slave Counterpoint*, pp. 455–8.

51. Peter Caron, 'Bambara Slaves'.

52. David Waldstreicher, 'Reading the Runaways'.

53. See RSCL 1766073106.

54. I use the word 'populuxe' to mean cheap, mass-manufactured versions of luxury goods, as defined by Cissie Fairchilds, 'The Production and Marketing of Populuxe Goods in Eighteenth-Century Paris', in *Consumption and the World of Goods,* ed. John Brewer and Roy Porter (London: Routledge, 1993), pp. 228–48.

55. John G. Clark, *New Orleans, 1718–1812: An Economic History* (Baton Rouge: Louisiana State University Press, 1970) p. 105.

56. See note 46. A visitor to Spanish New Orleans commented on the seeming cohesiveness of slaves in Spanish New Orleans, as observed during their weekly dances: 'form[ing] a single family united in their abjection … To the best of their ability they try to do each other as much good as they can'; see Claude-Cezar Robin, *Voyage to Louisiana, 1803–1805*, trans. and abridged by Stuart O. Landry Jr (1807, repr. New Orleans: Pelican, 1966), p. 248, quoted in Ingersoll, *First Slave Society*, pp. 192–3.

57. There are numerous references in Louisiana's records to the practice by blacks of distinctive habits, such as 'chanter negre', drinking rum but not wine (see RSCL 1743091001 and 1765090902 respectively), eating 'gombeau' (RSCL 1764090401) and using supernatural devices such as 'gris gris' (Le Page du Pratz, *Histoire* I, p. 334). On naming practices, see Appendix D: 'Evidence of Widespread Survival of African Names in Colonial Louisiana', in Hall, *Africans*, pp. 407–12.

58. The most comprehensive analysis of West African sources is provided by Helen Bradley Foster, *'New Raiments of Self': African American Clothing in the Antebellum South* (Berg Publishers, 1997). Examples from New Orleans of such features are documented in RSCL 1741011001, 1752032702 and the New Orleans Notarial Archives, Parish of Orleans, New Orleans, F4-02 [09427-28-29-30-31-32] 1738/02/25 (sale of effects, succession of Georges Amelot).

59. De Batz's images, owned by the Peabody Museum of Archaeology and Ethnology, Harvard, are reproduced in David I. Bushnell, *Drawings by A. De Batz in Louisiana, 1732–1735, With Six Plates* (Washington DC: Smithsonian Institution, 1927).

60. Morgan, *Slave Counterpoint*, pp. 598–99. Breech-clouts as staples of Indian garb are discussed by Robert S. DuPlessis in 'Circulation des textiles et des valeurs dans la Nouvelle-France aux xviie et xviiie siècles', in *Échanges et cultures textiles dans l'Europe pré-industrielle,* ed. Jacques Bottin and Nicole Pellegrin, *Revue du Nord*, special issue no. 12 (1996), pp. 73–89.

61. See White, 'Trading Identities', chap. 2 and 4. Examples of '*bricolage*' in African American culture are discussed in White and White, 'Slave Clothing', pp. 162–5, Shane White, 'It was a Proud Day', pp. 13–50, and Ann Smart Martin, 'Complex Commodities: The Enslaved as Producers and Consumers in Eighteenth-Century Virginia' (Paper presented at the Omohundro Institute of Early American History and Culture Annual Conference, Winston-Salem, June 1997).

62. RSCL 1766072904.

63. See Cynthia Adams Hoover, 'Music and Theater in the Lives of Eighteenth-Century Americans', in *Of Consuming Interests: The Style of Life in the Eighteenth Century,* ed. Cary Carson, Ronald Hoffman and Peter J. Albert (Charlottesville: University Press of Virginia, 1994), p. 333 for an assessment of the African precedents of the musical instruments pictured here.

64. Hugh Honour, *The Image of the Black in Western Art*, IV *From the American Revolution to World War* I (Cambridge MA: Harvard University Press, 1976), pp. 32–3; Beth Fowkes Tobin, *Picturing Imperial Power: Colonial Subjects in Eighteenth-Century British Painting* (Durham: Duke University Press, 1999), pp. 151–73

65. Agostino Brunias, 'Dancers, Dominica' ca. 1770s (present whereabouts unknown), reproduced in Lennox Honychurch, *The Dominica Story: A History of the Island* [Lennox Honychurch, 1975], p. 44.

8

Diasporic Brotherhood: Freemasonry and the Transnational Production of Black Middle-Class Masculinity

Martin Summers

In the 1930s, an important transatlantic relationship developed between D. K. Abadu-Bentsi, an Accra-born Fante in his thirties who was a sporadically employed teacher in the Gold Coast (colonial Ghana), and Harry A. Williamson, a middle-aged African American postal worker and writer in New York City. The half-decade long correspondence between Abadu-Bentsi and Williamson was not as ideologically motivated as communications between intellectuals and activists involved in the series of Pan-African congresses between 1900 and 1945. Nor was it as culturally and institutionally impacting as the transatlantic contacts that shaped the growth of Baptism and Methodism in western and southern Africa during the late-nineteenth and early-twentieth centuries. Neither were their exchanges as politically charged and tactically driven as those that marked the relationship between indigenous anti-colonial groups in Africa and their African American allies in the 1940s and 1950s.[1] Neither ideology, culture, nor politics – in the most conventional senses of those terms – were responsible for bringing Abadu-Bentsi and Williamson into each other's field of vision and, indeed, the two may never have met were it not for the fact that they were both Freemasons. The young Gold Coaster was made a Mason in the English constitution Victoria Lodge, No. 2392, located in Accra. At the time that his correspondence with Williamson began, he was affiliated with the Scottish constitution Lodge Morality, No. 1362, in Kumasi, where he was a schoolteacher. The older African American Mason was a charter member of a Brooklyn lodge, Carthaginian, No. 47, founded in 1904. By the 1930s, Williamson was somewhat of a Masonic luminary, having held several positions within the Grand Lodge of New York; he was generally recognised as one of the pre-eminent scholars and historians of Freemasonry among people of African descent.[2]

Abadu-Bentsi and Williamson were linked by a bond of fraternalism whose origins lay in early modern Europe but that, by the early twentieth century, existed in North and South America, Africa, Asia and Australia. 'Speculative', or symbolic, Freemasonry had its formal birth in early eighteenth-century Britain. Unlike the 'operative' masonry that constituted the core of guild-like lodges in medieval Europe, Freemasonry represented a fraternal tradition that incorporated the European and colonial élite and, by the late eighteenth century, members of an emergent bourgeoisie, petit bourgeoisie and artisan class. Through esoteric rituals that blended a Judeo-Christian belief system and a rational, scientific worldview, Freemasons constructed a collective identity based on the inculcation of producer values, bourgeois standards of morality, and respectability. On a more practical level, Freemasonry functioned as a mutual aid association, providing unemployment and death benefits, and serving as a profes- sional and business network. As such, the Craft was a route of upward mobility and the facilitator of the development of class-consciousness for many middle-class men.[3]

It is this latter characteristic – the role of Freemasonry in the formation of gender and class identities – with which this article is concerned. Most scholarship on Freemasonry, including scholarship that explores the gendered meaning of fraternalism, deals with the Order in its European and American manifestations. There is no corresponding literature on Freemasonry outside the European and American contexts and there is even less that examines how Freemasonry might have served as a conduit for the formation of collective identities that traversed national and geo- graphic boundaries.[4] This article explores the transatlantic links between Freemasons of African descent in general, and the relationship between Abadu-Bentsi and Williamson in particular, to suggest ways in which we might begin to look at fraternal voluntary associations as a crucial site for the formation of diasporic identity. To the extent that Freemasonry's 'significance resides not only in the social networks it created, reinforced or displayed, but in the meanings it articulated [and] the cultural context it provided for social action', we need to consider how those networks were constituted within a transnational context and how that context contributed to disparate, as well as similar, constructions of gender, class, race and ethnicity.[5] The key question that this article addresses is: To what degree did Freemasonry provide Abadu-Bentsi and Williamson (and other black Masons) a space in which, on the one hand, they could lay claim to a middle-class male subjectivity that was articulated within the universalist rhetoric and rituals and the social network capacity of the Craft and, on the other hand, construct a specifically racialised masculinity that paralleled their recognition of each other as fellow members of the African diaspora? In other words, I want to explore how men of African descent utilised a European cultural form to constitute themselves as men in conformity to bourgeois notions of manliness while also distancing themselves, to a certain degree, from white middle-class men. In doing so, I hope to illustrate the importance of recognising how diasporic identity formation is bound up in other processes of identity formation – specifically class and gender identities. If, as one historian has recently argued, the diaspora represents 'a stage for redefining one's social identity', then this article emphasises the importance of situating gender and class within these redefinitions.[6]

The correspondence between Abadu-Bentsi and Williamson began in the late fall of 1929. Williamson was not actually the African's first contact in the United States. Initially, Abadu-Bentsi had sent a letter to C. C. Hunt, a white Mason at the Iowa Masonic Library, inquiring about beginning an acquaintance with a graduate student at an American university. Hunt forwarded the letter to J. Hugo Tatsch, vice president of Macoy Publishing and Masonic Supply Company. Tatsch, like most other white American Masons, tended to conflate black Freemasonry in general with African American, or Prince Hall, Freemasonry. As such, in addition to answering Abadu-Bentsi's letter himself, he sent it on to his friend Harry Williamson who, at the time, was one of the most noted black Masons because of his scholarship and archival work on Prince Hall Freemasonry and Masonry in general. Williamson's first letter to Abadu-Bentsi, written in December 1929, set the stage for the 'education' that both would receive as diasporic subjects. His first communication began with an enumeration of his Masonic credentials but it quickly turned into a discussion of the state of black Freemasonry in the United States. 'Prejudice on account of color (black) permeates the nation in social, religious and political circles and has crept into secret societies', he explained to Abadu-Bentsi, 'so much so, we have organized societies identical to those of the whites but consisting of and governed exclusively by men of our own race'. By situating Prince Hall Freemasonry within the larger contours of anti-black racism in the United States, Williamson implicitly offered Abadu-Bentsi an explanation as to why Tatsch might have forwarded the African's letter to him in the first place. More importantly, he sought to establish a critical connection between the experiences of African Americans in general, and African American Masons in particular, with the experiences of people of African descent, both on the continent and elsewhere. 'Being an American Negro', he wrote, '[I] am in sympathy with the aims and aspirations of members of my race irrespective of their location and I assure you if it is possible for me to be of service to you in any particular, you have only to ask'.[7] The relationship that would unfold between the two was but part of a longer history of diasporic connections between black Masons.

Indeed, from its introduction into communities of African descent, Freemasonry was a diasporic project. Although his parentage and place of birth are unclear, black Masonic legend for years claimed that its 'father', Prince Hall, was a mixed-race Barbadian who immigrated to colonial British North America in 1765.[8] Shortly before hostilities broke out between England and the American colonies in April 1775, Hall and fourteen other free blacks were initiated into the Craft by members of Irish Military Lodge, No. 441, a lodge of Irish soldiers who were attached to the British regular army in Boston. After receiving the degree of Master Mason, the highest of the initial three degrees, they received a temporary dispensation to meet as Provisional African Lodge, No. 1. Because the temporary permit did not allow them to engage in certain activities – most importantly, the granting of degrees – Hall submitted a petition to the Provincial Grand Lodge of Massachusetts, the governing body of white Masons in New England. The Provincial Grand Master failed to act upon the petition and, because of the outbreak of the Revolution, Hall and his brethren did not pursue getting a regular warrant until after the war. Shortly after the war's cessation, Hall petitioned the Grand Lodge of England for a warrant and, in 1784, the Grand Lodge affirmed that 'Prince Hall, Boston Smith, Thomas Sanderson, and several other brethren residing in Boston, New England, in North America, do hereby constitute … a Regular Lodge of Free and Accepted Masons, under the title or denomination of the African Lodge'. Seven years later, African Lodge, No. 459 became a Grand Lodge in its own right, with Prince Hall as its first Most Worshipful Grand Master. Achieving the status of a Grand Lodge gave Hall and his brethren the authority to create subordinate lodges. Hall died in 1807 and, one year later, the African Grand Lodge was renamed Prince Hall in his honour.[9]

In the decades following the formation of African Grand Lodge, Prince Hall Freemasonry spread rapidly throughout the United States. Many of the black Masons who formed subordinate lodges under the auspices of Prince Hall were actually initiated in lodges in England and its Caribbean colonies. Several of the charter members of African Lodge in Philadelphia, which received a warrant from the African Grand Lodge in 1797, had received their Master Mason degrees in Golden Lodge, No. 22 in London. After their request for a charter was rebuffed by white Masonic authorities in Pennsylvania, they chose to affiliate with Prince Hall.[10] African American and African Caribbean seamen who were initiated in lodges in Liverpool, London and the British colonies in the Caribbean were responsible for introducing the higher degrees of Royal Arch and Knights Templar to black Masons within the United States in the early nineteenth century.[11] Just as black Freemasons circumnavigating the Atlantic brought rituals from English lodges back to the United States that augmented the fraternal tradition of Prince Hall, so Prince Hall (the institution, not the man) undertook the task of spreading Freemasonry beyond national borders. There were Prince Hall lodges in Bermuda as early as 1838 and in the early twentieth century, Royal Eagle Lodge, No. 45, located in Nassau, Bahamas, was a subordinate lodge under the jurisdiction of Prince Hall's New York Grand Lodge. By the 1940s, Prince Hall Grand Lodges of various states counted among their constituencies subordinate lodges in the Canadian provinces of British Columbia and Manitoba, Belize, The Netherlands Antilles islands of Aruba and Curaçao and Cape Town, South Africa.[12]

Individual Prince Hall lodges also evinced a particularly diasporic, pan-ethnic character. Because of the common custom and, in many cases, formal policies, of white American Masons not recognising the legitimacy of Prince Hall or prohibiting association with black Masons, Prince Hall became a virtual reservoir for Masons of colour in the United States, whether they were American or not. African Caribbean Masons migrating to the United States who wished to join white lodges, for instance, were often directed towards Prince Hall lodges. As such, Prince Hall lodges in large American cities tended to be ethnically diverse. For instance, African Caribbeans made up as much as a third of the proposed members of the lodge to which Williamson belonged, Carthaginian, No. 47, at a time when, by the best estimates, between 10 and 20 per cent of Brooklyn's black population was foreign-born.[13] Most, if not all, of the African Caribbeans in Carthaginian were from the British colonies and therefore English was their native language. In 1881, the Grand Lodge of New York issued a warrant to El Sol de Cuba, No. 38 in Manhattan. El Sol de Cuba was the initiative of Afro-Cuban Masons in New York who wanted to establish a lodge whose work 'could be conducted in the Spanish language'. El Sol de Cuba consisted primarily of Cuban and Puerto Rican émigrés who were fleeing the 'persecution by the Spanish authorities' on their home island. Due to the decrease of immigration from Cuba and Puerto Rico following the Spanish-American War in 1898, the lodge's membership increasingly became one whose native language was English. Consequently, the name of the lodge was changed to Prince Hall, No. 38 in 1914.[14]

Prince Hall's inclusiveness stretched beyond ethnicity and language. In the late 1920s, Puerto Rican and Cuban Masons who had immigrated to New York City established an interracial lodge, Hijos del Caribe, the members of which were sarcastically described 'as ranging in all shades of complexions – "from white as snow to two shades darker than midnight"'. The formation of this lodge, apparently not under the auspices of any North American Masonic governing body, led to the white Grand Lodge of New York's declaration that it was bogus or spurious. White Grand Lodge officials suggested that Hijos del Caribe disassemble and its white members affiliate with the Twenty-third Street Lodge, leaving the black members to join various Prince Hall lodges. Brothers of Hijos del Caribe flatly rejected this proposal and '[a] decision was unanimously reached to remain intact and stand uncompromisingly against the injection of the color issue and separation'. In December 1929, the lodge applied for a dispensation from the Prince Hall Grand Lodge of New York.[15] While it would be an exaggeration to suggest that the members of Hijos del Caribe who claimed European descent in their home islands assumed another ethnic identity through their membership in Prince Hall, their repudiation of the white Grand Lodge's proposal was clearly a rejection of the 'bi-racialist' logic of the dominant culture.[16]

Freemasonry in Africa took on a somewhat different cast than black Freemasonry in the western hemisphere, both in its proliferation and in the composition of its lodges. Outside of South Africa, Prince Hall did not have an official presence on the continent in the early twentieth century. Prince Hall Freemasons, however, were present in western Africa as early as the 1820s. For instance, Hiram Lodge, No. 3, in Providence, Rhode Island, became dormant for nearly a decade and a half because most of its members were among the initial wave of settlers to Liberia in 1822. In a pamphlet celebrating the centennial of the republic's independence, Liberian Masons pointed out that among the pioneers 'were a few who were craftsmen, hailing from coloured Lodges in the United States of America, working under the Prince Hall Grand Lodge Constitution of Boston, Massacheuttes [*sic*], U.S.A.'. Because of the hardships of settlement, however, these men 'deferred any formal setting up of Craft Masonry as such among their co-settlers'. Four decades would pass before Liberia had a Grand Lodge, one that was self-created outside of the auspices of any other existing Grand Lodges. As such, although Liberian Masons had relations with Prince Hall Freemasons, they were not under their jurisdiction.[17] Freemasonry made significant inroads into Africa in other ways. Agents of British colonialism – administrators, junior civil servants and army officers – established Masonic lodges in Sierra Leone throughout the nineteenth and twentieth centuries. Freemasonry existed in the Gold Coast as early as 1736. In the 1870s, British merchants, missionaries and army officers founded various Masonic organisations and similar fraternities in the Gold Coast, including the Masonic Club and the Good Templars. By the turn of the century, there were two lodges, Gold Coast, No. 773 and Victoria, No. 2392 in Accra.[18]

The ethnic composition of Masonic lodges and the degree of inter-action between black and white Masons in British West Africa also varied somewhat from black Masonic lodges in the United States. Prince Hall lodges reflected an ethnic diversity that was, in part, the product of biased non-recognition policies of white American Masons. In contrast,

Freemasonry among blacks in Sierra Leone was characterised by a certain ethnic exclusivity. Most of the Freemasons in Sierra Leone were Creoles, or descendants of liberated slaves and voluntary settlers who arrived in the British colony in the late eighteenth and early nineteenth centuries. As Abner Cohen argues, membership in Masonic lodges was one of the ways in which Creoles developed, and sustained, an 'elite culture' that separated them from the indigenous population of Sierra Leone. While there was certainly cooperation between Creole and white Masons in Sierra Leone, the Craft was dominated by Creoles by the twentieth century.[19]

From all indications, Freemasonry in the Gold Coast was more ethnically *and* racially integrated. Many lodges in the Gold Coast included African, European, Lebanese and Syrian members. The lodge with which Abadu-Bentsi affiliated while he was in Kumasi – the inland commercial entrepôt and administrative centre – counted among its members whites, blacks and Syrians. 'I have seen group photo of both White [and] Black when the Ashanti Chapter was founded', Abadu-Bentsi wrote to Williamson. 'The Blacks were some of the Brothers or Companions who formed its founders, as there were not sufficient white brothers here to carry it on'.[20] Abadu-Bentsi was most likely referring to Lodge Morality, No. 1362, which was founded in the summer of 1928 and consecrated in December of the following year. The observation expressed by Abadu-Bentsi is reinforced by the ceremonial programme of the lodge's consecration, in which names such as T. Biney Amissah, J. Evans Appiah, and J. A. G. Ansaah are alongside names such as J. O'Neil Cromwell, A. Martin Gottfried, and Johannes Welsing in the list of the lodge's founders. Moreover, Abadu-Bentsi handwrote 'Syrian' next to the names of three people who were listed among the lodge's 'Foundation Members', most likely the first individuals to be initiated into the lodge.[21]

Regardless of whether the Ashanti chapter to which Abadu-Bentsi referred and Lodge Morality were the same, the interracial and interethnic character of Freemason lodges and the interaction of white, black and Middle Eastern Masons in the Gold Coast is clear. Abadu-Bentsi, for instance, informed Williamson that the five lodges in Accra, some of which were racially exclusive and some of which were multiracial, all shared the same temple. Indeed, class and status were equal, if not greater, determinants of the composition of lodges. Comparing the racial politics of Freemasonry in the Gold Coast to that of the United States, Abadu-Bentsi pointed to the existence of class-based, rather than solely race-based, stratification among Gold Coast Masons. 'We are not badly placed as [far as] the Masonic Fraternity is concerned', he wrote, referring to Africans within the Craft. 'One has the right to visit any of the sister Lodges, except the Three-Pillar lodge in Accra which is solely for the high officials in the government Service, reckoning from the Governor of the

Gold Coast to those who are receiving not less than thousand pounds a year as salary and some well to do white merchants, but never black'. He went on to inform Williamson that 'some of the whites even are not granted admission'.[22] Although Africans may have held visitation rights, by the second decade of the twentieth century, lodges in the major urban areas – particularly on the coast – tended to be racially segregated in terms of their membership. According to Augustus Casely-Hayford and Richard Rathbone, this may have been the result of increasing competition between African and European merchants and the hardening of the power relationships that inhered in colonial administration.[23] The élitist policies of the Three-Pillar Lodge and the growing segregation of lodges in general notwithstanding, Freemasonry offered educated Africans – as it also did for blacks in the West – one venue through which to lay claim to, and perform, a putative middle-class status.

Throughout the late nineteenth and early twentieth centuries, the indigenous middle class in British West Africa was largely made up of Western-educated African professionals. Denied access to the entrepreneurial route to middle-class status through prohibitive colonial trade policies, discriminatory employment and promotion practices by European firms, and the presence of Lebanese and Syrian trading communities, African opportunities for social mobility were limited to the professional fields of law, medicine and journalism and employment in the civil service. This educated élite, which did include some entrepreneurs but was dominated by professionals, was concentrated in the coastal cities of Accra and Cape Coast and their surrounding areas. By the 1920s, this professional élite was augmented by the emergence of an educated class of Africans who could not claim an élite status but who, nonetheless, identified with the bourgeois bearings of Western culture. Facilitated by urbanisation and the need, on the part of the British, for the existence of an indigenous work force that would oil the wheels of the colonial bureaucratic machinery, this new 'social class', according to scholar Stephanie Newell, consisted of 'low-ranking civil servants, and also … merchants' clerks and mining clerks, catechists, cocoa-brokers, primary school teachers, and other members of the "white-collar" workforce, few of whom possessed the capital to trade or travel to Europe for professional training'.[24]

Abadu-Bentsi fell squarely within this emergent middle class. Born in 1893 in the Accra area, he either attended a missionary or government school as a child. His formalised education did not go beyond the primary level. However, Abadu-Bentsi continued to educate himself. 'My chief Studies are Comparative Religion, Science (both academic [and] occult) Philosophy [and] Literature', he wrote in his first letter to Williamson. 'I have not had any personal tution [*sic*] in these Subjects. I am trying to do the best I can with books I can get on the market [and] a[t] times by correspondence school'.[25] Although it is not clear what Abadu-Bentsi's occupation was at the time he was initiated in Victoria Lodge, No. 2392, he was most likely a primary school teacher. He eventually moved to Kumasi where he did teach although, again, it is not clear whether he taught at a mission or government school. Apparently, a majority of the members of Lodge Morality in Kumasi were teachers. The lodge also included other members of the emergent new middle class. According to agendas of lodge meetings in 1930, initiates and prospective initiates included a political clerk, a mercantile clerk, a reverend and a storekeeper.[26]

In *Literary Culture in Colonial Ghana: 'How to Play the Game of Life'*, Stephanie Newell maps the 'paracolonial networks' that constituted the collective identity of this new class. One of the ways in which members of this educated, semi-professional strata established 'their visibility and legitimacy' was through the formation of an associational life that included mutual aid and benevolent societies and literary and debating clubs. Moreover, these networks consisted almost exclusively of men. Within the literary clubs, especially, Western-educated African men engaged in intellectual exchanges that circulated and reinforced Western, bourgeois gender conventions regarding the assertion of manliness within the public sphere and the private world of feminine domesticity. These ideals of manliness were predicated on the models of manhood imported by missionary educators that placed an emphasis on industry, thrift, regularity and literacy.[27] Membership in Masonic lodges undoubtedly gave some credibility to their claims to middle-class status as well, a status that relied on the performance of appropriate models of manhood as much as anything else. What I want to suggest with the remainder of this article is that the 'paracolonial networks' of Freemasonry provided men of African descent, whose middle-class status – in terms of objective determinants such as occupation and income – was tenuous at best, a space in which to articulate a male subjectivity along the lines of the Western bourgeoisie. At the same time, the diasporic relationships that emerged out of the transatlantic links of Freemasonry allowed these men to articulate a gendered subjectivity that became self-consciously racialised.

Freemasonry facilitated the gender identity formation of middle-class men in a number of ways. Structurally, Freemasons belonged to associations that derived their collective sense of manliness as much from the absence – or, in the case of female auxiliaries, the subordinate positioning – of women as from the fraternal tradition's network of homosocial relationships. That corporate gender identity was rhetorically and performatively re-inscribed through the pervasive symbolism of the artisan in the Craft's ideology, myths and rituals, and the conceptualisation of the lodge as male space. On a more practical level, Freemasons existed within a web of social relationships that gave them an opportunity to experience upward mobility through the political and business contacts that the fraternal order nurtured. All of this was premised upon, and tied together through, a gendered ideology that equated manhood and production.

Because of the emphasis placed on the role of esoteric knowledge in shaping the lives and characters of men, Freemasons were loath to foreground the material advantages of belonging to the Craft. Masons tended to regard with some scepticism prospective initiates whose main goal in joining the Order, they felt, was to establish business and professional contacts.[28] Still, in addition to the provision of mutual aid and material support for families of deceased members, lodges provided networking opportunities for motivated men. It was somewhat common, at least in the case of Carthaginian, No. 47 in Brooklyn, for entrepreneurial members to solicit the patronage of their brethren or for members to request reference letters for employment. As Cohen argues in the case of Sierra Leone, there was a tight correlation between lodge membership and the civil service and professional élite and, indeed, one of the criticisms levelled by non-Masons was that 'all appointments and promotions in certain establishments are "cooked" in the lodges'.[29] This networking element of Freemasonry characterised much of the five-year long correspondence between Abadu-Bentsi and Williamson.

At the time that Abadu-Bentsi and Williamson began writing to one another, the former was a thirty-six year old husband and father of four children. Although he had been a teacher in Kumasi in the early 1920s, it is likely that he was unemployed in 1930. Like practically everywhere else, the Gold Coast was hit hard by the global depression of the early 1930s. The drastic decline in the price of cacao, and the concomitant decrease in government revenue that was generated from duties associated with the cacao trade, sent the Gold Coast into the economic doldrums. Without a substitute source of revenue, the colonial government was forced to make significant cuts in spending. Education was hit particularly hard. Teachers lost their jobs or had their salaries scaled back significantly and the teacher-training programmes within the colony experienced contraction.[30] Given that Abadu-Bentsi was a member of the emergent middle class that subscribed to Western, bourgeois gender conventions of masculine provider-hood and feminine domesticity, the economic uncertainty that accompanied the depression most likely adversely affected his sense of himself as a husband, a father, and a man. Abadu-Bentsi sought to exploit his fraternal relationship to Williamson to improve his employment and financial situation and, thus, claim a status as a provider for his family.[31]

Initially, Abadu-Bentsi expressed interest in furthering his studies in the United States and sought Williamson's assistance. His desire to study in the States was, in part, motivated by his familiarity with the experience of his 'late beloved countryman', Dr J. E. K. Aggrey, the famous Ghanaian educator who studied and taught at Livingstone College in North Carolina. But Abadu-Bentsi's desire was also the result of disillusionment with the colonial education system. In one of his first letters to Williamson, he delivered a subtle yet trenchant critique of colonialism that would characterise most of his letters. To his mind, the colonial education system was derelict in providing Gold Coast children the knowledge and skills necessary to enter the middle class. 'Education was brought to us here in order that we might be used as machines for the advantage of our white friends', he wrote to Williamson. 'Now that they have seen that we are doing more than they expected, the standard of education in our elementary school is lowered to such a pitch that boys and girls being turned out of School these days are good-for-nothing, as clerical matters are concerned'. He further criticised the top higher-education institution in the colony, Achimota College, as a conspiratorial effort on the part of the British to stem the flow of Africans seeking entry to universities in England.[32] Williamson was less than enthusiastic about trying to help Abadu-Bentsi, more out of a concern for his well-being than anything else. He informed his new friend that given the state of the economy, the United States was not an ideal destination, particularly for blacks. 'I sincerely regret I am unable to favor such a proposition at this time', he responded to Abadu-Bentsi's request, 'because of the great economic depression existing all over the country and the hundreds of thousand[s] of persons who are out of employment, together with a movement to give preference in employ-ment to natives in place of foreigners'. Williamson warned Abadu-Bentsi that, given that 'most of our people in the large northern cities are employees rather than employers' in addition to the wage disparity between whites and non-whites, it would be hard for the Gold Coaster to make a living wage for himself, much less enough money to support his family. Williamson suggested that if he was determined to make it to the United States that he come alone, try to establish himself, and then send for his family.[33]

Abadu-Bentsi did not make it across the Atlantic. It would have been difficult, if not impossible, for someone who had so little disposable in-come that he occasionally could not afford to buy postage, not to mention the barriers presented by American immigration policy. Sometime between August 1930 and March 1931, Abadu-Bentsi moved to Cape Coast – the former capital and, along with Accra and Sekondi, one of the Gold Coast's major urban areas. He indicated in a letter to Williamson that due to the depression, he left Kumasi 'penniless'. It is not clear what brought him to Cape Coast. He might have secured another teaching position as his return address was in the care of a D. Jackson Davies, Esq., at St. Nicholas Grammar School. In any event, shortly after arriving in Cape Coast, Abadu-Bentsi decided to go into business for himself. If he could 'only get few pence as capital', he informed Williamson, he wanted to go into farming – primarily poultry – and palm oil-based soap manufacture. As in his letter to Williamson requesting assistance to come to the United States for educational purposes, Abadu-Bentsi framed his entrepreneurial desire in the context of colonial economic exploitation. 'Our position is too bad to talk of', he wrote. 'It requires an open-minded African to tell you of our present standing. Almost everything we are using here all come to us from foreign lands with exception of food stuff ... We are absolutely dependent on the Europeans. We cannot manufacture anything worthy of the name'. He chalked up this dependence to the fact that the British did not encourage the development of indigenous industries or educational training that would foster such development. 'And the reason for not allowing them', he wrote, referring to industrial schools, 'is we will be taught how to make use of our own raw products and other things which will close down some of the English commercial [and] manufacturing houses. They want to have us in subjection as long as they reign over us'. Abadu-Bentsi wanted to counter this dependency by engaging in agricultural and industrial production and sought Williamson's assistance in obtaining literature on poultry farming and soap making.[34] For his part, Williamson supported Abadu-Bentsi's entrepreneurial efforts and did so not only as a fellow Mason but as a fellow diasporic subject. 'It is a very sad story you write about the conditions of the natives in your country', he wrote to Abadu-Bentsi. 'The only way out appears to be the method adopted by you in obtaining the necessary information from race brethren in other countries, to enable the African to learn of the up-to-date methods in business in foreign countries. To follow up such methods will be the only salvation in view'.[35]

Abadu-Bentsi's attempt to improve his and his family's financial situation through agricultural production and manufacturing was unsuccessful. It is unclear how much work he actually put into his new venture for there is nearly a three-year gap in the record of correspondence between the two. Abadu-Bentsi wrote a brief letter to Williamson in January 1932 in which he did not mention anything related to farming or soap making. The next letter from Abadu-Bentsi in Williamson's personal correspondence is dated 27 December 1934. At that point, Abadu-Bentsi was in Monrovia, Liberia. He indicated that he had left Kumasi in September 1934, which suggests that at some point between January 1932 and September 1934, he decided to give up his plan to farm and make soap out of palm oil in order to go back to teaching. Abadu-Bentsi arrived in Monrovia alone. He felt 'obliged to leave the poor kiddies behind until such time that I should find a foothold in this country'. His plan was to find a teaching job in one of the mission schools. By April 1935, he was teaching at St. Thomas School in the Krutown area of Monrovia.[36]

Having never been to Liberia, Abadu-Bentsi's Freemason membership undoubtedly gave him advantages that other non-Mason immigrants did not have. He knew practically no one in Monrovia – only a few students that he had taught while in Kumasi – but he visited one of the local temples on St. John's Day, one of the high holy days in Freemasonry, in order to establish contacts with the Monrovian middle class. Abadu-Bentsi also met Dr. Nathaniel Cassell, the former president of Liberia College and the Past Master of the Grand Lodge of Liberia, fairly soon after arriving in Monrovia. It is possible that Williamson facilitated the initial contact, as Williamson and Cassell had known each other since the latter came to the United States on a tour with the Liberian president, C. D. B. King, in 1919. Abadu-Bentsi might also have met Cassell in church, in which case all he would have to do is indicate – through a handshake or the simple pin on the lapel – that he was also a Mason. It is unlikely, however, that this was the scenario given that he also had the chance to meet King in this manner and failed to do so. 'Bro. King, ex President of this country', he informed Williamson, 'though I have seen him several times in church, I have not as yet have [*sic*] the occasion of meeting him as a brother'. It is clear that Abadu-Bentsi did not meet Cassell by visiting the latter's lodge. 'I have not visited the Lodge here since my arrival', he further wrote to Williamson, 'though Dr. Cassell has been asking me several times to do so. I hear the people in this country have quite peculiar ways of going about everything they do and one has to go slowly at things'.[37]

Regardless of how Abadu-Bentsi met the acquaintance of Cassell, Williamson sought to serve as a broker between the two men. Williamson wrote to Cassell in the summer of 1935, most likely inquiring if there was anything Cassell could do to help Abadu-Bentsi in his career. Cassell responded that there was little he could do. 'He is engaged in teaching as he informed you', Cassell said of Abadu-Bentsi:

> however, under some disadvantages, it not affording him an income of any size. In fact, teaching at no time in Liberia has brought much of an income, indeed, like the Minister of the Gospel, it has been a kind of salary, causing one to live from hand to mouth, especially has that been the case since the depression, the depression fell very hard on Liberia. I am rather sorry for the brother, but am not in a position to help him to do better. He has not complained as I know of, yet I happen to be in the secret of the fact that his service at teaching is not bringing him a living wage.[38]

In addition to requesting Cassell's assistance on behalf of Abadu-Bentsi, Williamson suggested that the young teacher contact the incoming African American US ambassador to Liberia, Lester A. Walton. Williamson offered to facilitate this introduction as Walton was an 'old friend' and a Mason. Although Walton was no longer 'an active member of the Craft',

Williamson clearly believed that he would assist a fellow Mason in any way that was within his capacity.[39]

Unfortunately, we do not know whether Abadu-Bentsi was able to benefit from Walton's acquaintance. Indeed, we do not know what came of the remainder of Abadu-Bentsi's stay in Liberia, for the correspondence between him and Williamson stopped in the fall of 1935 – or at least there is no record of correspondence beyond this point. The outcome of Williamson and Abadu-Bentsi's relationship – that is, whether or not Abadu-Bentsi was able to materially benefit from the fraternal connection he made with Williamson – is less important than what the relationship represented and how it functioned. Thrown into economic instability by the Great Depression, Abadu-Bentsi availed himself of his membership in an august organisation with a global reach to attempt to travel to the United States for further education and, that having failed, obtain assistance in his career as a teacher and entrepreneur in Africa. Masonic affiliation allowed the sporadically employed teacher to rub elbows with the Liberian élite, including government officials such as the former president and secretary of state of the country. This is not surprising, given that Freemasons typically used the networking capacity of the Order to socially and economically advance themselves.[40] Williamson's mediation of Abadu-Bentsi's networking gave this particular aspect of Freemasonry a diasporic dimension.

Abadu-Bentsi's attempts to exploit the relationships that emerged out of his involvement in the Craft illustrate the ways in which his status as a Freemason informed his gender identity. As the depression made it more difficult for Abadu-Bentsi to occupy the position of breadwinner for his family, his relationship with other Freemasons, especially Williamson, became instrumental in his efforts to secure a living, and a family, wage. Of course, in addition to his identity as a breadwinner being compromised by the economic exigencies of the time, Abadu-Bentsi's sense of his own manhood was probably also militated against by the larger socio-historical meanings of marriage and women's economic agency in colonial Ghana.[41] There is simply not enough information about his family in Abadu-Bentsi's correspondence to speak authoritatively on this issue. However, it is reasonable to infer that his involvement in Freemasonry – which was fundamentally tied to the temperance movement in the Gold Coast – contributed to a conceptualisation of self that revolved around an equation of masculinity with production and femininity with domesticity.[42] Shortly after their correspondence began, for instance, Abadu-Bentsi expressed gratitude for a copy of the 'Prince Hall Primer' Williamson had sent to him. In that same letter, he voiced the desire to receive more material that would deepen his education about Masonry and about his role in the public sphere of production. 'I shall be thankful for anything that will come from you', he wrote, 'that may be of help to me as a Mason and man of the busy world'.[43] As Abadu-Bentsi's statement of appreciation suggests, he associated his identity as a Freemason with an aspirational identity as a productive participant in the marketplace. While this was articulated through his efforts to utilise the business and professional networks of the Craft, it was reinforced by the discursive and performative conflation of manhood and production in the rhetoric, prescriptions, and rituals of Freemasonry.

Within the homosocial space of the lodge room, Freemasons engaged in a number of activities that consolidated their identities as members of the Order and as middle-class men. Masons attended regular meetings in which they voted to accept or reject applicants, initiated new members, imparted the secrets of the Craft to existing members, and raised their worthy brothers to higher degrees. These rituals were bound up in, and reinforced, producerist models of manhood. The first three degrees, collect-ively known as the Blue Lodge degrees, were figurative representations of the various stages of the working life of an artisan. New Masons were initiated into the Craft as Earned Apprentices. Possessors of the second degree were called Fellow Craftsmen while those who were raised to the third degree became Master Masons. Upon initiation, Earned Apprentices received a leather or lambskin apron, an indispensable part of the artisan's uniform. As they advanced to higher degrees, their aprons were embellished with various insignia, they were presented with the 'working tools' appropriate to the degree, and learned different passwords that solidified their position within the hierarchy of the Order.

But it was not merely the symbolic association with the artisan that underpinned the producerist model of manhood to which Freemasons adhered. The commitment to the producer values of industry, thrift, regu-larity, abstemiousness and the public display of those values – respectability – were constituent elements of the collective male subjectivity that Freemasonry cultivated. Producer values and respectability structured the criteria for determining who could become a member and who moved up the ladder of organisational leadership. An individual had to exhibit these qualities before he could hope to become a lodge officer, especially the Worshipful Master, the highest position of authority on both the local and supra-local levels. The Worshipful Master 'should be punctual and methodical in all things', one Mason wrote, 'and, both by his character and conduct command the respect, the esteem and good will of all men, for as Master is supreme in his Lodge, and distinguished by his position in the Craft, so should he also be distinguished as the possessor of an irreproachable character, a dignified demeanor, an expanded intellect, and a liberal education'.[44]

In addition to regularity, industry, intelligence, and, in general, overall character, temperance was considered a critical component of manliness.

The charge to the Junior Warden, third in line behind the Worshipful Master and Senior Warden, outlined by the Grand Lodge of Arkansas, for instance, included the following instruction: 'To you is committed the superintendence of the craft during the hours of refreshment. It is therefore indispensably necessary that you should not only be temperate and discreet in the indulgence of your own inclinations, but carefully observe that none of the craft be suffered to convert the purpose of refreshment into intemperance and excess'.[45] Moderation was the watchword of Masons. Indeed, while some Masonic lodges tolerated moderate use of alcohol during the period of refreshment, others sought to banish it completely from their midst. In 1890, for instance, the Grand Lodge of Illinois prohibited subordinate lodges from initiating any men who owned establishments serving liquor.[46]

The dearth of evidence with respect to the internal workings of lodges in Africa makes it difficult to determine whether Africans and European colonials placed a similar emphasis on temperance. There is evidence, however, that there were strong links between Masonic lodges and temperance societies in the Gold Coast in the late nineteenth and early twentieth centuries. Moreover, like membership in Freemasonry, 'to join the temperance movement was an indication of social mobility' because of its association with 'social progress' and 'modernity'.[47]

Although less is known about the dynamics of Freemasonry in Africa, it is clear that the rituals associated with craftsmanship, the relationship between Masons and temperance advocates, and the more practical function of the lodge as a network for the professional élite and the emergent middle class represented the ethos of production as a central organising principle in the gender identity formation of African Masons. This was a shared ethos among Masons of all racial, ethnic and national backgrounds. With the remainder of this article, I shall explore how this universally shared ethos – or group consciousness – facilitated the development of another, more racialised group consciousness.

Over the course of their correspondence, Williamson and Abadu-Bentsi engaged in a series of conversations that shared their attitudes about the racial politics of their respective societies, and, in the process, formed a relationship that was guided as much by their common racial positions as it was guided by their common ties to a fraternal tradition. Thus, the shared sense of belonging that these men felt as Freemasons facilitated a means through which to question and condemn the marginalisation – the opposite of belonging – that they experienced as a result of, in the case of Abadu-Bentsi, colonialism, and, in the case of Williamson, Jim Crow. Through the letters they exchanged, and the supplementary material they enclosed within the letters, Abadu-Bentsi and Williamson educated each other about their respective social environments. In doing so, they engendered a diasporic consciousness in each other.[48]

For instance, Abadu-Bentsi sent Gold Coast newspapers to Williamson that were of a revelatory nature to the older African American. 'The two Coast newspapers reached me', Williamson wrote in the fall of 1930, 'and I found their contents in some instances rather strange but interesting and note the Africans have their racial troubles similar to what we have over here'. This was undoubtedly the intention of the young Gold Coaster. He prefaced one dispatch of issues of local papers with the following statement: 'You will find in the papers am sending today how poorly we are being treated by the whitemen [*sic*]. They style themselves as being civilized but they are worse than the so-called savages'.[49] For his part, Williamson sent Abadu-Bentsi copies of the *National Fraternal Review*, the National Association for the Advancement of Colored People's journal, *The Crisis*, and various black newspapers. As in the case of the African newspapers Williamson received, the material sent from the States was enlightening for Abadu-Bentsi and increasingly solidified his diasporic consciousness. Interestingly, this consciousness positioned African Americans as the 'older siblings', vis-à-vis Africans, in what he perceived to be the global struggle against white supremacy. 'The newspapers which you send me at times are full of interest', Abadu-Bentsi expressed to Williamson. 'They always give me the push to be up and doing. The only people we at this end have got to set before us as example for copying are the American Negroes; because they had passed through or almost through the indignities which we are harbouring now'.[50] As Abadu-Bentsi's observations illustrate, he was developing a critique of colonialism and situating it within a larger history of European and white American injustice toward people of African descent. Much of this critique incorporated essentialist ideas of blackness and whiteness. Furthermore, his racial essentialism was gendered in the sense that it focused on an overly aggressive and morally bankrupt imperial white masculinity.

As his requests of Williamson to assist him in his further education and economic ventures indicate, Abadu-Bentsi's assessment of life in the Gold Coast did not lack a negative appraisal of Britain's imperial presence. Abadu-Bentsi was astutely aware of the political economy of colonialism and his letters to Williamson were replete with keen assessments and criticisms. 'Again, they have got us in their grip because we do not know how to make any war implement', he wrote of the British. 'Nothing on that line is being taught. The commonest things as matches [and] sugar we cannot make them because the process of turning the raw materials into these things are not known to us. We are not being treated as the Romans taught them. We are just like tools in their hands'.[51] Abadu-Bentsi's critical evaluation of colonialism was underpinned by a certain belief in the essential differences between blacks and whites. Europeans and white Americans, he argued, were deceitful, materialistic, power-hungry, and,

as suggested by his comment on the savagery under the veneer of civilisation, hypocritical when it came to religion and morality. 'It is not only
the White Americans who come out here with their prejudices[;] the Europeans do the same particularly the English people with their craftiness.
They are more than wolves in sheep['s] clothings'.[52] His inclusion of
Americans of European descent in his unsympathetic depiction of the
forces of colonialism, reinforced by Williamson's account of Jim Crow in
the United States, marked all whites, in Abadu-Bentsi's estimation, as
inimical to the progress of blacks in Africa as well as the diaspora.

What is interesting about Abadu-Bentsi's collapsing of whiteness, white
people and colonialism is the way in which it took on a gendered cast. In
addition to using the sardonic moniker, 'white friends', Abadu-Bentsi
tended to use the term 'whiteman' or 'whitemen' as a signifier of European
imperialists. This may have been merely his universal use of the male-
gendered subject to stand in for all Europeans. Yet I would argue it was
more than that. Many of the essentialist characteristics he attributed to
whites – duplicity, materialism, aggressiveness – were extreme forms of
the acumen and ambition needed to succeed in the market place. Indeed,
Freemasonry, through its emphasis on character and brotherhood, was
envisioned as the mediation between a producerist manhood and its
evil twin. White Masons on the whole, Abadu-Bentsi felt, failed to live up
to the highest ideals of civilised manliness. In a letter to Williamson, he
compared Tatsch, the progressive white American Mason, with his fellow
white 'brethren' in the colonies. 'The tone of Bro[.] Tatsch's letter seems
to be giving the real man, his very self in words', he wrote. 'One hardly
hears our white friends speaking or writing so favourably of our kind – the
Blacks. His letters speak creditedly [*sic*] of him as a REAL Freemason,
one who does understand Freemasonry not as the nominal Masons one
meets with'.[53] In his criticism of the moral bankruptcy of Europeans,
and specifically the British, then, Abadu-Bentsi juxtaposed the ideals of
manliness as articulated by the doctrine and rituals of Freemasonry –
a manliness that was not only oriented around production but was
characterised by altruism, benevolence and a belief in the equality of man
– against what he perceived to be the reality of an aggressive, overly
acquisitive, racially intolerant imperial white masculinity. Furthermore, in
doing so, he inferred the existence of an oppositional black masculinity
that was more docile, more spiritual.

Along with his reproach of the 'whiteman', Abadu-Bentsi articulated
an essentialist evaluation of the natural spirituality and humanitarianism
of black people. His very assessment of the colonial order and Africans'
place within it reinforced this essentialism. 'My brother', he opined in a
letter to Williamson, 'the average Negro on the whole is [a] loving and
Sympathetic Creature, if it were not so, no whiteman would dare come

to the Gold Coast'. His attitude toward the British presence in the Gold Coast and, consequently, his thoughts on how Africans should relate to it, was deeply informed by a religiously-inspired pacifist sensibility. He pointed to the anti-colonial movement coalescing around Gandhi as a model for Africans and invoked the words of Annie Besant, the English theosophist and reformer, as a guiding principle for Africans under the imperialist thumb of the British: 'If you cannot love your enemies, you can at least stop hating them. This I have quoted merely to give me the courage to wink over the ill-treatment our white friends are always ready to measure to us'. Yet Abadu-Bentsi's apparent comfort with the docility of Africans did not translate into an acceptance of dependence. Rather, his letters to Williamson evinced a nascent nationalist consciousness. This emergent consciousness turned on the distinction he posited between a moral, humanitarian black masculinity and an avaricious, depraved white masculinity. This is perhaps best captured in one of the more nationalist statements Abadu-Bentsi made to Williamson. 'Though Mother Africa has had and [is] still having ill paintings [*sic*], but that cannot make us disloyal or forsake our dear old mother, Africa', he argued. 'She will one day recover her kingdom but for that Kingdom to stand it will require her sons ruling with a loving heart and not the tyrannical heart of our white friends and brothers'.[54]

Abadu-Bentsi's gendering of the continent as feminised space – and the gendering of those who would ultimately liberate it as male – was a tactic that was similar to the rhetoric of African redemption that characterised the nationalism of Marcus Garvey and the Universal Negro Improvement Association. Along with his condemnation of imperialism as a product of an ersatz civilised white manliness, Abadu-Bentsi's expressions of anti-colonialism reflected a masculinist understanding of the power relationships between Europeans and Africans and what would be necessary to disrupt those relationships. In this sense, the ethos of production was more than just an organising principle for his gender identity as an individual and a Mason; it was the organising principle around which people of African descent would liberate themselves.[55] Yet Abadu-Bentsi's version of redemption went beyond merely being able to produce things such as agricultural and industrial goods and 'war implements.' He continued to hew to the idea that black men were the true inheritors, and practitioners, of civilised manliness. In doing so, he elevated the role of spirituality and altruism as constituent values of bourgeois ideals of manhood.

What began as a friendly communication between fraters, the correspondence between D. K. Abadu-Bentsi and Harry A. Williamson eventually developed into a transatlantic dialogue that encompassed not only the esoteric minutiae of Freemasonry, but the weightier topics of colonialism, racism and liberation as well. Several connections linked these two men together. Initially brought together by their membership in a fraternal order that had its origins in early modern Europe, Williamson and Abadu-Bentsi, like scores of thousands of men of all races, ethnicities and nationalities, shared an identity that was rooted in a tradition that celebrated the manly artisan; this tradition held forth productive engagement in the market place and commitment to bourgeois values and respectability as the cornerstones of male character and authority. But the relationship that developed between these two represented much more. While their common membership in the Craft was reflective of their respective efforts to constitute themselves as middle-class subjects, the brotherhood that emerged out of that common membership was productive of an emergent diasporic consciousness. Their shared identity as Free-masons contributed to the maturation of a shared identity as marginalised individuals within a web of social, economic and political structures and relationships that connected Africa, the Americas and Europe. The development of this diasporic consciousness is perhaps best illustrated in a sentiment expressed by Abadu-Bentsi when Williamson informed him that, because of his deteriorating eyesight, he would curtail the scholarly work he was doing on black Masons. 'Your leaving off the Masonic work as you are doing at present', Abadu-Bentsi wrote to his friend:

> will, indeed, be a terrible blow to the fraternity in general and the Negro Mason in particular. Because all whom I have had the honour of corresponding with in America, speak so highly of you and your work as being the outstanding authority in Free-masonry with regard to the Negro Mason in the United States of America. *Where shall we be?*[56]

Abadu-Bentsi's inclusion of himself within the sphere of Prince Hall Freemasonry, given Prince Hall's relative absence on the continent of Africa, is a significant example of how his transatlantic relationship with Williamson contributed to a new articulation of a diasporic identity.

Abadu-Bentsi and Williamson's correspondence offers scholars a way of thinking about the formation of diaspora community and diasporic identity. To the extent that the formation of diasporic identity is a dynamic, ongoing process, as Paul Gilroy and others have argued, recognising its fluidity allows us to situate it alongside other dynamic processes of identity formation, including class and gender identities.[57] What the relationship between Williamson and Abadu-Bentsi suggests is that the formation of diasporic, class and gender subjectivities are mutually constitutive. Addition-ally, as study of the dispersal of peoples from the African continent and the far-flung communities that emerged out of that dispersal continues to consume significant amounts of energy within academic circles, we need to examine how the interrelatedness of these processes of identity formation is riddled with tensions and contradictions. In the case of Abadu-Bentsi and Williamson, I have tried to show how one group consciousness based on a European cultural form facilitated the development of another group consciousness grounded in its exteriority to Europe (and white America). Yet both of these collective identities were circumscribed by gender and class. In this sense, the diasporic consciousness that was nurtured through the correspondence between an African and an African American Mason re-inscribed class and gender boundaries even as it laid the potential groundwork for more progressive and collective social action.[58]

Notes

Versions of this article were delivered at the Hobart and William Smith Colleges' Fisher Center for the Study of Women and Men and the Baobab Series at the University of Oregon. I wish to thank those who commented on the paper in those venues – especially Laura Fair, Anthony Foy, Dennis Galvan, Jim Mohr, Lisa Wolverton, and Stephen Wooten – and the anonymous readers for *Gender and History*.

1. Imanuel Geiss, *The Pan African Movement*, trans. Ann Keep (London: Methuen, 1974); Sandy D. Martin, *Black Baptists and African Missions: The Origins of a Movement, 1880–1915* (Macon: Mercer, 1989); James T. Campbell, *Songs of Zion: The African Methodist Episcopal Church in the United States and South Africa* (Chapel Hill: University of North Carolina Press, 1998); Penny Von Eschen, *Race Against Empire: Black Americans and Anticolonialism, 1937–1957* (Ithaca: Cornell University Press, 1997); James H. Meriwether, *Proudly We Can Be Africans: Black Americans and Africa, 1935–1961* (Chapel Hill: University of North Carolina Press, 2002).
2. D. K. Abadu-Bentsi to Harry A. Williamson, 3 March 1930, box 8, fol. 5; Harry A. Williamson, *The Story of Carthaginian Lodge No. 47, F. & A. M.* (Brooklyn: The Carthaginian Study Club, 1949), Printed Material, New York. Both in Harry A. Williamson Collection on Negro Masonry, Schomburg Center for Research in Black Culture, New York Public Library, New York.
3. Steven C. Bullock, *Revolutionary Brotherhood: Freemasonry and the Transformation of the American Social Order, 1730–1840* (Chapel Hill: University of North Carolina Press, 1996), pp. 9–15; Mark C. Carnes, *Secret Ritual and Manhood in Victorian America* (New Haven: Yale University Press, 1989), p. 24; William A. Muraskin, *Middle-class Blacks in a White Society: Prince Hall Freemasonry in America* (Berkeley: University of California Press, 1975), pp. 19–20; Lynn Dumenil, *Freemasonry and American Culture, 1880–1930* (Princeton NJ: Princeton University Press, 1984), pp. xii–xiii.
4. Carnes, *Secret Ritual and Manhood*; Mary Ann Clawson, *Constructing Brotherhood: Class, Gender and Fraternalism* (Princeton NJ: Princeton University Press, 1989); William D. Moore, 'Structures of Masculinity: Masonic Temples, Material Culture, and Ritual Gender Archetypes in New York State, 1870–1930', (Ph.D dissertation, Boston University, 1999). For gendered studies of Freemasonry among African Americans, see Craig Steven Wilder, *In the Company of Black Men: The African Influence on African American Culture in New York City* (New York: New York University Press, 2001); Maurice Wallace, '"Are We Men?" Prince Hall, Martin Delany, and the Masculine Ideal in Black Freemasonry, 1775–1865', in *Constructing the Black Masculine: Identity and Ideality in African American Men's Literature and Culture, 1775–1995* (Durham: Duke University Press, 2002), pp. 53–81; Martin Summers, *Manliness and Its Discontents: The Black Middle Class and the Transformation of Masculinity, 1900–1930* (Chapel Hill: University of North Carolina Press, 2004). On Freemasonry outside of a strictly European and/or white American frame, see Augustus Casely-Hayford and Richard Rathbone, 'Politics, Families and Freemasonry in the Colonial Gold Coast', in

People and Empires in African History: Essays in Memory of Michael Crowder, eds. J. F. Ade Ajayi and J. D. Y. Peel, pp. 143–60 (London and New York: Longman, 1992); Abner Cohen's work on Sierra Leone: *The Politics of Elite Culture: Explorations in the Dramaturgy of Power in a Modern Society* (Berkeley: University of California Press, 1981) and 'The Politics of Ritual Secrecy', *Man* 6:3 (1971), pp. 427–48. Also see Jesse Hoffnung-Garskof, 'The Migrations of Arturo Schomburg: On Being *Antillano*, Negro, and Puerto Rican in New York, 1891–1938', *Journal of American Ethnic History* 21 (2001), pp. 3–49; Valid J. Fozdar, 'Constructing the "Brother": Freemasonry, Empire, and Nationalism in India, 1840–1925', (Ph.D dissertation, University of California, 2001); Frank K. Karpiel, 'Mystic Ties of Brotherhood: Freemasonry, Royalty and Ritual in Hawai'i, 1843–1910', (Ph.D dissertation, University of Hawaii, 1998).

5. Clawson, *Constructing Brotherhood*, p. 11.
6. Emmanuel Akyeampong, 'Africans in the Diaspora: The Diaspora and Africa', *African Affairs* 99 (2000), p. 186. Also see Sidney Lemelle and Robin D. G. Kelley, 'Imagining Home: Pan-Africanism Revisited', in *Imagining Home: Class, Culture and Nationalism in the African Diaspora,* ed. Lemelle and Kelley (London: Verso, 1994), pp. 1–16; Barbara Bair, 'Pan-Africanism as Process: Adelaide Casely Hayford, Garveyism, and the Cultural Roots of Nationalism', in *Imagining Home*, pp. 121–44; Robin D. G. Kelley, 'How the West Was One: On the Uses and Limitations of Diaspora', *Black Scholar* 30 (2000), pp. 31–5.
7. Williamson to Abadu-Bentsi, 17 December 1929, Williamson Collection, box 8, fol. 5.
8. The history of Hall as a free, mixed-race Barbadian, first put into circulation by William Grimshaw, was later debunked by Charles Wesley. See Grimshaw, *Official History of Freemasonry Among the Colored People in North America* (1903; reprint, New York: Negro Universities Press, 1969), pp. 69–72; Wesley, *Prince Hall: Life and Legacy* (Washington DC: United Supreme Council, Southern Jurisdiction, Prince Hall Affiliation, 1977), pp. 34–5.

    I use the term 'father' of black Freemasonry somewhat hesitantly. Prince Hall Freemasonry cannot be reduced to black Freemasonry since many Masons of African descent, particularly outside of the United States, did not belong to Prince Hall lodges. Still, as we will see, there was a conflation of Prince Hall Freemasonry and black Masonry within the minds of not only blacks but whites as well.
9. Harry E. Davis, *A History of Freemasonry Among Negroes in America* (Charles T. Powner, 1946), pp. 21–39; Grimshaw, *Official History*, pp. 69–72, 84–6, 90; Wesley, *Prince Hall*, pp. 27–43.
10. Davis, *History of Freemasonry Among Negroes*, pp. 73–5, 94–7.
11. Grimshaw, *Official History*, pp. 336–42; Davis, *History of Freemasonry Among Negroes*, pp. 166–7, 218–20. For an excellent discussion of the role of sailors in the formation of diasporic consciousness, see W. Jeffrey Bolster, *Black Jacks: African American Seamen in the Age of Sail* (Cambridge MA: Harvard University Press, 1997).
12. Loretta J. Williams, *Black Freemasonry and Middle-Class Realities* (Columbia: University of Missouri Press, 1980), p. 44; 'Review of the Subordinate Lodge Reports of the M. W. Grand Lodge of the State of New York for 1912 and 1913', in Minutes of the Grand Lodge, June 1913, Williamson Collection, Masonic Records, vol. 2; Davis, *History of Freemasonry Among Negroes*, pp. 80–1.
13. 'Negro Masons Eager to Aid in Fight on Frauds', *New York World*, 13 June 1925, in Williamson Collection, clipping file. The statistics regarding Carthaginian are drawn from Hall of Carthaginian Record Book, 1904–1930, Williamson Collection, Masonic Records, vols. 1–6. The statistics on the foreign-born black population in Brooklyn cover the period between 1910 and 1930 and are drawn from Craig Steven Wilder, *A Covenant With Color: Race and Social Power in Brooklyn* (New York: Columbia University Press, 2000), p. 125; Harold X. Connolly, *A Ghetto Grows in Brooklyn* (New York: New York University Press, 1977).
14. 'History of Prince Hall Lodge No. 38', *Seventy-fifth Anniversary of Prince Hall Lodge, No. 38, F. & A. M. P. H.*, souvenir program, 4 November 1956; Harry A. Williamson, 'Arthur A. Schomburg: The Freemason', typescript, 13 March 1941. Both in Williamson Collection, Printed Material-New York. For a more detailed discussion of El Sol de Cuba lodge, see Hoffnung-Garskof, 'The Migrations of Arturo Schomburg', pp. 29–32.

15. 'Lodge Problem of Color Settled', *The World*, 22 June 1930, in Williamson Collection, clipping file; 'Report of Special Deputy Grand Master for Hijos del Caribe, U.D.', *Eighty-fifth Annual Session Proceedings of the Most Worshipful Grand Lodge of the Most Ancient and Honorable Fraternity of Free and Accepted Masons Prince Hall of the State of New York For the Year 1930*, 53–4, Williamson Collection, Printed Material-New York.

16. On 'bi-racialist' thought and the logic of 'race as color' in the early twentieth century, see Matthew Pratt Guterl, *The Color of Race in America, 1900–1940* (Cambridge MA: Harvard University Press, 2001).

17. Davis, *History of Freemasonry Among Negroes*, pp. 83–4; 'A Brochure Issued Under the Authority of the Most Worshipful Grand Lodge of Masons, Republic of Liberia, Commemorative of the One Hundredth Year of the Independence of the Republic of Liberia, 1847–1947', in Williamson Collection, Printed Material, box 19, fol. 2.

18. Cohen, *Politics of Elite Culture*, p. 154; Cohen, 'Politics of Ritual Secrecy', p. 429; Casely-Hayford and Rathbone, 'Freemasonry in the Colonial Gold Coast', pp. 146–7; David Kimble, *A Political History of Ghana: The Rise of Gold Coast Nationalism, 1850–1928* (Oxford: Oxford University Press, 1963); J. B. Anaman, *The Gold Coast Guide* (London: Christian Herald, 1902), pp. 135–6.

19. Cohen, *Politics of Elite Culture*, esp. pp. 89–125; Cohen, 'Politics of Ritual Secrecy', p. 429.

20. Abadu-Bentsi to Williamson, 26 May 1930, Williamson Collection, box 8, fol. 5.

21. Lodge Morality No. 1362, S.C., Kumasi, Ashanti, Gold Coast, 'Programme of the Erection, Consecration & First Installation Meeting', 20 December 1929, in Williamson Collection, Printed Material, box 19, fol. 2.

22. Abadu-Bentsi to Williamson, 26 May 1930, Williamson Collection, box 8, fol. 5.

23. Casely-Hayford and Rathbone, 'Freemasonry in the Colonial Gold Coast', pp. 153–4.

24. Rhoda E. Howard, *Colonialism and Underdevelopment in Ghana* (New York: Africana Publishing Co., 1978), pp. 181–93; Michael Crowder, *West Africa Under Colonial Rule* (Evanston: Northwestern University Press, 1968), pp. 293–307, 335–42; Newell, *Literary Culture in Colonial Ghana: 'How to Play the Game of Life'* (Bloomington: Indiana University Press, 2002), pp. 32–41 (quotes on pp. 40–41). Also see Stephan Meischer's work on Akan masculinity: 'Becoming a Man in Kwawu: Gender, Law, Personhood and the Construction of Masculinities in Colonial Ghana, 1875–1957', (Ph.D dissertation, Northwestern University, 1997), esp. pp. 111–12.

25. Abadu-Bentsi to Williamson, 3 March 1930, Williamson Collection, box 8, fol. 5.

26. Abadu-Bentsi to Williamson, 27 August 1930 and 27 December 1934, Williamson Collection, box 8, fol. 5; Agendas for regular meetings of Lodge Morality, No. 1362, S. C., 17 May 1930, 16 August 1930, and 18 October 1930, Williamson Collection, Printed Material, box 19, fol. 2.

27. Newell, *Literary Culture in Colonial Ghana*, pp. 39, 53–63; Meischer, 'Becoming a Man in Kwawu', pp. 111–12, 360, 389. Also see Crowder, *West Africa*, pp. 341, 384–7.

28. Muraskin, *Middle-class Blacks*, pp. 168–9.

29. Hall of Carthaginian Record Book, 6 and 20 December 1921, Williamson Collection, Masonic Records, vol. 3; Cohen, 'Politics of Ritual Secrecy', pp. 434–5.

30. Crowder, *West Africa*, pp. 322–3; Newell, *Literary Culture in Colonial Ghana*, p. 14. Also see Meischer, 'Becoming a Man in Kwawu', pp. 332–5. For biographical information on Abadu-Bentsi, see Abadu-Bentsi to Williamson, 26 May 1930, 1 August 1930, and 27 December 1934, Williamson Collection, box 8, fol. 5.

31. On the role that salaried income played in the development of 'new self-images as important family providers' among Yoruba men, see Lisa A. Lindsay, '"No Need … To Think of Home"? Masculinity and Domestic Life on the Nigerian Railway, c.1940–61', *Journal of African History* 39 (1998), pp. 44–53.

32. Abadu-Bentsi to Williamson, 26 May 1930, Williamson Collection, box 8, fol. 5. On Aggrey, see Magnus J. Sampson, *Gold Coast Men of Affairs (Past and Present)* (1937; reprint, London: Dawsons of Pall Mall, 1969), pp. 58–71.

33. Williamson to Abadu-Bentsi, 7 August 1930, Williamson Collection, box 8, fol. 5.

34. Abadu-Bentsi to Williamson, March 1931, Williamson Collection, box 8, fol. 5.
35. Williamson to Abadu-Bentsi, 1 June 1931, Williamson Collection, box 8, fol. 5.
36. Abadu-Bentsi to Williamson, 23 January 1932 and 27 December 1934, Williamson Collection, box 8, fol. 5.
37. Abadu-Bentsi to Williamson, 27 December 1934 and 22 April 1935, Williamson Collection, box 8, fol. 5.
38. Cassell to Williamson, 17 September 1935, Williamson Collection, box 8, fol. 5.
39. Williamson to Abadu-Bentsi, 2 August 1935, Williamson Collection, box 8, fol. 5.
40. See Abadu-Bentsi to Williamson, 22 April 1935, Williamson Collection, box 8, fol. 5. On networking, see Cohen, 'Politics of Ritual Secrecy', p. 433.
41. See, for instance, Claire C. Robertson, *Sharing the Same Bowl: A Socioeconomic History of Women and Class in Accra, Ghana* (Bloomington: Indiana University Press, 1984), esp. pp. 183–4; Jean Allman, 'Rounding Up Spinsters: Gender Chaos and Unmarried Women in Colonial Asante', *Journal of African History* 37 (1996), pp. 195–214; Emmanuel Kwaku Akyeampong, *Drink, Power, and Cultural Change: A Social History of Alcohol in Ghana, c. 1800 to Recent Times* (Portsmouth, NH: Heinemann, 1996), pp. 62–7.
42. Casely-Hayford and Rathbone argue that the temperance movement and, by implication, Freemasonry, 'stressed the notion of family responsibility and by this it meant the nuclear rather than the extended family, for the former was felt by the society's adherents to be somehow more obviously Christian.' See 'Freemasonry in the Colonial Gold Coast', p. 149.
43. Abadu-Bentsi to Williamson, 3 March 1930, Williamson Collection, box 8, fol. 5.
44. Grimshaw, *Official History*, pp. 325–6.
45. *Masonic Handbook of Most Worshipful Grand Lodge, F. & A. M. of the State of Arkansas*, n.d., pp. 32, 34, in Williamson Collection, Printed Material, box 15, fol. 1.
46. Grimshaw, *Official History*, p. 228. Also see Dumenil, *Freemasonry and American Culture*, p. 24.
47. Casely-Hayford and Rathbone, 'Freemasonry in the Colonial Gold Coast', pp. 149–50; Akyeampong, *Drink, Power, and Cultural Change*, pp. 71–2. Also see Cohen, *Politics of Elite Culture*, on the importance of drinking within Creole lodges in Sierra Leone.
48. For a discussion of letter writing, identity formation, and self-representation, see Earl Lewis, 'Invoking Concepts, Problematizing Identities: The Life of Charles N. Hunter and the Implications for the Study of Gender and Labor', *Labor History* 34 (1993), pp. 292–308.
49. Williamson to Abadu-Bentsi, 12 October 1930; Abadu-Bentsi to Williamson, 15 December 1930. Both in Williamson Collection, box 8, fol. 5.
50. Williamson to Abadu-Bentsi, 1 August 1930; Abadu-Bentsi to Williamson, March 1931. Both in Williamson Collection, box 8, fol. 5. I do not want to overstate the impact that his exposure to the historical and contemporary manifestations of anti-black racism in the United States had on Abadu-Bentsi's emergent nationalist consciousness. Laura Chrisman's caution regarding the relationship between African Americans and black South Africans in the early twentieth century is instructive. 'The fact of a transatlantic relationship', she writes, 'cannot be prematurely converted into the conclusion that Africans were uncritically modeling themselves on African-Americans, nor that African America supplies a vanguard global class'. See Chrisman, 'Rethinking Black Atlanticism', *The Black Scholar* 30 (2000), p. 14.
51. Abadu-Bentsi to Williamson, 26 May 1930, Williamson Collection, box 8, fol. 5.
52. Abadu-Bentsi to Williamson, March 1931, Williamson Collection, box 8, fol. 5.
53. Abadu-Bentsi to Williamson, 26 May 1930, Williamson Collection, box 8, fol. 5. For the definitive study of the relationship between discourses of manliness and civilisation around the turn of the twentieth century, see Gail Bederman, *Manliness and Civilization: A Cultural History of Gender and Race in the United States, 1880–1917* (Chicago: University of Chicago Press, 1995).
54. Abadu-Bentsi to Williamson, 26 May 1930, 1 August 1930, March 1931, Williamson Collection, box 8, fol. 5.
55. Abadu-Bentsi was hardly alone in this respect. African Americans throughout the early twentieth century, radical and conservative alike, equated production with progress or

liberation. John E. Bruce, both a Mason and a supporter of Garvey, serves as an example: 'We are a race of consumers. We can be if we will a race of producers, but in order to attain to this position in the social progression we must organize!' Bruce, 'Untitled typescript', n.d., pp. 4–6, in John E. Bruce Papers, file B.9-107, Schomburg Center for Research in Black Culture.

56. Abadu-Bentsi to Williamson, March 1931, Williamson Collection, box 8, fol. 5 (emphasis added).

57. Gilroy, *The Black Atlantic: Modernity and Double Consciousness* (Cambridge MA: Harvard University Press, 1993). On class identity and class consciousness as process, see E. P. Thompson, *The Making of the English Working Class* (1963; reprint: London: V. Gollancz, 1980); Daniel J. Walkowitz, *Working With Class: Social Workers and the Politics of Middle-Class Identity* (Chapel Hill: University of North Carolina Press, 1999). On gender identity as process, see Bederman, *Manliness and Civilization*; Judith Butler, *Gender Trouble: Feminism and the Subversion of Identity* (New York: Routledge, 1990).

58. My thinking on the complexities of diaspora has been influenced by Sandra Gunning, 'Nancy Prince and the Politics of Mobility, Home and Diasporic (Mis)Identification', *American Quarterly* 53 (2001), pp. 32–69.

9

Gender in the African Diaspora: Electronic Research Materials

Patrick Manning

Research agendas for studies of the African Diaspora encompass a wide-range of themes, including patterns of enslavement; life under slavery; abolition and emancipation; the development of post-emancipation societies; life under colonialism; the creation of postcolonial societies; and, debates over present-day social issues ranging from education to clitoridectomies. For all of these issues, the study of male and female roles (but particularly the latter) is now of key importance. Furthermore, scholars are paying particular attention to gendered analyses that include but also reach beyond specific locales, to encompass the broadest possible geographic understanding of the African Diaspora. The speedy development of such innovative approaches to the field can only be enhanced by the use of electronic materials.

Electronic resources provide new and exciting materials that can facilitate social science and humanities scholarship on the African Diaspora. These resources are particularly valuable in locating connections across the regional, disciplinary and social boundaries of earlier research.[1] The very newness of studying gender and the African Diaspora, however, means that the basic materials to be searched and linked electronically are neither highly organised nor well funded. This overview of electronic materials surveys those that are readily available as well as techniques for locating and exploring additional items. It principally addresses the World Wide Web, but also electronic discussion groups, CD-ROMs and other forms of electronically stored data.

Both historical and contemporary documents are of course found primarily in archives rather than online: online, one mainly locates research reports rather than documents themselves. Despite this limitation, an advantage of Internet searches is that they provide information on scholars and research groups that are currently active. Electronic resources also provide good places to display data and drafts, and to announce programmes and locate collaborators. The liveliness and activity of the web makes it possible to get beyond treating the African Diaspora as a static object of analysis, creating greater possibilities for conveying the significance of gender roles in the constitution and reproduction of diaspora.[2]

The negative side of online materials is the 'digital divide'. That is, the expansion of electronic resources has tended to privilege those well supplied with training in and access to previous information systems. Internet resources have been somewhat slow in reaching people of colour generally, women in particular, and most of the geographic terrain of the African Diaspora, including Africa, Latin America and the Caribbean.[3] On the other hand, a concerted campaign to reverse or limit this digital divide has emerged. For instance, some excellent materials and effective collaborative structures are beginning to balance the overall shortage of electronic resources addressing gender and the African Diaspora.[4] Given the web's significant slant towards finished research or discussion-group announcements about research, it is a particularly valuable resource when beginning a research project or formalising a research question. Above all, this article suggests recommendations for making good use of electronic materials in these early stages of research.

Research issues

As noted above, the issues addressed in studies of gender and the African Diaspora are numerous and overlapping. The examples presented here reflect the wide scope of this field, as well as some of the current priorities. Given that slavery and the slave trade are fundamental issues in African Diaspora studies, the temporal scope of the African Diaspora is usually taken as the past five centuries, starting with the opening of regular Atlantic maritime contacts in the fifteenth century, and moving to analyses of emancipation and the development of post-emancipation society in the nineteenth and twentieth centuries. The social issues of the African Diaspora are viewed through both modern and postmodern lenses.

In geographic scope the African Diaspora encompasses historical and societal interaction involving many regions. Opinion has varied on whether to include the African continent – the homeland – in studies of the African Diaspora. The approach taken here includes the continent, since Africa comprises not only the point of departure for millions of migrants, but also a large and vibrant zone of continuing interaction among communities within and beyond the continent.[5] A further point on geography is the need to give adequate attention not only to the Diaspora in North America, but also to Atlantic communities of the African Diaspora in South and Central America, the Caribbean, Canada and Europe.[6] In the same vein, one must also note the significance of the African Diaspora in the Middle East, North Africa and the Indian Ocean.[7]

In social scope, African Diasporic communities, created by early modern migrations, maintained and reproduced connections among various social strata and between often-distant territories. Labour migration included initial and subsequent movements of slaves and indentures, and new migrations of wage labourers in the nineteenth and twentieth centuries.[8] At the same time, cultural interaction, facilitated initially through travel and trade and more recently through electronic media, has brought developments in religion, dress, music and philosophy. In addition, movement and modification of familial patterns have resulted in changing gender roles; these roles have also been affected by shifting boundaries of race, ethnicity, class and religion. The result has been the creation of highly complex diasporic communities.[9] At every level, collective memory has kept alive community recollections of past oppression, of life without oppression, of the sounds and tastes of childhood and of the idea of an African homeland.[10] These issues arise in conjunction with the broader social processes of colonialism and nationalism, struggles over civil rights and human rights, and development of new, vibrant and contested forms of popular culture.

With these complexities in mind, the African Diaspora is best seen as a social and geographic totality, not just a collection of regions and nationalities.[11] What is distinctive in studies of the African Diaspora – as contrasted for instance with nationally-based African-American studies in the USA – is the emphasis on trans-regional connections, and also the additional emphasis on the multiple perspectives of the communities under study, as well as the multiple analytical frameworks used by scholars. Thus, if one gives particular focus to the gendered dimensions of diasporic connections, one undertakes a complex study that is likely to reveal social relationships that have escaped previous notice.

Available technology and research techniques

The techniques for online research are only now being developed, and the rules and conventions of research online have yet to be established. One of the strengths of online analysis, however, is that many guides and handy hints are placed online by public-spirited individuals and by organisations supporting online linkages. For instance, the H-Net group of electronic discussion groups provides an Internet citation guide and suggestions for the critique of websites.[12] Because the quantity of online materials is growing rapidly, any current list of resources soon becomes obsolete. Thus, my survey emphasises techniques of research and assessment, as much as lists of resources.

When it comes to locating quick answers to factual questions, the World Wide Web and its search engines are particularly strong tools. Search techniques are especially adept at enabling the user to go from general to specific, and to learn more and more about any given topic.[13] More difficult than fact-checking is using the web to make connections among different areas of knowledge and to develop a larger picture and a wider under-standing. With persistence and imagination, however, one can access information with depth and breadth, and not just speed and specificity. In this regard, it may be helpful to think of the structure of the web itself. On one hand, it consists of millions of distinct files, created and mounted separately; on the other, the individual files are linked electronically into one huge network, and they are further linked by many intermediate structures, of which the search engines are only the most obvious.[14] As a subject of study the larger patterns of life in the African Diaspora are paralleled by the broad patterns in the knowledge and assemblage of files on the web.

The researcher begins work with a search for particular types of information: certain kinds of documents; subject areas; authors; pub-lishers; factual specifics; or, links and references. A 'keyword' search, in which the search engine decides on the selection of authors, subjects and so forth, simply involves inputting a term. By using 'advanced search' functions, the researcher can also search separately by author, subject, and so on. It is useful to keep in mind the analogy between the Internet and a library: that is, once you find an interesting reference, it is good to browse the nearby files for other good finds.[15] Researchers should also be sure to investigate various formats. For instance, one might explore the implications of a slaving voyage through a combination of CD-ROMs, web simulations, image databases and discussion lists.[16]

Taking notes becomes a critical issue in electronic research for all but the smallest of projects. How does one retrieve and retain the results of electronic research? When bookmarking websites becomes unwieldy, one option is to copy URLs and downloaded text into text files, which are searchable within the word processing program.[17] One can also paste references and other data to a spreadsheet file, in order to keep track of categories. A further step that I have found useful is the creation of a data-base that includes both selected evidence and my own analytical categories.[18] Still, the biggest problem for note-taking comes in the long run: unfortu-nately, since platforms and operating systems change every few years, one is often put in the position of updating and translating notes periodically so as not to lose access to them.

Structure of electronic publication

Creators of Internet files must first select a language of presentation. Although English has become the prevailing language of international scholarship, the web enables scholars to develop thriving resources for documentation and debate in any language. French-language websites provide materials on the Caribbean, francophone Africa, Canada and Europe, including numerous international organisations.[19] Spanish-language materials on the African Diaspora address Cuba and Puerto Rico, mainland countries including Venezuela, Colombia, and Mexico, plus Spain.[20] Portuguese-language materials centre on Brazil, but also include Angola, Mozambique and other countries of Africa, as well as Portugal.[21] Materials in other languages may not be central to the web, but nonetheless they benefit from the technology.[22]

Websites have come to dominate the electronic media of research and publication. Publishers operate at a number of levels, including international organisations, corporate conglomerates, small groups and individuals,[23] and many of these maintain excellent websites. The United Nations and World Bank maintain websites relevant to the African Diaspora,[24] while national governments publish guides and documents.[25] Some non-governmental and non-profit organisations also publish actively.[26] Certain university presses emphasise topics in the African Diaspora, as do certain trade presses.[27] In addition, scholarly associations sponsor publications and sometimes publish directly (CODESRIA, NCBS).[28] CD-ROMs, though less accessible, provide some excellent resource materials and are more easily explored once obtained.[29] Standard reference sources, now online, include dictionaries, encyclopaedias, bibliographic references and writing and publishing guides.[30]

Forms of electronic resources

Regardless of how they reach the web, electronic resources are published in a variety of forms. For instance, they can be classified into conferences, symposia, discussion lists, academic programs, organisational websites, resource lists and individual websites. Conference websites are a useful place to begin, because they reveal the development of research and scholarly discourse. For instance, sites from three international conferences on Women in the African Diaspora that took place in 1992, 1998 and 2001 have maintained a continual presence on the web.[31] The Canadian conference on mothering in the African Diaspora and the Dartmouth conference on gender in the African Diaspora are just two more of the many conferences whose traces may be retrieved.[32] Such conference sites provide excellent markers of the developments in the field. In addition to past conferences, calls for papers are also well represented on the web.[33] Conference notices provide a good way to identify research topics and individual researchers in studies of gender and diaspora, and they provide an informal way to start thinking about cross-disciplinary connections through the exploration of conferences organised outside one's own formal training. In addition to major conferences, smaller symposia are often advertised on the web; pursuit of these leads may give indications of new research on its way to publication.[34]

Though they do not focus exclusively on gender issues and are not as numerous as conference sites and calls for papers, research programme websites are significant sources of information. For instance, the website of the ongoing African Diaspora Research Project directed by Dr Ruth Simms Hamilton at Michigan State University is a place to start; the Harriet Tubman Center at York University in Ontario is also a major centre.[35] Another relevant and ongoing research project at UCLA focuses on cultural studies.[36] In addition, the web lists announcements of new research projects, such as the one in progress on women and religion at Princeton.[37] CODESRIA, the research collaborative for African scholars, publishes results of its agenda-setting conferences.[38] Meanwhile, the Stanford University library has constructed a detailed list of research projects, including a list of projects on the African Diaspora.[39]

One should also note that online journals, discussion lists and bulletin boards were early forms of electronic communication, and they continue to thrive and evolve. Currently, at least fifteen active discussion lists exist that are relevant to the study of gender and the African diaspora.[40] Unless they have a website to anchor them, discussion lists and bulletin boards are not indexed by search engines; however, cross-posting is common, so by reading one list carefully it is often possible to learn about several others.[41] There has also been an increase in online publication of established print journals, as well as newer ventures,[42] although unfortunately, not all electronic journals are able to sustain publication.[43] In addition, the websites of university-based academic programmes can offer valuable information: though such sites are of course aimed at publicising their own programmes, they do provide materials of interest, such as symposia, curricula, syllabi,[44] bibliography and resource lists.[45] One can also visit the sites of major museums, which often summarise their exhibits online, providing useful materials for both teaching and research.[46] International para-governmental organisations, beginning with the United Nations, are particularly important for indicating cross-national connections.[47] Also, non-governmental organisations, especially those centred around women's interests, give attention to gender issues.[48]

Resource lists developed by active groups and energetic individuals reflect the value of the democratised side of the Internet. These eclectic lists are essential to locating and nurturing links among topics. Historian Lynn Nelson maintains an exceptional list of Internet resources in history at the University of Kansas.[49] Bibliographies posted by individuals, while rarely exhaustive, often yield new ideas.[50] Electronic resource lists, the favourites posted by individuals or groups, reveal the approach of investigators as well as their findings.[51] By the same reasoning, sites maintained by individuals provide not only autobiographies of the authors, but also their ways of approaching Internet materials.[52] For all such non-organisational sites, the patient use of search engines, plus the copying and saving of links, can be very beneficial.

Examples: researching electronically

A discussion list devoted specifically to either the African Diaspora or to gender issues within the diaspora does not yet exist. Thus far, the Internet has served as a nexus of debate rather than as a repository of data. Nevertheless, the available tools do provide an excellent basis for framing and pursuing research. Covering three main sets of issues, the following section provides illustrative recommendations for investigators addressing research questions associated with the role of gender in the interpretation of the African Diaspora and diasporic connections.

Slavery and abolition. An expanding Atlantic and then global system of slavery did much to create the African Diaspora, launching forced migrations to the north, west and east of sub-Saharan Africa.[53] For the era in which slavery remained in force, the associated issues of work, family and cultural transformation have retained substantial attention as research priorities.[54] Resistance to slavery, the development of free communities of colour and the processes of individual and collective emancipation gain particular attention for the eighteenth and nineteenth centuries.[55] The development of racial categorisation, including ideologies of racial discrimination on the one hand and the identification of hierarchies of racial mixture on the other, provide a further arena of discussion across the full range of African Diaspora history.[56] For all the work that has been done, much more is needed to clarify the gender relations and cultural patterns of the diaspora for this formative period. The centrality of interactions across the diaspora is reflected in the significance that issues of slavery and emancipation had for the African continent as well. How does the interpretation of the African Diaspora change when one integrates into the analysis the expansion of slavery in Africa and the divergent gendered proportions brought to the continent and diaspora by slave trade?

Post-emancipation society. The struggle to recover from the experience of slavery and gain positions of social dignity is a central trope in African Diaspora studies.[57] Analyses emphasise developments in political identity, and the challenges faced by freed black populations as they encountered new forms of racial discrimination – with distinct though related forms in the USA, the Caribbean, South America and the various regions of Africa. Numerous studies on gender and colonialism in post-emancipation societies focus particularly on the late nineteenth and early twentieth centuries. These cultural and political changes were accompanied by expanding migrations, now of free people. The redirected migrations of black people were part of an expanding global mobility that in turn responded to industrialisation.[58] Despite its tumult, this era resulted in an outpouring of cultural creativity in communities throughout the African Diaspora. Scholarship has focused especially on black literary output.[59] Parallel studies in other media have addressed visual art and music, as well as their combination in an influential popular culture. Most analyses in print and online, however, have presented society and culture in national contexts.[60] How did gender roles change around the Atlantic in post-emancipation society? How can the study of gender serve to reframe our understanding of the 'double consciousness' of this historical moment?

Postcolonial society. The second half of the twentieth century brought decolonisation and major advances in civil rights throughout the African Diaspora. Establishment of many new national units and greater ease of travel brought an expansion in pan-African connection and identity. Yet conflicts exploded between black communities and hegemonic power structures; between black communities and white communities; and within black communities themselves. How were African Diaspora societies to define their own identity, yet at the same time gain integration into global power structures?

Struggles with the state over civil rights broadened into struggles over human rights within civil society. Issues of class conflict, ethnic conflicts and individual assaults took new forms in the late twentieth century, each with gendered implications.[61] Families, complex and contested social units in every era, became at once stronger and weaker. As schools and work-places gradually displaced families as sites of formation for young people of colour, males and females of all ages took on new roles. Conventional rites of passage to adulthood were contested.[62] New studies of masculinity, now in the context of an updated understanding of gender dynamics, have expanded the scope of traditional analysis.[63] How have contemporary migrations affected family patterns? In the current era, spectacular developments in popular culture such as South African music, Brazilian capoeira and Michael Jackson's tours have reverberated throughout the African Diaspora. They respond, arguably, not simply to new technology but also to the experiences of diasporic communities.[64] The great expansion and continuing debates on education throughout the diaspora affect gender roles in popular culture, but also in work, politics, and other areas.[65]

Directions of study

To conclude, researchers should not only make use of electronic resources, but also interrogate them. How does the Internet represent gender? How does it represent racial designations? How does it represent geographic space? In some ways the web does not represent gender directly. In other ways, as with sexually explicit sites, it represents gender all too blatantly. Racial identifications, similarly, are at once invisible and omnipresent on the web. There is much to be done in sorting out the meanings of information in electronic form.

The research emphasis on gender in the African Diaspora is significant not only for advancing the understanding of specific social issues and populations. By extending across boundaries of gender, race and region, this research strategy exemplifies the new scholarship developing in many contexts across the globe. It contrasts sharply with earlier positivistic scholarship, where the emphasis was on researching a few variables within a given set of categories. Studies of gender in the African Diaspora link research agendas across categories and address the interactions of a wide variety of factors.

Electronic resources can be used for research in both old and new styles, and are certainly valuable for the detailed analysis of specific topics.[66] But they can also contribute to locating and nurturing interdisciplinary and interregional ties. Scholars interested in global, transnational and trans-cultural analysis can be creative in identifying and developing electronic resources that facilitate their research needs, using the breadth and rapidity of electronic communication to support new and innovative research agendas.

What will happen next? Will there be a growth in collaborative research? An expansion in cross-national, multilingual studies? New developments in theory? Will graduate students be linked to inter-campus and inter-national networks, rather than studying within the confines of their own departments? Research with electronic materials can help advance all of these possibilities. Furthermore, the Internet is repositioning the ivory tower in the social landscape. Through the Internet, scholarly specialists and general audiences encounter each other more readily than before. Electronic media, while eliciting new analytical insights in the gendered dimensions of the African Diaspora, will also play a role in the public discourse that sustains and develops the communities of the African Diaspora. The Internet reminds us that all scholarship has a social conscience of one sort or another.

Notes

The author expresses thanks to Stacy Tweedy and Tiffany Trimmer, doctoral candidates in world history at Northeastern University, for their research assistance and critique in preparation of this review.

1. The websites and other resources cited here, while recommended as good examples, are of necessity only a tiny proportion of the total available materials. Many other fine resources remain for the reader to locate and use.
2. Gender roles shifted drastically in the forced creation of the African Diaspora, and shifted again in association with the diaspora-wide transformations of emancipation, industrialisation and nation-building.
3. For the principal site on the digital divide, directed by Craig Smith, see <www.digitaldivide.org>. See also the Public Broadcasting System site, at <www.pbs.org/digitaldivide>; and the Benton Foundation site at <www.digitaldividenetwork.org/content/sections/index.cfm>.
4. The World Bank symposium on the digital divide reflects, at once, research projects funded by the bank and the political pressures to which the organisation must respond. <www.worldbank.org/gender/digitaldivide/diaspora.ppt>.
5. See the site of the Université Cheikh Anta Diop, Dakar, Senegal, <www.ucad.sn>.
6. For a substantial print journal on the African Diaspora, published in Colombia from 1991 through 1996, see *America Negra*, <www.javeriana.edu.co/Humana/negra.html>. The library at the Mona Campus of the University of the West Indies in Kingston, Jamaica, is a major collection, and its website provides links to research institutions of the English-speaking Caribbean, at <wwwlibrary.uwimona.edu.jm:1104/history.htm>.
7. On the African diaspora in North Africa, see the website of John Hunwick, <pubweb.acns.nwu.edu/~jhunwick/diaspora.html>.
8. Kim Richardson, 'From Slaves to Immigrants,' <www.brazzil.com/p36mar01.htm>.
9. For visual art from Congo-Kinshasa, see <www.congonline.com/Peinture/peintres.htm>.
10. The Schomburg Center of the New York Public Library supports substantial exhibits in African-American and African diaspora history in addition to its role as a major research center: see <www.nypl.org/research/sc/sc.html>. The Ecole du Patrimoine Africain, in Porto-Novo, Bénin, is a leader in the development of historical museums throughout the African continent: see <www.epa-prema.net/>.
11. The Association for the Study of the Worldwide African Diaspora (ASWAD) is forming under the leadership of Michael Gomez of New York University: see <www.aswadiaspora.org/>.
12. An Internet citation guide created in 1996 by Melvin Page, co-editor of H-AFRICA, is still the most widely cited: see <www2.h-net.msu.edu/~africa/citation.html>. Columbia University Press and Bedford-St. Martin's have also posted citation guides, at <www.columbia.edu/cu/cup/cgos/idx_basic.html> and <www.bedfordstmartins.com/online/citex.html>. For guides to evaluating sites, see 'Evaluating Internet Sources', <twist.lib.uiowa.edu/resources/evaluate.html> and 'The Web as a Research Tool: Evaluation Techniques', <www2.widener.edu/Wolfgram-Memorial-Library/webevaluation/webeval.htm>.
13. Among the major search engines are: Google, <www.google.com>; Alta Vista, <www.altavista.com>; and Yahoo, <www.yahoo.com>.
14. On the development of nodes and hubs in the Internet and other complex networks, see Albert-László Barabási and Eric Bonabeau, 'Scale-Free Networks,' *Scientific American* (May 2003), pp. 60–69.
15. A comparison of the 'advanced search' function of AltaVisa with that of an online library catalogue such as the Hollis catalog of Harvard University libraries reveals numerous organisational parallels. See <www.altavista.com>; and <lib.harvard.edu/>.
16. See notes 53 and 54 below.
17. Similarly, it is usually possible to copy or download texts or images from CD-ROMs.
18. I have found Filemaker Pro to be a useful and flexible program for creating databases of research notes.
19. Université des Antilles et de la Guyane, Centre d'Etudes et de Recherches Appliquées aux Langues, Littératures et Cultures Comparées, <www.univ-ag.fr/labos.php?code=305>; African Societies Online is published in English, French, and Italian, at <www.africansocieties.org/>.
20. For Afro-Cuban links, see <www.afrocubaweb.com/>. For links throughout Latin America, see 'The African Diaspora' (University of Texas), <lanic.utexas.edu/la/region/african>.

21. On Brazilian women, see 'Mulheras negras,' <www.mulherasnegras.org>.
22. See the site for the Pulaar (or Fulbe) language of West Africa, 'WebPulaaku,' <www.pulaaku.net/>. For access to writings in Afrikaans, including its two million Coloured speakers, see 'Afrikaans crows nest,' <www.geocities.com/Paris/2920/medialinks.html>. Amharic, Hausa, Swahili, Yoruba, and Zulu languages also have a significant presence on the web.
23. Dieudonné Gnammankou, <www.gnammankou.com>.
24. The UNESCO site (<www.unesco.org/>) is very rich, including such materials as links to national libraries <www.unesco.org/webworld/portal_bib/Libraries/National/>) and the site of its diaspora-wide Slave Route project, at <www.unesco.org/culture/dialogue/slave/>. See also the World Bank Group, <www.worldbank.org/>.
25. The files of South Africa's Truth and Reconciliation Commission provide an important source of data on gender issues in the midst of social crisis: <www.doj.gov.za/trc/>. See also the sites of Angola (<www.angola.org/); Trinidad (<www.gov.tt/>); and the Brazilian governmental site, 'Portal Palmares' (<www.palmares.gov.br/index.html>).
26. Women's Rights Watch, <www.hrw.org/women/index.php>.
27. University of Warwick Centre for Caribbean Studies (<www.warwick.ac.uk/fac/arts/CCS/>) is associated with the university's active publishing program in Caribbean studies. See also Yale University Press at <www.yale.edu/yup/subjects/womens.htm>; and for books published in Africa see the Africa Book Centre, <www.africabookcentre.com/acatalog/index.html>.
28. National Council for Black Studies, <www.cas.gsu.edu/ncbs/>.
29. Gwendolyn M. Hall, *Databases for the Study of Afro-Louisiana History and Genealogy, 1699–1860* [CD-ROM] (Baton Rouge: Louisiana State University Press).
30. Schomburg Center of the New York Public Library, <www.nypl.org/research/sc/sc.html>. Encyclopaedia Britannica has two websites: <www.britannica.com/>; and <www.eb.com/>.
31. First International Conference on Women in Africa and the African Diaspora (WAAD), 'Bridges across Activism and the Academy,' Nsukka, Nigeria (1992), <www.iupui.edu/~aaws/waad/conf.htm> (see also <www.iupui.edu/~aaws/waad/proceeds.htm>); Second conference on women in the African Diaspora, Nsukka (1998), <csf.colorado.edu/forums/ecofem/may98/0010.html>; Third International Conference on Women in Africa and the African Diaspora (WAAD III), 'Facing the New Millennium: Gender in Africa and the African Diaspora – Retrospection and Prospects,' Antananarivo and Tamatave, Madagascar (2001), <www.sas.upenn.edu/African_Studies/Current_Events/waad1001.html>.
32. 'Mothering in the African Diaspora: Literature, History, Society, Popular Culture and the Arts,' York University, Toronto (2000), <www.yorku.ca/crm/Conferences/African%20Mothering/africpro.htm>; 'Gendering the Diaspora,' Dartmouth College (2002), <www.dartmouth.edu/~jbyfield/diaspora/schedule.html>.
33. 'CFP: Black Women and The Making of a New Diaspora,' University of Pennsylvania (2002), <www.english.upenn.edu/CFP/archive/Gender-Studies/0051.html>.
34. 'Bridging the African diaspora,' University of Nebraska – Lincoln (2001), <www.unl.edu/unlies/symposium/schedule.html>.
35. 'African Diaspora Research project,' Michigan State University, <www.msu.edu/unit/uap/africa.html>; Harriet Tubman Resource Centre on the African Diaspora, York University, <www.yorku.ca/nhp/>.
36. Cultural Studies in the African Diaspora Project, UCLA, <www.sscnet.ucla.edu/caas/diaspora/index.html>.
37. This is a three-year project (2001–04) on Women and Religion in the African Diaspora at Princeton University, funded by the Ford Foundation, <www.princeton.edu/~csrelig/prrg.htm>.
38. CODESRIA (Council for the Development of Social Science Research in Africa), <www.codesria.org/>.
39. Stanford Library, Social Sciences Data Service. <www-sul.stanford.edu/depts/ssrg/ssds/main.htm>.

40. Based at H-Net (<h-net.msu.edu>) are over a hundred discussion lists, including over a dozen relevant to gender in the African diaspora: H-Afro-Am, H-Africa (a total of seven associated lists), H-AmStudy, H-Caribbean, H-Ethnic, H-LatAm, H-Women, and H-World. Archives of current and past messages are searchable.

41. The discussion list on 'The history of slavery, the slave trade, abolition and emancipation,' based at the University of Houston, accepts messages at <Slavery@listserv.uh.edu>.

42. The History Cooperative publishes several major journals online (<www.historycooperative.org/journals.html>); a larger number of online journals are made available through JSTOR (<www.jstor.org/>). Newer ventures online include *African Studies Quarterly*, <web.africa.ufl.edu/asq/v6/v6i3a7.htm>; and African Societies (with French and Italian versions) <www.africansocieties.org/>. For a resource list of ejournals, see <www.library.miami.edu/ejournals/african.html>.

43. World History of Slavery, Abolition, and Emancipation, <h-net.msu.edu/~slavery>.

44. Lynette Jackson, 'Black Nationalisms,' Barnard College (1998), <www.barnard.columbia.edu/history/old%20files/jackson/3101/3101y.html>; Robert Tempelman, 'Music of the African Diaspora, U of Cincinnati (2002), <www.worldmusic.uc.edu:8000/WorldMusic/Classes/AfricanDiaspora/Syllabus.htm>.

45. Stanford University Libraries, African Studies Programs Worldwide, <www-sul.stanford.edu/depts/ssrg/africa/asp.html>; Bard College African and African Diaspora studies and Gender Studies, <www.bard.edu/academics/undergrad/inter_multi/aads/>, and <www.bard.edu/academics/undergrad/inter_multi/gender/>; Spelman College, Women and African Diaspora Studies Program, <pages.towson.edu/ncctrw/publications/diaspo.html>; Centre for Study of the African Diaspora, University of Amsterdam, <users.fmg.uva.nl/iverheij/program.html>; African Diaspora at Indiana University's Department of History, <www.indiana.edu/~histweb/pages/graduate/african_diaspora.htm>; New York University, Africa and African Diaspora, <www.nyu.edu/gsas/dept/history/african_and_african_diaspora.htm>.

46. 'African Voices,' Smithsonian Institution, <www.si.edu/africanvoices>; 'American Memory,' Library of Congress, <www.loc.gov>.

47. UN Economic Commission for Africa, <www.uneca.org/aknf/aknf2001/srength.htm>; UNESCO slave route, <www.unesco.org/culture/dialogue/slave/html_eng/diaspora.shtml>.

48. Pan African Women's Liberation Movement, <www.wougnet.org/Profiles/pawlo.html>; Women's Human Rights Net, <www.whrnet.org/>. Another developing intellectual collaborative is that of world historians, with a web presence and resource catalogue at the World History Network, <www.worldhistorynetwork.org>.

49. World Wide Web Virtual Library, based at the University of Kansas, <www.ku.edu/history/VL/index.html>.

50. 'Questia, the online library' (<www.questia.com/>), provides bibliographic lists in response to searches; bibliographies from the 1998 'Roots' summer seminar at the University of Virginia are posted at <cti.itc.virginia.edu/~roots/site/biblios.html>.

51. Internet Resources: Women of Color & Women Worldwide (Stanford Libraries), <www-sul.stanford.edu/depts/ssrg/kkerns/wcolor.html>; African Studies Page of the International and Gender Studies Resources Website, <globetrotter.berkeley.edu/GlobalGender/africapage.html>; Africa South of Sahara (Karen Fung, Stanford Libraries), <www-sul.stanford.edu/depts/ssrg/africa/women.html>; Smithsonian Institution, <www.si.edu/history_and_culture/african_american/>; African Diaspora Central, Herbert Ruffin II, History, Claremont Graduate University, <www.grad.cgu.edu/~ruffinh/african_diasporacentral/>; Everythingblack.com, <www.everythingblack.com>; African Philosophy resources, <www.augustana.ab.ca/~janzb/afphil/afamres.htm>; Educational Development Center links, <www.edc.org/GDI/links_education.htm>; African Americans in Media, <www.uiowa.edu/~commstud/resources/GenderMedia/african_txt.html>; Suggestions, Comments or Corrections to Karla-Tonella@uiowa.edu,

<www.uiowa.edu/~commstud/resources/bordercrossings/diaspora.html>; Universities in Nigeria (Robert-Jan Bulter list of universities of the world), <www.bulter.nl/universities/ng.html>.

52. Filomena Steady, <www.wellesley.edu/PublicAffairs/Profile/sz/fsteady.html>.
53. Users may explore age and gender distribution of captive populations on CD-ROM for the Atlantic slave trade, and by web simulation for the African continent, Atlantic and the Americas. David Eltis et al. (eds) *The Transatlantic Slave Trade: A Database on CD-ROM* (Cambridge University Press, 1999); Patrick Manning, 'The Atlantic Slave Trade: Demographic Simulation', <www.migrationsim.neu.edu/>.
54. For an online collection of hundreds of images of life under slavery and slave trade, see Jerome S. Handler and Michael L. Tuite Jr., 'The Atlantic Slave Trade and Slave Life in the Americas: A Visual Record', <gropius.lib.virginia.edu/Slavery/index.html>.
55. 'Women and Slavery in the Caribbean' (Penny Welch, University of Wolverhampton), <pers-www.wlv.ac.uk/~le1810/slavery.htm>.
56. Encyclopedia Africana (Harvard Afro-American Studies) <www.africanaencyclopedia.com/>. A separate project for a 20-volume Encyclopaedia Africana (based at the University of Ghana), has closed its website, previously located at <www.endarkenment.com/eap/>.
57. The distinction between slavery and emancipation cannot, however, be expressed through straightforward periodisation: the emancipation of black slaves, rather than occurring at a given moment, was a process extending from the eighteenth into the twentieth centuries.
58. For a collection of documents and analyses emphasising connections across the African diaspora and their links to other migratory movements, see Patrick Manning et al., *Migration in Modern World History, 1500–2000* [CD-ROM] (Wadsworth, 2000).
59. Project on the History of Black Writing, <www.ku.edu/~phbw/>; the University of Virginia Electronic Text Center includes a substantial number of texts by African-American authors: <etext.lib.virginia.edu/uvaonline.html>.
60. American Memory, <memory.loc.gov/>.
61. In the extremes of Central African warfare, children became heads of household as well as refugees, and girls were drafted as soldiers as well as rape victims.
62. Female Genital Mutilation Network <www.fgmnetwork.org/>.
63. For studies of masculinity, see Herman Gray, <muse.jhu.edu/quick_tour/18.2gray.html>; Gerald Butters on Oscar Micheaux in Journal for MultiMedia History, <www.albany.edu/jmmh/vol3/micheaux/micheaux.html>; and the *Journal of Southern African Studies*, special issue on masculinities in southern Africa <www.tandf.co.uk/journals/archive/c-archive/jss-con.html>.
64. See the website of singer Angelique Kidjo, <wwwusers.imaginet.fr/~kidjo/index.html>.
65. The Women of Uganda Network provides examples of these changes, at <www.wougnet.org/Links/education.html>.
66. Harlem, in the era of its Renaissance, is often labelled as 'capital of the black world.' Of the many excellent exhibits and websites on this topic, a growing number address gender issues. It is perhaps time for some to address relations between Harlem and the 'provinces' of the black world throughout Africa and the diaspora.

Index